Let Truth Prevail

LET TRUTH PREVAIL

*An Introduction to European
Christian Renewal Movements*

R. Allen Diles

LET TRUTH PREVAIL
An Introduction to European Christian Renewal Movements

Copyright © 2021 by R. Allen Diles

ISBN 978-1-68426-241-0
LCCN 2021010634

Printed in the United States of America

ALL RIGHTS RESERVED

No part of this publication may be reproduced, stored in a retrieval system, or transmitted in any form by any means—electronic, mechanical, photocopying, recording, or otherwise—without prior written consent.

Scripture quotations noted ESV are from The ESV® Bible (The Holy Bible, English Standard Version®) copyright © 2001 by Crossway, a publishing ministry of Good News Publishers. ESV® Text Edition: 2016. The ESV® text has been reproduced in cooperation with and by permission of Good News Publishers. Unauthorized reproduction of this publication is prohibited. All rights reserved.

Scripture quotations noted NASB are taken from the New American Standard Bible® Copyright © 1960, 1971, 1977, 1995, 2020 by The Lockman Foundation. All rights reserved.

LIBRARY OF CONGRESS CATALOGING-IN-PUBLICATION DATA
Names: Diles, Allen, 1966- author.
Title: Let truth prevail : an introduction to European Christian renewal movements / Allen Diles.
Description: Abilene, Texas : ACU Press, 2021. | Includes bibliographical references.
Identifiers: LCCN 2021010634 (print) | LCCN 2021010635 (ebook) | ISBN 9781684262410 (trade paperback) | ISBN 9781684269419 (ebook)
Subjects: LCSH: Reformation—Early movements. | Christian sects, Medieval. | Church history—Middle Ages, 600-1500. | Reformation—Europe. | Church renewal—Europe. | Europe—Church history.
Classification: LCC BR295 .D55 2021 (print) | LCC BR295 (ebook) | DDC 274/.6—dc23
LC record available at https://lccn.loc.gov/2021010634
LC ebook record available at https://lccn.loc.gov/2021010635

Cover design by ThinkPen Design, LLC
Interior text design by Strong Design, Sandy Armstrong

For information contact:
Abilene Christian University Press
ACU Box 29138
Abilene, Texas 79699

1-877-816-4455
www.acupressbooks.com

21 22 23 24 25 26 27 / 7 6 5 4 3 2 1

To Laurie, Andrew, and Luke, and to my students.

"Because we love God's church, we take seriously its history."
—**John Mark Hicks and Bobby Valentine**, Kingdom Come

"Truth conquers only if one is willing to lay down one's life for the sake of the truth."
—**Craig Atwood,** The Theology of the Czech Brethren from Hus to Comenius

Contents

Preface 9
Introduction 13
    The Concept of Restoration

Chapter 1 25
    Setting the Stage: The Medieval Church and the Need for Reformation
    "in Head and in Members"

Chapter 2 39
    "To Obey God Rather than Men": The Waldensians

Chapter 3 61
    "Truth Prevails over All": The Czech Reformation Part 1

Chapter 4 77
    "Jesus Christ, the Best Lawgiver": The Czech Reformation Part 2

Chapter 5 93
    "Faith, Love, and Hope": The Unity of the Brethren *(Unitas Fratrum)*

Chapter 6 115
    "For the Greater Glory of God": The Protestant and Catholic Reformations
    of the Sixteenth Century

Chapter 7 139
    "Given, Surrendered, and Sacrificed Wholly to God": Evangelical Anabaptists Part 1

Chapter 8 163
    "Overthrowing Religion and Civil Order": Evangelical Anabaptists Part 2

Chapter 9 181
    "A Personal Religion of the Heart": Pietism, Schwarzenau Brethren,
    and the Moravian Brethren

Chapter 10 209
    "No Such Thing as a National Church": Scottish Restorationists

Afterword 229
    "Yet More Truth to Break Forth from His Holy Word"

Selected Bibliography 235

Preface

Having been raised within the restorationist heritage of the US Restoration or Stone-Campbell Movement, I have always appreciated the plea of calling the church of Jesus Christ to return to its New Testament norms and ideals as a means of achieving unity among followers of Jesus, even when the reality often fell short of the plea. Graduate instruction at Abilene Christian University under Everett Ferguson, Doug Foster, and Leonard Allen whetted my appetite for further studies in church history, and I had the opportunity to pursue them at Charles University while I was stationed as a missionary in Prague, Czech Republic. At the beginning of my doctoral studies there, my major professor, Noemi Rejchrtová, suggested I read an anthology of excerpts of primary sources and commentary from the era of the Hussite movement in the Czech lands. The title of the recommended work was *Slovem obnovená*,[1] which struck me because the Czech word *obnovit* can be translated into English as both *restore* and *renew*—thus, *Restored [or Renewed] by the Word*. From my own heritage, Alexander Campbell had once made the astonishingly incorrect claim that "not until within the present generation did any sect . . . unite and build upon the Bible alone." He continued, "Since that time, the first effort known to us to . . . restore primitive Christianity, or to build alone upon the Apostles and Prophets, Jesus Christ himself the chief corner-stone, has been made."[2] Yet Professor Rejchrtová's book was introducing me to

Czech thinkers who had prized restorationist ideals hundreds of years before the time of Alexander Campbell. In particular, this book introduced me to the Taborite restorationist priest Nicholas Biskupec of Pelhřimov, and Professor Rejchrtová encouraged me to pursue a comparative study of Alexander Campbell and Nicholas Biskupec. This became the subject of my dissertation, but it also became the launching pad for my interest in exploring additional restorationist movements from European history.

After accepting a position teaching church history at Harding University, I was assigned to develop and teach a course called "History of Renewal Movements" for which I could not locate a suitable text. Thus was born the dream of a volume that would introduce significant European restoration-type movements to my students—the volume you now hold in your hands. This volume is intended for nonspecialists, particularly undergraduate college students and laypersons in a church Bible class or small-group setting. The choice of which movements to survey was based entirely upon my own interests and areas of study. Many other movements, such as the English Baptists and Plymouth Brethren, to name two, could have and probably should have been included in a volume such as this, but the limitations of time, space, and interest dictated the focus of this volume. Perhaps a future volume could explore additional movements, including examples from Africa and Latin America.

In the present volume, all translations of biblical texts, save those within quotations of other works, are my own, as are translations directly from sources written in Czech. In addition to thanking professors Ferguson, Foster, Allen, and Rejchrtová for their inspiration and encouragement, I would also like to thank Professor David Holeton, who mentored me through much of the dissertation process at Charles University. Thanks are also due to my colleagues in the College of Bible and Ministry at Harding University, several of whom read chapters and made suggestions for this present volume and all of whom have encouraged my work.

I am grateful to Tina Rogers of the L. M. Graves Memorial Library at the Harding School of Theology for aid in acquiring some important sources at the last minute.

I also wish to express appreciation to Jason Fikes and Mary Hardegree of Abilene Christian University Press for their suggestions and guidance in bringing this work to completion, and to the reviewers who provided valuable feedback.

I want to thank my wife, Laurie, and my boys, Andrew and Luke, for bearing with me through this project. Finally, I want to say thank you to my parents, Bob and Mary, for raising me in a home of faith.

NOTES

[1] Amedeo Molnár, Noemi Rejchrtová, and Luděk Rejchrtový, eds., *Slovem obnovená: čtení o reformaci* (Prague: Kalich, 1977).

[2] Alexander Campbell, *The Christian System: In Reference to the Union of Christians, and a Restoration of Primitive Christianity, as Plead in the Current Reformation* (Joplin, MO: College Press, 1989), ix.

INTRODUCTION

The Concept of Restoration

A twelfth-century merchant in France, captivated by the story of the rich young ruler, throws his money in the street and begins an itinerant life of preaching the Word to people who rarely hear gospel preaching. Thousands of fifteenth-century men, women, and children to whom Communion in both kinds has been prohibited trek up steep mountain slopes in the Czech lands to hear the gospel proclaimed and to receive the Lord's Supper. A sixteenth-century former priest huddles with like-minded friends in a small house in Zurich and cries out to be baptized with true Christian baptism, even though he knows what he will suffer because of it. Small groups of men and women interested in spiritual renewal and holy living gather in unauthorized meetings throughout seventeenth-century Germany to read and discuss the Bible for themselves. An eighteenth-century band of religious refugees committed to prayer and living out the teachings of Scripture experiences a revival that leads to an explosion of mission work. After an in-depth personal study of biblical baptism, an eighteenth-century Scottish preacher holding a gospel meeting in London asks the Baptists there to immerse him into Christ.

What do these stories have in common?

Each is representative of multitudes of people throughout history who, in their search for truth as revealed in the Word of God, concluded that within the church of their day, things were not as God intended. Indeed, not only did they conclude that things were not as they should be, but they were also willing to do something about it—even at the cost of great personal sacrifice. They hoped to bring about spiritual renewal among God's people.

This impulse was nothing new. As early as the second century, the Montanist movement, known variously as the New Prophesy or the Phrygian heresy, had arisen, calling the church back to a more rigorous morality and the apostolic power of the Holy Spirit. Again, in the fourth century, the Donatist movement arose to challenge what it perceived as an illegitimate partnership between church and state and a corrupt priesthood, even rejecting the validity of sacraments performed by unworthy priests. Both of these movements represented efforts to renew the church, and they sprang from the impulse that true Christianity was what most closely imitated the teachings and practices of the apostles.[1]

This volume will trace several later movements of renewal that sprang up throughout Europe from the late medieval period to the eighteenth century. In every case, these movements were seen as a threat to the establishment churches of their time, whether it was the Roman Catholic Church or, for example, the established Lutheran or Presbyterian state churches. These movements, like the Montanists and Donatists before them, were usually even considered heretical. To quote Carlos M. N. Eire, "One of the traits shared by all those who were branded as heretics was their belief that the Catholic Church [established church] could not reform itself, or was corrupt beyond hope."[2] While it could be argued that this belief may have been misguided, each of these groups drew attention to aspects of the church in which they believed correctives were in order. Sometimes these movements focused their renewal efforts on ecclesiology, particularly in terms of church organization and its authority. Other times the focus was related to doctrine or practice. Still other times the focus was moral in terms of Christian living and mission. Often, the focus was some combination of these various concerns.

While each movement discussed in this book called the church to renewal, most of them can best be classified in some sense as restoration or restitution movements.[3] Doug Foster explained that "restorationism assumes a sharp break between the way things are now and the way things used to be or ought to be." He continued, "All restoration movements, however, seek to make things 'right again.' True Christian restoration focuses on areas in which the church has departed from its intended ideal in belief and practice . . . [and] restoration movements often call for radical change."[4] According to Leonard Verduin, "Restitutionists sought to recover the Church of the New Testament; their ambition, early and late, was to return the Church of Christ to its New Testament format."[5]

Sometimes the line between reformation and restoration is blurry. What distinguishes restoring from reforming? Perhaps the metaphor of a stream can be useful in distinguishing between the two. The reformer believes that the stream has become polluted, and it is therefore necessary to try to purify the water. The restorationist believes that the water has become so polluted that it cannot be purified. The only way to restore pure water is to go back to the original spring. In other words, the reformer tries to purify or reform the existing church, whereas the restorationist tries to restore the original church. Often, for the restorationist, this "polluting of the stream" or "fall" occurred with the union of church and state that began during the time of Constantine the Great. Thus, one distinction between reformers and restorationists has been that reformers, such as Martin Luther, Ulrich Zwingli, John Calvin, and John Knox, have generally accepted a concept of Christian society that assumed cooperation between church and state, and they relied on civil authorities and legal measures to advance their reforms.[6] In other words, they worked from within the establishment. Restorationists, such as, for example, the Anabaptists (Chapters Seven and Eight), Schwarzenau Brethren (Chapter Nine), and Glasites/Sandemanians (Chapter Ten), on the other hand, tended to reject the role of the state in church affairs and reform, and this often put them outside the establishment and on the fringe of society.[7]

It has also been claimed that those known as reformers tended to focus their efforts on a return to doctrinal purity but gave less emphasis to the actual life of the believer, whereas restorationists insisted on both doctrinal purity as well as purity of life, such that "the idea of restitution is a return to the lifestyle as well as to the doctrine of the apostolic church."[8] Certainly, several movements discussed below, such as, for example, the Waldensians (Chapter Two), the Unity of the Brethren (Chapter Five), evangelical Anabaptists, and Pietists (Chapter Nine), gave significant emphasis to the moral life of the disciple, and by so doing offered a critique of what they viewed as the moral laxness of the established church. A point of discussion for readers of this text might be whether, and to what degree, each of the movements portrayed represent a restorationist versus a reformationist approach to church renewal and where there might be overlap between the two concepts.

There have been objections to or critiques of the whole concept of restoration as a valid enterprise. For example, there is the charge that because restorationists desire to return the church to a supposed primitive ideal, there is a loss of a sense of historical connection to all that has happened since the time of the early church, which produces among restorationists a sense of "historylessness."[9] Certainly, this has been the case with some restorationists. For example, many Waldensians had the mistaken historical notion that their movement originated in the time of Constantine and survived in an unbroken line until the Middle Ages. "Historylessness" is not, however, a necessary component of restorationism. Many restorationists have been keen students of the history of the church and its development, thereby discovering "truths" that need to be restored. For example, the Hussites (Chapters Three and Four) were aware that the practice of Communion in one kind (withholding the cup from the laity) was a relatively late development in the history of the church, and they sought to restore the earlier apostolic practice of Communion in both kinds. The Unity of the Brethren theologian Luke of Prague was well versed in both the early church fathers and the scholastic theologians. Several of the Anabaptist leaders knew the ancient church fathers well and referred to their writings. Restorationists must learn to take history seriously if they wish to distinguish between spiritually healthy developments in the life of the church and developments within the church that represent unhealthy departures from the ancient practice or belief of the church.[10]

Another objection to the restorationist approach is that restorationists are inevitably schismatic.[11] Given the propensity of non-restorationist groups to divide, this may not be a fair critique; at least, it is not something that is unique to restorationists.[12] Nevertheless, if restorationists wish to be serious about obedience to Jesus, they certainly must take seriously his call to unity (John 17:21–23). Having said that, it must be admitted, and we shall see, however, that many restorationists have been schismatic, divisive, and sectarian in both their approach and tone. Schism has frequently occurred when restorationists have come to believe that their approach is the only valid expression of Christian faith and practice. However, it must also be remembered that, in many cases, restorationists did not intend to be schismatic but were given the unfortunate choice of either violating their conscience or being expelled from the establishment churches of their time. On the other hand, it is also important to remember that many restorationists, such as the Unity of the Brethren, many Pietists, and the Haldane brothers (Chapter Ten), have envisioned their program as a means for achieving Christian unity. As Everett Ferguson has noted, a failure to fully implement an ideal does not in and of itself invalidate the ideal.[13]

A third objection to the restoration approach is that, due to various factors of historical development, a restoration of the primitive church is simply neither desirable nor possible. This objection is often based on the understanding that the goal of restoration is to reproduce in modern times an anachronistic copy of the primitive church. Although there have been some restorationists who have contributed to this understanding, if this is the goal, it is neither desirable nor possible.[14] Rather than an anachronistic copy of the primitive church, the proper goal of restoration is to restore the ideals that God intended for his church. Of course, this approach does not assume that such an ideal ever existed in any actual New Testament congregation. It is an aspiration to aim for. In the words of Gary Holloway and Doug Foster, restorationists "want to be the kind of church that the first century churches *should have been*."[15]

Ferguson has provided a cogent defense of the restoration principle and has demonstrated that restoration is intellectually reasonable: (1) It has a theological basis in the concept of authoritative revelation. (2) It has historical justification as a recurring motif throughout Christian history. (3) Its implementation is practical—that is, it can be attempted without requiring instruction in any particular denomination's specific doctrine. (4) Its plea can be ecumenical, taking positions that stand on the undivided ground of historic Christianity.[16] The assumption of this volume is that while there may be legitimate concerns regarding faulty approaches to restoration, the enterprise in itself is worthy of consideration, and we certainly have something to learn from those who have attempted it.

Because restoration movements have tended to operate from the outside and have even been persecuted by the establishment, they have often been seen as mere footnotes to the main story of Christian history. John Howard Yoder addressed this when he asked, "Is restitution a story of its own or merely a recurrent recalcitrant note to the main story?"[17] He maintained that professional historians, trained in the mainstream, tend to see restorationist movements as side notes to the more important events and figures shaping the history of the church, but he pointed out that some others have seen these movements as making a significant contribution to the story.[18] Alfred DeGroot pointed out that the restoration principle "appears in all religions and ages," and Stephen Lawson recognized the "ubiquity of this method of renewal throughout Christian history."[19] Jarold K. Zeman had already provided an answer to Yoder's question when, regarding restorationists, he claimed that "the motif of renewal . . . serves as the organizing principle of the unfolding of the story of the Church."[20] Although few would likely agree with Zeman, this volume suggests that his claim is worth considering.

The approach of this volume is intentionally more narrative and descriptive than analytical, and it does not attempt to plow new ground in research or advance new arguments. Each of the movements addressed in this volume are themselves the subjects of vast amounts of scholarly material, and much of that material has been consulted. Many of those works are noted or listed in the bibliography. The debates that occupy the energies of scholars, however, are not likely to interest the novice. Instead, the aim of this book is to collect and make available to the reader the stories and aims of several minority groups in one volume and perhaps to instill curiosity for further study. The method pursued in this volume is to first provide a narrative overview of each movement, highlighting important persons and events, followed by an introduction of important teachings and emphases of each movement, and concluding by suggesting some of the enduring legacies of each. Although this volume is generally sympathetic to the aims of these movements, it also draws attention to some of the weaknesses with which these movements struggled.

There have been those who, committed to the ideas of a fall of the church and a faithful minority that has always survived and managed to keep the "true faith" alive, have attempted to trace an unbroken chain of minority groups back from the present to the apostolic age.[21] From a historical perspective, these attempts are doomed to failure. Nevertheless, without suggesting genetic links between them, we shall see some interesting connections and intersections between the various movements discussed in this book. For example, the Waldensians influenced and were influenced by the Taborites and the Unity of the Brethren. The Unity of the Brethren were in many ways the spiritual heirs of the Taborites and were the spiritual forerunners of the Moravian Brethren. Several Anabaptist groups had contacts with the Unity of the Brethren and influenced Pietistic groups such as the Schwarzenau Brethren. The Pietists influenced the Moravian Brethren and the eighteenth-century evangelical missions movement of which the Haldane brothers became a part.[22] The early leaders of the Scotch Baptists were defectors from the Glasites and influenced the Haldanes. In pointing out connections and intersections, however, it would be inaccurate to draw the conclusion that these movements led one to another in any sort of unbroken genetic chain. In most cases, they did not.

Our survey calls attention to four significant points that become apparent when considering these movements. The first is that although each of these movements was attempting to be faithful to God's revealed truth, the movements were dissimilar in significant ways. Each movement was particularly shaped by its own unique historical context, which determined against what the movement was reacting and what would be the particular emphases of each movement. Thus, for example, the Waldensians were reacting against what they perceived as an incompetent clergy and a neglect of preaching, the Pietists were reacting against what they perceived as stale and lifeless doctrinal minutiae, and Scottish restorationists were reacting against the concept of the National Covenant. Taborites were reacting against what they perceived as illegitimate distinctions between clergy and laity that manifested themselves in practices such as Communion in one kind, while Anabaptists reacted against a concept of the church that encompassed all society in ways that exploited commoners.

A second and related point is that although various restorationists might believe and even claim that their movement was the only visible manifestation of the true church, our survey will illustrate that this is not tenable. No single movement fully grasps all the truth of God's will, and each has its own weaknesses and blind spots. Many restorationist groups have a tendency to be, from the perspective of outsiders, idiosyncratic in some of the practices they emphasize, such as infant Communion, foot washing, the holy kiss, communitarian living, triune immersion, or the casting of lots. Although restorationists tend to assume that God's truth as it is revealed in Scripture is plain and clear to all who read it honestly, the inability of restorationists to convince a majority of other believers and the reality of schisms among restorationists themselves demonstrate that Scripture may not always be as clear as restorationists assume.

A third point that becomes apparent from a study of these movements is that restoration is an ongoing process rather than an accomplished fact. No restoration movement begins with all of its conclusions already in place. Instead, each movement evolves,[23] both as its circumstances change and as its leaders come to recognize additional biblical truths through further interaction with the Word of God. For example, it was only after significant controversy that the Unity of the Brethren concluded that the expectations of leaving urban centers and requiring nobles to give up their rights was going beyond the demands of the gospel. The practice of community of goods evolved in several different ways among various Anabaptist groups. It took the Moravians several years to recognize their role in world missions, and it took the Haldanes time to conclude that weekly Communion and believers' immersion were proper New Testament practices.

A fourth point is that although there is significant dissimilarity between the various movements covered in this book, there is also sometimes a surprising similarity in many aspects of these movements. Everett Ferguson claimed, "There seems to be something about the nature of Christianity that nurtures the restitution motif among its adherents and something about the nature of the biblical record that produces churches of the same general type when the effort is made to take it as normative for church life."[24] Additionally, he identified several common characteristics of restorationist groups, including "believers' membership, separation from the world, discipline, the Great Commission, religious liberty, and mutual aid."[25] The astute reader will recognize several of these characteristics in the movements covered by this book.

Chapter One of this volume gives a brief description of the ways the medieval church had changed since its first-century beginnings. It particularly highlights issues that became important and against which the renewal movements treated in this book reacted. The chapters that follow are the heart of the volume and deal with specific renewal movements that, each in their own way, reacted against the religious establishment of their own time. In each case, the movement arose when men and women compared the church of their day with the church about which they read in Scripture and found the church of their day to be lacking. Believing that God's truth as revealed in Scripture would ultimately prevail, they called for renewal.

Chapters Two through Five deal with movements that originated prior to the sixteenth-century Reformation, though two of these movements ultimately connected with Protestantism in significant ways. Specifically, Chapter Two addresses the Waldensian movement that originated in the late twelfth century and then struggled to survive, often underground, until it joined forces with the sixteenth-century Reformed movement in Switzerland. Chapters Three and Four explore the fifteenth-century Bohemian or Czech "First Reformation."[26] Although this reformation is best known for the martyr John Hus, we will especially focus on the Taborite restoration movement. Chapter Five traces the tragic story of the Unity of the Brethren, a movement that sprang up in the mid-fifteenth century from the ashes of the Taborites and survived, in spite of severe persecutions, until its seventeenth-century demise that was largely a result of the Thirty Years' War.

Chapter Six addresses the major wings of the sixteenth-century reformations (Lutheran, Reformed, English, Scottish, and Catholic). Because these movements are generally more familiar than the other movements in this volume, and because these movements would not be classified as restoration movements per se, this volume treats them in only the most general terms, highlighting those aspects that are most relevant to the issues otherwise addressed in this volume. Nevertheless, the Reformation leaders of the sixteenth century, working in cooperation with the civil magistrates, also sought to achieve purity in the church by returning it to its intended ideal.

The remaining chapters introduce movements that became possible because of the Protestant Reformation. In many ways, these movements were reactions against it and the religious establishments it fostered. Chapters Seven and Eight trace the saga of various segments of the so-called radical reformers known as Anabaptists. Chapter Nine addresses the rise of Pietism, with particular emphasis on Pietistic offshoots, the little-known Schwarzenau Brethren, and the more renowned Renewed Unity of the Brethren, known more commonly as the Moravian Brethren. Chapter Ten wraps up our survey with three Scottish restoration movements, the Glasites/Sandemanians, the Scotch Baptists, and the Haldane movement, each of which originated in the eighteenth century. An afterword concludes with some general observations.

Each chapter includes items that invite the reader to think about, or discuss in a small group or classroom setting, aspects of each movement and to compare each with the other movements in the book.

Questions for Thought or Discussion

1. Why might each generation of Christians find itself in need of renewal?
2. How would you define *restoration*?
3. How would you distinguish between restoration and reformation?
4. What do you think of the objections to the restorationist approach and the responses to those objections?
5. What other objections and responses can you think of?
6. Do you think restoration is a valid enterprise? Why or why not?

NOTES

[1] Both movements were ultimately judged as heretical schismatics.

[2] Carlos M. N. Eire, *Reformations: The Early Modern World, 1450–1650* (New Haven, CT: Yale University Press, 2016), 60.

[3] The terms *restoration, restorationist,* and *restorationism* are interchangeable with *restitution, restitutionist,* and *restitutionism.*

[4] Douglas A. Foster, *Will the Cycle Be Unbroken? Churches of Christ Face the 21st Century* (Abilene, TX: Abilene Christian University Press, 1994), 177–78.

[5] Leonard Verduin, *The Reformers and Their Stepchildren* (Grand Rapids: Baker, 1980), 40.

[6] "The practical goal followed by all the great Reformers has always been to convince the holders of governmental authority to take in hand the reform of the church," Amedeo Molnár, in Giovanni Gonnet, "The Influence of the Sermon on the Mount upon the Ethics of the Waldensians of the Middle Ages," *Brethren Life and Thought* 35 (1990): 38. See also the discussion in William R. Estep, *The Anabaptist Story*, 3rd ed. (Grand Rapids: Eerdmans, 1996), 241–43.

[7] Jarold K. Zeman, "Restitution and Dissent in the Late Medieval Renewal Movements: the Waldensians, the Hussites and the Bohemian Brethren," *Journal of the American Academy of Religion* 44, no. 1 (1976): 26–27; cf. Gunnar Westin, *The Free Church Through the Ages*, trans. Virgil A. Olson (Nashville: Broadman, 1958), who demonstrates that this tendency has existed within the church since its inception. In some ways, the Taborite movement discussed in chapters Three and Four is an exception to this general rule. While the Taborites did operate outside the establishment, they also tried to enact a new establishment.

[8] Everett Ferguson, *The Early Church and Today,* vol. 2: *Christian Life, Scripture, and Restoration* (Abilene, TX: Abilene Christian University Press, 2014), 271.

[9] For example, "Primitivism rejects historical conditioning, claiming instead to bring the normative past into the present without historical mediation," and these approaches "remain historically incoherent and theologically catastrophic," Stephen D. Lawson, "Resisting the Primitivist Temptation," in *Scripture First: Biblical Interpretation that Fosters Christian Unity*, ed. Daniel B. Oden and J. David Stark (Abilene, TX; Abilene Christian University Press, 2020), 115, 117. Lawson acknowledges that restorationism and primitivism may be different, but he suggests that they both rely on the same approach to the past—"one that begins in purity and is followed by a subsequent fall into corruption, which is followed by the recent return to the pristine state of things," 6.

[10] In spite of his overall hostility to the primitivist/restorationist approach, as the title to his article suggests, Lawson, nevertheless, recognizes that as "a call to question the beliefs and practices of Christians in the present by judging them against ancient norms," it "is good and necessary" and "an essential part of the way that Christians should appeal to the past," Lawson, "Resisting," 104.

[11] Lawson points out that the sheer number of those groups who claim to have restored the pure church argues against the idea that any one of them has, "Resisting," 117–18.

[12] This is even a propensity of adherents of non-Christian religions as well (e.g., various sects of Judaism and Islam). Perhaps it is more of a human propensity than a propensity of any one particular religious approach. "Disagreement is as much a part of human experience as breathing. Religion is not exempt from this rule," Eire, *Reformations*, 62.

[13] Ferguson, *Early Church*, 259.

[14] For a critique of this approach to restoration, see, for example, Alfred T. DeGroot, *The Restoration Principle* (St. Louis: Bethany, 1960). DeGroot suggests that "a valid restorationism must take its rise, and create its formal expressions, in the realm of New Testament attitudes, ways of life, and spiritual convictions," 45.

[15] Gary Holloway and Doug Foster, *Renewing God's People: A Concise History of Churches of Christ* (Abilene, TX: Abilene Christian University Press, 2006), 10 (italics mine).

[16] Ferguson, *Early Church*, 261–66.

[17] John Howard Yoder, *The Priestly Kingdom* (Notre Dame, IN: University of Notre Dame Press, 1984), 132–33.

[18] Yoder, *Priestly Kingdom*, 133.

[19] DeGroot, *Restoration Principle*, 127; Lawson, "Resisting," 104.

[20] Zeman, "Restitution and Dissent," 7.

[21] Examples would include Gottfried Arnold, *Unpartheyische Kirchen- und Ketzerhistorien biss auf das jahr Christi 1688* (Frankfurt am Main: Thomas Fritschens sel. Erben, 1729); nineteenth-century Landmarkism; and to a lesser degree, the previously cited Gunnar Westin, *The Free Church Through the Ages*. See the discussion in Murray L. Wagner, *Petr Chelčický: A Radical Separatist in Hussite Bohemia* (Scottdale, PA: Herald Press, 1983), 47–48. On Landmarkism, see Richard T. Hughes and C. Leonard Allen, *Illusions of Innocence: Protestant Primitivism in America, 1630–1875* (Chicago: University of Chicago Press, 1988), 79–82, 92–101.

[22] On the connections between Pietism and the eighteenth-century evangelical missions, see James L. Gorman, *Among the Early Evangelicals: The Transatlantic Origins of the Stone-Campbell Movement* (Abilene, TX: Abilene Christian University Press, 2017).

[23] Indeed, sometimes the evolution is negative, such as, for example, when the Hussites determined that it was acceptable to take up arms to defend their cause.

[24] Ferguson, *Early Church*, 264.

[25] Ferguson, *Early Church*, 264. Not all of these characteristics were present in all the movements covered by this volume. Believers' membership in particular was not necessarily a characteristic of several of the movements covered—initially, the Unity of the Brethren was characterized by believers' membership, but later it accepted the baptism of infants into membership.

[26] The "First Reformation," which began more than one hundred years prior to Martin Luther, is a common term that Czechs and even scholars such as Thomas Fudge (*The Magnificent Ride: The First Reformation in Hussite Bohemia* [Brookfield, VT: Ashgate, 1998]) use to refer to the reform movement that preceded and included John Hus and his disciples. I will usually use the term *Czech Reformation*. The term *Bohemia* is from the Latin name of the western geographic region of the modern Czech Republic, sometimes now referred to as Czechia. I prefer to refer to this historical region as the Czech lands.

CHAPTER 1

SETTING THE STAGE

The Medieval Church and the Need for Reformation
"in Head and in Members"

By late medieval times, the church in Western Europe looked different from the one established in the first century. The monepiscopacy[1] that had become the norm by the end of the second century had developed into a complex hierarchy, and after the Great Schism of 1054 that permanently separated Eastern Orthodoxy from Roman Catholicism, the Roman Catholic Church held a virtual monopoly on faith in Western Europe. This church had developed into a sophisticated and highly structured organization that brooked no competition, and the church was also competing with the state for political power and influence. The bishop of Rome, known as the pope, functioned as the practical head of the church, and the College of Cardinals made up the body of the church. Although officially the pope functioned as Christ's vicar on earth, for the common person, the pope was not simply the vicar but the supreme leader. As such, it came to be considered heretical for anyone to question the headship of the pope. As a result of this highly developed hierarchy, there was a strong and clear distinction between clergy and laity. Only those who were ordained or were part of a recognized religious order could perform the functions and ministries of the church.

Over the centuries, a complex system of sacraments had developed.[2] A sacrament can be defined as a visible act by or through which the grace of God is conveyed to the person receiving the act. By the late medieval period, the Roman Catholic Church commonly recognized seven sacraments: baptism, confirmation, penance, Eucharist, extreme unction (final anointing), ordination, and marriage. The sacraments were controlled and administered by the clergy and became a source of great power for the church. Because the sacraments were the means of receiving God's grace and because they were accessible only through the clergy, the clergy held the keys to the kingdom and salvation. People believed this and respected it, and the sacraments became a means that elevated priests above the rest of society. Developments relating to the sacraments of baptism, the Eucharist, and penance became major issues against which several of the movements surveyed in this book were reacting, so it is necessary to go into some detail about them.

Baptism was the sacrament of incorporation into the church and was understood to be the point at which the recipient received forgiveness of sins. Since the time of Tertullian (c. 155–c. 240), infant baptism had been practiced, though it did not become common until the mid-third century.[3] By the fifth century, the linking of infant baptism to the doctrine of original sin caused infant baptism to become, with rare exceptions, the universal practice.[4] The practice of baptizing infants, however, caused baptism to become disassociated from faith and repentance. Another change in the practice of baptism was that the original practice, well-documented linguistically and archaeologically, of immersion, or burial in water, was gradually replaced by the practice of affusion—that is, pouring of water.[5]

Over the centuries, a number of changes had occurred in the celebration of the Eucharist as well.[6] These major changes had to do with the development of the Eucharist into the Holy Sacrifice of the Mass.[7] From early times, the elements of the Lord's Supper had been closely identified with Jesus's actual body and blood, and sacrificial language was often used to describe the ritual. By the late Middle Ages, Thomas Aquinas's (1225–74) understanding of the doctrine of transubstantiation was generally accepted, holding that the substance of bread and wine was changed mysteriously into the real substantial body and blood of Jesus, though still retaining the accidents or characteristics of bread and wine.[8] This change took place at the moment the priest elevated the host and pronounced the words of consecration. *Host* comes from the Latin word *hostia* and means *sacrifice*. This reflected the understanding that in the Mass, Jesus was literally being offered again as a propitiatory sacrifice, though in an "unbloody manner." Thus, because the elements of the Mass were really and mysteriously Jesus, it was considered not only permissible but also obligatory to offer worship to the elements.[9]

Another medieval change in eucharistic practice had to do with the reception of the elements themselves. Communion "in both kinds" (*sub utraque specie*) was the practice of receiving both the bread and the wine during the Eucharist, as had been the practice of the primitive church. Communion in one kind (*sub una specie*) was the receiving of only the bread. Since about the twelfth century, the common practice in the Roman Catholic Church had been to withhold the wine from the laity.[10] The priest could place the unleavened wafer,[11] transubstantiated into the body of Christ, directly on the tongue of the communicant, but with the wine, transubstantiated into the blood of Christ, it was a bit more complicated. There was always the danger that some of the blood might be spilled or trickle onto the floor and be stepped in, thus literally causing the sacrilege of trampling on the blood of Christ. A philosophical theory called concomitance, developed by Aquinas, provided a solution. The idea was that since the literal body and blood of Christ could not be separated one from the other, when the elements were transubstantiated, the whole Christ, body and blood, were contained in each of the elements. Thus, partaking of the part gave the benefit of partaking of the whole; the laity could be given only the bread and yet would still be receiving both body and blood, and this could be done without the risk of spilling the blood of Christ.[12] Because, however, the priests continued to drink from the chalice, this practice accentuated the difference between clergy and laity.[13]

Frequency of Communion was another way the Eucharist had changed by the Middle Ages. Although it was offered not only each Sunday but at other times as well, most people no longer received Communion every

Lord's Day. Ordinarily, before one could receive the Eucharist, one was required to submit to the sacrament of penance, which involved several steps. First, the sinner needed to feel contrition for his or her sin. Then the sinner would make private auricular confession of sin to the priest, who would pronounce absolution or forgiveness of sin and its guilt and prescribe some act of satisfaction that must be performed—for example, going on a pilgrimage or attending a certain number of Masses. Satisfaction was for the purpose of obtaining purification or remission of the temporal punishment demanded by the sin, while absolution removed the eternal punishment. Because penance was required before a person received the sacrament of Communion, and since most people chose to confess infrequently, this meant that most people rarely participated in the Lord's Supper, some even going for years without partaking. On the other hand, many people participated in a form of "spiritual or ocular Communion," that is, they gazed reverentially at the elevated host in order to receive spiritual benefit. Benefit could be gained from this practice precisely because of the belief that at the moment of the elevation of the host, the elements were transubstantiated into the body and blood of Christ. Thus, one was gazing not at bread and wine, but at Jesus himself. Moreover, this could be done without the risk of partaking unworthily, which was a matter of grave concern. The infrequency with which many people received the Eucharist was recognized as so problematic that the Fourth Lateran Council (1215) prescribed that every Catholic Christian should do penance and receive the Eucharist at least once a year.[14]

In the developing sacramental system, baptism was the sacrament for dealing with inherited sin and any other sin that might have been committed prior to baptism, and penance was the sacrament for dealing with post-baptismal sin. As mentioned, part of dealing with post-baptismal sin was the practice involved in penance of making satisfaction to erase the temporal penalty of sin. But what if a person who had received baptism and who had done penance had failed to make complete satisfaction for sin? The guilt of sin had been erased by the blood of Christ, but the temporal penalty had not yet been paid. Was that person saved or lost? In other words, how could a saved person who was not entirely pure enter into the eternal bliss of the presence of God? This conundrum was solved by the doctrine of purgatory. It seemed logical that before a person could come into the presence of God, he or she would have to be purified from any remaining taint caused by unsatisfied temporal penalties for sin. This would take place not in heaven or hell, but in a place of preparation—purgatory. In distinction from hell, which was a place of eternal suffering, purgatory was conceived of as a place of temporary suffering, where a soul could be purged and made ready to enter into heaven. A soul's time in purgatory, however, could be exceedingly long, even thousands or millions of years. The thought of spending many years in purgatory filled many a medieval mind with anxiety and terror.[15]

The church had also conceived of a way to reduce one's time in purgatory. Just as it was likely that most people had not fully paid the temporal punishment due for their sins, it was also certain that some people had done enough good things to create a surplus of merit beyond what they owed in terms of temporal punishment. For example, surely the apostles and some of the saints had a surplus of merit, and Christ himself had accumulated an infinite supply of merit. This led to the idea of a treasury of merit from which merit could be tapped to offset temporal penalties owed. By withdrawing from the treasury of merit, the church could grant indulgences, which was relief from temporal penalties owed due to sin. Not only that, but the church could also grant indulgences to people who had died and were already suffering in purgatory. Such indulgences could shorten one's time in purgatory or even release the soul from purgatory altogether. Church officials began to grant indulgences for the performance of various good works, such as going on a Crusade. In time, indulgences were also granted to people who had made significant gifts of alms to the church. Although it was not technically a correct understanding of what transpired, it would not be a great leap for a person to assume that by "purchasing" an indulgence, one could, in effect, "purchase" the forgiveness of sins.[16]

In addition to changes regarding the Lord's Supper mentioned above, medieval worship had changed significantly in other ways from that of the early church. Much of the simplicity that characterized the early Christian assemblies had been replaced by a precisely structured and complex system of ritual. The order of the liturgy was carefully prescribed and was conducted only by the clergy. Proper Christian worship in the medieval period did not even require the presence of the laity in order for it to take place! In the West, the liturgy was usually conducted in Latin, a language that few of the laity could understand. Preaching often received little emphasis, and since few could understand the Latin sermons anyway, this is understandable.[17] In addition, preaching could only be done by those who had been expressly authorized by the local bishop. Because so few people could understand the sermons and the other phrases of the liturgy, many people relied on the imagery that came in the form of statues (or icons in the East) for their understanding of biblical stories. Often, people venerated these statues and images, believing that the saint depicted could intercede directly with God. Clerical vestments were an aspect of the ancient imperial court protocol that was incorporated into Christian worship. These were the special robes the priests were required to wear in order to properly conduct the worship; like other practices, the robes helped emphasize the distinction between clergy and laity. A fairly late addition to Christian assemblies in the West, though never in the East, was that of instrumental accompaniment (usually organs) to the singing. Like other changes in Christian liturgical practice, organs also were borrowed from the imperial court ceremonials of an earlier time. They do not appear to have been used regularly in the liturgy of the church until around the thirteenth century.[18] Choirs were incorporated into the music of worship, which meant that the regular attendees had little occasion to join in the singing themselves. These and other changes resulted in a worship atmosphere that was shrouded in mystery and in which the laity were, in effect, simply observers rather than participants.

The medieval understanding of Christian life was another area of church life that had undergone significant change. Because, in the medieval world, membership in the Roman Catholic Church coincided with membership in society, there was no longer much sense of the Christian life as being that of aliens and strangers in the world. After all, "everyone" was a Christian by virtue of the fact that, under normal circumstances, shortly after birth everyone would have been baptized. The idea of Christendom or Christian society played an important role in how people viewed discipleship. Of course, it was obvious that not everyone lived, nor could be expected to live, according to the demands of the New Testament in terms of ethics and morality. This led to the common acceptance of the idea that the actual ethical demands of the gospel—for example, the Sermon on the Mount—were not for the everyday Christian but were for a special class of Christian—the religious, that is, those in holy orders. Or another understanding was that many of the teachings of Scripture were simply "counsels" that one could take or leave rather than commands that one was obliged to obey. The common person could satisfy his or her religious obligations not by living an actual life of discipleship but by receiving the sacraments. Thus, for many medieval Christians, ritual became far more important than actual discipleship or morality in determining one's status before God. A life of holiness was no longer the expectation for the day-to-day Christian. Not only was holiness not expected much of everyday Christians, but there was immorality even among the clergy. For example, in principle, the ideal of clerical celibacy was honored, but what "celibacy" meant in practice was abstinence from marriage, not abstinence from sexual relations, and many clergymen kept concubines by whom they had numerous children.[19]

Additionally, by the later medieval period, other than along the borders of Christendom, much of the missionary commitment that had characterized the early Christian centuries had waned, since "everyone" was already Christian. There were still some vestiges of missionary work to the "heathen," such as the work of the Franciscans, but the form of mission that involved the most people in the Middle Ages was that of participating in a Crusade.

The Medieval Mendicant Orders

As people in the Middle Ages came to recognize that much about the church did not seem to be the way it ought to be, there were various efforts at renewal. Some of these efforts, such as those of the Bogomils or Cathars (also known as Albigensians), would have been judged heretical from any standard Christian or biblical perspective. Others, such as those of the Waldensians or John Hus and his followers, were seen as heretical primarily because they did not submit to the Roman Catholic Church and its hierarchical authority, even though their theology was technically "orthodox." Within monastic movements, there were periodic attempts at renewal. For example, the monastery at Cluny in eastern France led a major monastic renewal during the eleventh century, and the order of Cistercians led an important twelfth-century renewal movement.[20] Other groups, such as the great mendicant orders like the Dominicans and Franciscans, were embraced by the Roman Catholic Church and accomplished much good within the bounds in which they were allowed to operate. Unlike traditional monasticism, the mendicants were not restricted to living in monasteries, but they were expected to preach among the people. Three forces were probably at work in the rise of the mendicant orders. First, they were in many ways a reaction against the unauthorized Waldensian and Cathar movements. Second, they satisfied the great need for preaching among the people. Third, they fulfilled a deep spiritual longing among many for a life of "apostolic poverty" without the isolation that came from monastic life.

The most important of these new orders were the Franciscans, the Dominicans, the Carmelites, and the Augustinians. All of these groups were interested in spiritual renewal, but they all sought that renewal within the bounds of the Roman Catholic Church. Due to space limitations, as an example of a renewal movement that Roman Catholicism considered legitimate, let us give attention here only to the most popular mendicant order, the Franciscans.

Francis (d. 1226) was born in Assisi, Italy, in the winter of 1182–83 to Peter and Pica Bernardone.[21] His parents, having become wealthy in the cloth trade, were able to send Francis to the St. George Parish School near their home. Francis was educated to be a successful merchant like his father, but he was known for being kind and generous, often giving food to the poor from his own family's table.

When Francis was about twenty years old, he enlisted to fight in the army of Assisi in its struggle against Perugia. Assisi was defeated, and Francis was taken prisoner for about a year, during which time his health was greatly weakened. Nevertheless, Francis impressed his fellow prisoners by remaining joyful and rarely complaining. Finally, Francis was ransomed by his father and returned home. Once he regained his strength, Francis again enlisted in the military, still hoping to find the proverbial fame and fortune that such a career might bring. However, on his way to the military encampment, he had a vision in which he was instructed to return to Assisi.

Francis obeyed the instruction of the vision and returned to determine what the next steps would be.

Francis began spending a great deal of time in prayer, and as he did so, his calling began to become clear. After hearing a sermon from Matthew 10:1–13 in which Jesus sent out his apostles instructing them to take nothing with them, and in spite of opposition from his father, Francis began the life of a wandering hermit, going about attempting to do good to those he met. Soon, three other young men joined Francis, and they began to go out preaching about the kingdom of God and attempting to convert the world. Their message of poverty and proclamation was attractive to others, and their group grew to twelve. Francis and his eleven companions then went to Rome in order to receive papal approval for their new mission. Eventually, in 1210, Pope Innocent III approved the new Order of the Friars Minor (*fratres minores*), and in 1215, at the Fourth Lateran Council, he announced them as an existing order.[22]

In addition to the young men who were attracted to Francis and his way of life, by 1212, two sisters from Assisi, Clare and Agnes, had chosen to follow the example of Francis and take up a life of poverty and discipleship. Eventually, their mother, Ortolana, and a third sister, Beatrice, joined them, and the movement developed into the Poor Clares, a female branch of the Franciscan movement known as the Second Order. Instead of serving in mendicant ministry, however, the women lived as nuns in convents and were served by friars acting as their chaplains. Clare wrote a rule for her order, which became the first order written by a woman to receive papal approval.[23]

The order grew rapidly, and in 1217, at Porziuncola, the Friars Minor, or Franciscans as they came to be called, held their important fraternal gathering known as a chapter. These meetings later took place regularly and provided an opportunity for the friars to get to know one another, report on how God had been working in their lives, encourage one another, and pray together. At the Chapter of 1217, the Franciscans made the decision that the order would begin to attempt mission work, in which they became heavily involved, often to Muslims; the first five Franciscan martyrs died while attempting to spread the gospel to Muslims of Morocco. Francis himself went to Egypt in 1219 and met with Sultan Melek-el-Kamil.

Unfortunately, this was during the time of the Fifth Crusade, so there was little opportunity for actual evangelism. Wherever he went, however, Francis was known for his gentleness and his message of peace based on Jesus Christ. For Francis, there was no difference between proclaiming redemption and proclaiming peace.[24]

An important phenomenon related to the growing popularity of the Franciscan Order was the development of an order for laypersons, both men and women, known as the Brothers and Sisters of Penance, or the Third Order. This order allowed the laity to minister with the friars and participate in a life of prayer, fasting, worship, and devotion while still marrying, remaining with their families, and going about their everyday work. Because of the large number of people who chose this vocation, the so-called Third Order gave the Franciscans significant influence.

The Franciscans were not interested in questions related to the reforming of the organization, worship, or doctrine of the church, but they were interested in calling people to lives of devoted discipleship, which is their enduring legacy.

Prelude to the Sixteenth-Century Reformations

In the fourteenth century, Europe was shaken by the Hundred Years' War and the outbreak of the plague. In the same century, the church was unsettled by the so-called Avignon Papacy, brought about when, in 1309, the weak French pope, Clement V (1305–14), moved the seat of the papacy from Rome to Avignon, where it remained until 1377. During this almost seventy-year period, all of the popes were French, and they were all under the influence of the French kings.[25] For many people throughout Europe, the control of the papacy by the French monarchs was an unsatisfactory state of affairs.

What was merely an unsatisfactory state of affairs developed into a full-blown crisis in 1377, when Pope Gregory XI (1370–78) returned to Rome and suddenly died. With the Roman populace demanding that the cardinals elect an Italian pope, the cardinals elected Urban VI (1378–89). Four months later, however, twelve of the sixteen cardinals, safely away from Rome, declared Urban's election invalid because the election had been held under duress and the threat of mob violence. They held another election and elected Clement VII (1378–94), who promptly returned to Avignon. This marked the beginning of the Great (Western) Schism, with two men claiming to be the legitimate pope. Europe was divided in loyalty between the two competing popes, as each monarch chose, often along political lines, to which pope he would give his support.[26]

It was in the context of both the Avignon Papacy and the Great (Western) Schism that the English reformer John Wyclif (1325[?]–84) came on the scene. Wyclif, sometimes referred to as "the Morning Star of the Reformation," advocated several positions that became controversial. For example, he believed that God, as the supreme Lord, granted possessions and powers, whether civil or ecclesiastical, to rulers as stewardships, held only on condition of faithful service. Those church officials living in mortal sin therefore forfeited their claims. He taught that Christ, rather than the pope, is the head of the church, thus rejecting the absolute authority of the papacy. Wyclif believed that Scripture was the highest authority for Christians in matters of faith and morals and that everything in the church not supported by Scripture was a human innovation. He also opposed the sale of indulgences and rejected the theory of transubstantiation, replacing it with a view known as *remanence*, holding that the bread and wine remained in the consecrated elements while the body and blood of Christ were received by faith. Wyclif was also instrumental in the translation of the Bible into English. Though church authorities eventually condemned twenty-four propositions from Wyclif's works, they were unable to prosecute him personally, and he died peacefully following a stroke suffered while celebrating the Mass. Wyclif's followers, called Lollards, continued to propagate his ideas for generations after his death. In the fifteenth century, however, Wyclif's influence would also be felt in the Czech lands of Central Europe, to which we shall return.[27]

In the meantime, people were anxious that the problem of the schism be resolved and that unity be restored to the church. Concerned theologians, such as Cardinal Pierre d'Ailly (1350–1420) and his disciple and fellow cardinal Jean de Gerson (1363–1429), advocated that papal authority should be subject to the authority of a general council of the church, which could bring about needed reform of the church "in head and members."[28] By this, they meant reform in the papacy and clerical hierarchy. This idea of the church being governed by general councils with authority over the pope came to be known as conciliarism. Under the leadership of the cardinals, several important councils met during the fifteenth century. The first was held in Pisa in 1409, but it simply resulted in three men claiming the papacy. Although the Council of Constance was ultimately able to resolve the schism with the election of Martin V (pope, 1417–31), his successor, Eugenius (pope, 1431–47), had a falling out with the Council of Basel, at the conclusion of which the pope's authority was once more firmly established. In the words of Carlos M. N. Eire, "Conciliarism had flared up, suddenly, in a glorious display, much like a firework shot into the night sky. But it fizzled out just as quickly too, and along with it vanished its plan for ongoing reform."[29]

Questions for Thought or Discussion

1. What were some of the ways the medieval church differed from the early church?

2. What was the relationship between ritual and morality for many in the Middle Ages?

3. What were the emphases of the Franciscans and of Wyclif?

4. What were strengths and weaknesses of the Franciscans and of Wyclif?

5. What do you find particularly attractive about the Franciscans and Wyclif?

6. What lessons or applications can you draw from their efforts?

NOTES

[1] Rule by one bishop over an area or region, known as a diocese.

[2] For an excellent discussion of the medieval understandings of the sacraments, see Norman Tanner and Sethina Watson, "Least of the Laity: The Minimum Requirements for a Medieval Christian," *Journal of Medieval History* 32, no. 4 (2006): 395–423.

[3] Tertullian opposed the practice. See his *On Baptism* 18, cited in Everett Ferguson, *Early Christians Speak: Faith and Life in the First Three Centuries*, 3rd ed. (Abilene, TX: Abilene Christian University Press, 1999), 54–55.

⁴In discussions on the doctrine of original sin, a synod in Carthage in 418 ruled that infants should be baptized for the remission of sins.

⁵The simple sprinkling of water also became common. Thus, what had originally been an exceptional emergency procedure came to be the norm. It appears that affusion was not commonly practiced until at least the eighth century. See David N. Bell, *A Cloud of Witnesses: An Introduction to the Development of Christian Doctrine to AD 500*, rev. ed. (Collegeville, MN: Cistercian Publications, 2007), 198.

⁶An excellent discussion of medieval eucharistic practice is found in Amy Nelson Burnett, "The Social History of Communion and the Reformation of the Eucharist," *Past and Present* 211 (May 2011): 77–119.

⁷The origin of the term *Mass* is unclear, but it likely derives from the phrase "*ite missa est*," with which the priest dismissed the people at the end of the liturgical service. See Everett Ferguson, *Church History*, vol. 1: *From Christ to the Pre-Reformation*, 2nd ed. (Grand Rapids: Zondervan, 2013), 325.

⁸The term *transubstantiation* was used by the Fourth Lateran Council of 1215.

⁹See the *Catechism of the Catholic Church*, part two, "The Celebration of the Christian Mystery," 1322–1419, but especially 1367, accessed May 5, 2020, https://www.vatican.va/archive/ccc_css/archive/catechism/p2s2c1a3.htm.

¹⁰Ferguson, *Church History*, 432.

¹¹The church in the West had begun using unleavened bread sometime around the eighth or ninth century, and it was introduced in Rome in the eleventh century. In the East, leavened bread was used, often dipped in the wine. See John H. Erickson, "Leavened and Unleavened: Some Theological Implications of the Schism of 1054," *St. Vladimir's Theological Quarterly* 14, no. 3 (1970): 155–76; and C. E. Pocknee, "The Bread of the Eucharist," *Church Quarterly Review* 162 (1961): 59–62.

¹²Ferguson, *Church History*, 433.

¹³Burnett, "Social History," 85–90.

¹⁴Burnett, "Social History," 81–85; Tanner, "Least of the Laity," 408.

¹⁵Carter Lindberg, *The European Reformations*, 2nd ed. (Malden, MA: Wiley-Blackwell, 2010), 31. The idea of purgatory was sometimes biblically supported by reference, for example, to Matthew 5:26 or 1 Corinthians 3:13–15, but the most explicit passage was found in the Apocrypha, 2 Maccabees 12:38–45.

¹⁶On indulgences and popular understandings of them, see Carlos M. N. Eire, *Reformations: The Early Modern World, 1450–1650* (New Haven, CT: Yale University Press, 2016), 146–53.

¹⁷Though the Fourth Lateran Council of 1215 had encouraged local bishops to establish at least one school in each diocese in the hopes of improving priestly education and preaching in vernacular languages, this suggested reform was poorly implemented. For a discussion of priesthood in the Middle Ages, see Greg Peters, ed., *A Companion to Priesthood in the Middle Ages* (Boston: Brill, 2015).

¹⁸Ferguson, *Church History*, 372, 464. The Byzantine court used organs during court functions, but not during the liturgy, and had given organs to both Pippin III and to Charlemagne. Eventually, in the West, the organs made their way into the monasteries and then into the liturgy.

¹⁹Although concubinage was fairly common, most clergy appear to have respected their vows, Jonathan W. Zophy, *A Short History of Renaissance and Reformation Europe: Dances over Fire and Water*, 2nd ed. (Upper Saddle River, NJ: Prentice Hall, 1999), 27.

[20] Henri de Lubac noted that the desire of the medieval monasteries was to restore a life "according to the imitation of the Apostles" or "in the fashion of the primitive church," *Medieval Exegesis: The Four Senses of Scripture*, 2 vols., trans. Mark Sebanc and E. M. Macierowski (Grand Rapids: Eerdmans, and Edinburgh: T & T Clark, 1998, 2000), 2:148.

[21] A fascinating account of Francis's life written by his contemporaries is found in E. Gurney Salter, trans., *The Legend of Saint Francis by the Three Companions* (London: J. M. Dent & Co., 1902). I draw primarily from Gianmaria Polidoro, *St. Francis of Assisi* (Gorle, Italy: Velar, 2006).

[22] Their recognition as an existing order was important because after the decree of the council banning new religious orders, the only future outlet for renewal seemed to be heresy. See Jarold K. Zeman, "Restitution and Dissent in the Late Medieval Renewal Movements: the Waldensians, the Hussites and the Bohemian Brethren," *Journal of the American Academy of Religion* 44, no. 1 (1976): 8.

[23] Ferguson, *Church History*, 482.

[24] See Polidoro, *St. Francis*, 31–33.

[25] This era has also been known as the "Babylonian Captivity of the Papacy." Just as Israel was in captivity in Babylon for seventy years, so the papacy was in "captivity" in Avignon for almost seventy years.

[26] France and its allies supported the Avignon pope, while England, the Holy Roman Empire, and their allies supported the Roman pope—Eire, *Reformations*, 54.

[27] For a summary of Wyclif's views and career, see Eire, *Reformations*, 51–52.

[28] John D. Woodbridge and Frank A. James III, *Church History*, vol. 2: *From Pre-Reformation to the Present Day* (Grand Rapids: Zondervan, 2013), 45.

[29] Eire, *Reformations*, 62.

CHAPTER 2

"To Obey God Rather than Men"
The Waldensians

In many ways, the twelfth century was a time of religious fervor. It was ushered in by the Crusaders' conquest of Jerusalem in 1099, and it witnessed two additional Crusades to the Holy Land. The Cistercians, under Bernard of Clairvaux (1090–1153), led a significant monastic revival, and there was a burgeoning of houses for the Austin canons and the Premonstratensian canons. The twelfth century also brought educational developments that led to the founding of universities and what has been termed the "twelfth-century renaissance."[1] This was the age of great Scholastic scholars such as Anselm of Laon (d. 1117), Peter Abelard (1079–1142), Hugh of St. Victor (d. 1142), and Peter Lombard (1100–1160). There was also a growing idealization of the concept of "nakedly following the naked Christ"[2] in "apostolic poverty" and preaching in the vernacular language.

Valdes and the Early Spread of a Movement

It was in this context that, around 1170, a rich merchant of Lyon named Valdes or Waldo (1140[?]–1218[?]) went through a sudden conversion that led him to a radical new way of following Christ.³ As the story goes, Valdes was moved by the story of St. Alexis, who had given up everything, including his wife, to follow Jesus. Valdes asked a local member of the clergy the best way to ensure his salvation and was referred to Jesus's teaching to the rich young ruler to sell all he had and follow Jesus (Matt. 19:21). After arranging for his wife to live on the income from his properties and for his daughters to be placed in a cloister, Valdes sold his business and gave the proceeds to the poor. Supposedly, he threw some coins into the street, saying, "I am avenging myself upon these enemies of my life who have enslaved me, so that I cared more for gold pieces than for God and served the creature more than the Creator."⁴

Valdes persuaded two scribes to translate much, if not all, of the New Testament and sections of the Old Testament into the local language, and he soon gathered several followers who called themselves the Poor in Spirit, later becoming known by outsiders as the Poor of Lyon. He and his followers were convinced that the contemporary priesthood was morally deficient and not competent to preach the gospel.⁵ Sensing a call to remedy this through their own preaching, his followers went out preaching two by two, according to what they perceived to be the apostolic pattern. They became committed to two important principles: The Bible and its interpretation should be made known to the people in their own language, and no later than 1184, they were proclaiming that the Bible is the final authority for the Christian in faith and practice.⁶ A generation before the rise of the Dominican and Franciscan mendicant movements, Valdes's message of voluntary poverty and his challenge to become imitators of Christ and his apostles attracted a large number of followers, particularly from among the poor. The Waldensian movement, however, was not limited to the poor, ultimately reaching people of all social classes from both rural and urban areas.⁷

Valdes had every intention of remaining within the Roman Catholic Church. According to the practice of the church at the time, however, one could only preach with approval from the local bishop, and this Valdes and his followers did not have. In 1179, two representatives, including perhaps Valdes himself, went to Rome and attended the Third Lateran Council under Pope Alexander III, hoping to be granted permission to preach.

One of their examiners criticized these early Waldensians for assuming that "ancient times" were better than present times,[8] which probably indicates that, from the beginning, the Waldensians were looking to the early church as a corrective for what they saw as deficiencies in the church of their day. The result of their examination was that, absent the permission of their local authorities, their preaching was forbidden. At this point, the Poor of Lyon chose to obey God rather than men (Acts 5:29) and continued to preach.[9]

The following year, Valdes presented an orthodox profession of faith in which he affirmed, among other ideas, the Trinity, the creeds of the church, the Old and New Testaments, the incarnation and human physical nature of Christ, his death and resurrection, and the bodily resurrection at final judgment. In addition, Valdes rejected the teachings of the Cathar heretics.[10] Not only that, but Waldensians also continued to learn and use the Apostles' Creed throughout their history. In other words, as far as their beliefs went, Waldensians were not heretical. Nevertheless, at the Council of Verona in 1184, the movement was formally condemned and placed under eternal anathema, resulting in official persecution.[11] Then, an edict from about the year 1194 decreed punishment (confiscation of property and prosecution) for anyone giving Waldensians shelter, food, or drink or even listening to them. Because the Waldensians were defying church authority, they could be punished in any form other than death or mutilation. Three years later, burning was decreed for those convicted of the Waldensian heresy.[12]

In 1208, Pope Innocent III (1160/61–1216) declared a Crusade in southern France against the Cathars, also known as the Albigensians. The Crusade began in 1209 and led to fighting that lasted until 1229. Although the Waldensians were strongly opposed to the teachings of the Cathars, the Crusaders did not bother to distinguish between the two, and many Waldensians suffered persecution and martyrdom during this period. In 1215, the Fourth Lateran Council issued another decree officially condemning Waldensianism as heresy.[13]

In spite of persecution, or perhaps because of it,[14] the Waldensians spread rapidly throughout Europe, reaching almost all levels of society. Much of their growth came from their conviction that preaching was the duty of every Christian, and in the words of Amedeo Molnár, "He who does not freely proclaim the truth is a traitor to the truth."[15] On the other hand, Valdes himself resisted efforts to organize as a separate church, and for much of their history, Waldensians often continued to accept the sacraments from the Roman priests. This practice was as much for practical reasons as for theological ones. As long as they were continuing to attend services and receive the sacraments in Catholic churches, they might avoid drawing obvious attention to themselves as religious nonconformists.[16] On the other hand, persecution drove the Waldensians to reconsider their relationship to the church and ultimately to develop their own theological positions, often in direct opposition to and in rejection of Roman Catholic teaching.[17]

As the movement spread, it came into contact with a similar-thinking group in northern Italy called the Humiliati or the Poor of Lombardy.[18] After some initial contacts, six representatives of each group met in May 1218 in Bergamo, Italy, to seek grounds for unity between the two movements. Although the movements had much in common, there were also significant differences.[19] For example, those from France considered evangelism to be the most important priority, whereas those from Italy considered the life of the community to be the most important. Those from Lyon favored electing leaders for specific terms, while those from Lombardy believed that leaders should be elected for life. Both groups, however, agreed that they were not dependent on the Roman Catholic apostolic succession for their leadership. The French rejected work as means of earning a living, believing that it would distract from preaching, while the northern Italians believed work performed in the context and for the benefit of the community was important and worthy of respect. As it turned out, with increasing persecution, even the French Waldensians eventually had to adopt various trades simply to avoid detection. Those from Lyon were more lenient toward divorce, believing it to be permissible for a just cause (remember that Valdes himself had left his wife) and even sometimes without the consent of a spouse. The Lombards held that divorce was permissible only with the consent of both spouses or on grounds of fornication or adultery. Regarding the sacraments, the Poor of Lyon generally accepted the doctrine of transubstantiation and practiced infant baptism, though they disagreed among themselves on some points regarding baptism, but the Poor of Lombardy questioned transubstantiation and apparently baptized adults. Additionally, prior to Bergamo, at least some of the Lombards celebrated their own Eucharist. While those of Lyon accepted the Roman church hierarchy and seemed more interested in inner renewal, those of Lombardy rejected the Roman church hierarchy and advocated more open separation from it, including a Donatistic rejection of the validity of sacraments performed by unworthy priests.

Although the two sides were unable to come to full agreement on all issues, they did reach agreement in some areas, especially in affirming pacifism and in recognizing the need for calling ministers from among the community instead of depending on those ordained by the Roman church. A question remained as to whether baptism must be performed exclusively by a priest or whether a layman could legitimately perform the rite. The Lombards received assurances from the French that they would not be forced to practice anything for which they could not find clear biblical directives. This implied a willingness to reexamine Scripture and give up even well-established traditions or customs if they were discovered to be unsupported by the Bible. In other words, renewal was to be an ongoing process. Ultimately, as both groups continued to spread throughout Europe, even those from Lombardy came to be known as Waldensians.

As the two groups spread, each continued its own unique emphases. Thus, although the connections between various Waldensian groups is not always certain, we can recognize at least three major groupings of Waldensians in the thirteenth century. Throughout France and north of the Alps were those who generally maintained the emphases of the original Poor of Lyon;[20] south of the Alps in Italy were those who generally maintained the emphases of the Poor of Lombardy; and north of the Alps, but spreading eastward through Germany and central Europe, were those who most often maintained the emphases of the Poor of Lombardy.

An "Underground" Movement

Eventually, persecution at the hands of such inquisitors as Conrad of Marburg (c. 1180–1233),[21] Moneta of Cremona (d. 1260),[22] Bernard Gui (c. 1261–1331), and Peter Zwicker (d. 1403) drove the Waldensians underground, and, at times, entire communities migrated together from one area to another. Zwicker was probably the greatest opponent of Waldensians, serving as inquisitor for more than ten years. His goal seems to have been to win converts rather than to create martyrs, and he brought hundreds back into the Catholic fold, primarily through persuasion instead of torture. The constant pressure, rejection, and persecution by the church led to the Waldensians' view of the Roman Catholic Church as fallen. They dated this fall of the church to the so-called "Donation of Constantine," when "poison" was poured into the church as Pope Sylvester accepted the wealth and temporal authority the emperor Constantine bestowed on it.[23] This view of the church as fallen led, in turn, to the reevaluation and radicalization of Waldensian beliefs, including the necessity of some sort of organization. As time passed, they developed a complete underground structure, becoming, in effect, a church within the church that in some places rivaled the Roman Catholic Church.[24]

One consequence of the persecution was that from the mid-thirteenth century to the mid-fourteenth century, Waldensians in many places lost much of their evangelistic and missionary fervor and began to turn inward, withdrawing into secrecy and clandestine activities.[25] The preachers were no longer able to proclaim the gospel openly in public, and the rapid spread of the movement came to an end; in many cases, the Waldensians became a movement simply passed down from parents to children and from generation to generation rather than growing through reaching new converts. Preaching was now done mainly in the homes of friends and to select acquaintances. While secrecy, particularly that of the traveling preachers, may have seemed to be necessary for survival, it also damaged the credibility of the movement. After all, how could Waldensians claim to possess the truth and yet keep it secret? Their opponents argued that if their message really were true, they had an obligation to proclaim it publicly, no matter the risk, and that their preachers had an obligation to remain with their flock in time of persecution rather than flee at the first sign of the inquisitors.[26] This is not to say, however, that Waldensians completely gave up on evangelism. Although the brethren themselves no longer openly sought out new converts, followers would identify potential converts, and once they had discovered someone with true interest, they would introduce the potential convert to the brethren, who would then proceed with the teaching.[27]

Another difficulty faced by the Waldensians in the fourteenth century had to do with their inaccurate historical memory of their origins as described in a document referred to as the "Book of the Elect." This document claimed that the Waldensian movement dated from the time of the Donation of Constantine, when Pope Sylvester accepted the "poison" of wealth and power poured into the church but a companion of his did not and broke away to lead a church committed to the ideals of poverty. Allegedly, this group had then survived eight hundred years until the time of "Peter" Valdes, himself an ordained priest, who rose up to lead and spread the movement.[28] Waldensian opponents could easily demonstrate the falsity of the claims of this document and thus were effective at winning many converts back to the Roman Catholic Church.

In the fifteenth century, Waldensians in the Czech lands came into contact with the Hussite movement. The extent to which the Waldensians influenced the Hussites and to which the Hussites influenced the Waldensians is a complex question, but it is likely that both movements mutually influenced each other to some degree. Particularly significant is the interrelationship between the Waldensians and the more radical Taborite branch of the Hussite movement.[29] One important Waldensian leader at this time was the German Friedrich Reiser (1402[?]–58). Reiser, whose father had been a Waldensian follower, began training in Freiburg, Switzerland, to become a Waldensian itinerant preacher in the early 1420s and began his actual preaching ministry around 1423. Around 1429, he visited the Czech town of Tabor and then moved to Prague to explore a relationship with the Hussites, primarily with their more radical Taborite wing. He was hoping for unity between the Waldensians and Hussites. While in Prague, Reiser learned Latin from a priest and received a German copy of the New Testament that he, in turn, copied for one of his disciples. Sometime before 1433, the Taborite bishop Nicholas Biskupec visited Reiser in Prague and ordained him as a priest; possibly later in Basel, Biskupec ordained him as a bishop.[30] On the one hand, this represented a rejection of the idea of the unique apostolic succession passed down by the Roman church, while, on the other hand, it demonstrated that some sort of appropriate episcopal succession was still necessary for legitimate ordination. After returning to Germany, Reiser ordained at least six other Waldensian priests/servants of the Word through the laying on of hands, and he spent several years in pastoral and organizational work throughout Germany. Reiser helped introduce the theological views of the Taborites to the various Waldensian communities he served. In particular, Reiser appears to have introduced the practice of celebrating the Eucharist of both kinds into these Waldensian communities.[31] Though Reiser disguised himself as a traveling merchant and was careful to meet secretly at night with his followers, he was finally discovered and arrested in Strasbourg in January 1458. Under torture, Reiser, like many both before and after him, recanted and also divulged the names of many of his brethren. Finally, he and a woman named Anna Weiler were bound together to a stake and burned on March 6, 1458. Interestingly, in 1467, a follower of Reiser ordained a priest in the newly formed Unity of the Brethren that emerged following the demise of the Taborite movement.[32]

In 1487, Pope Innocent VIII authorized a Crusade against the Waldensians in northwestern Italy and southeastern France in the regions of Savoy, Piedmont, and the Dauphine. Waldensians responded by appealing that they were prepared to defend their positions from Scripture before a general council of the church, but that "we refuse to follow those who betray the rule of the gospel and who forsake the tradition of the apostles."[33] The appeal was to no avail. The Crusade was violent, and many captured Waldensians were killed in gruesome ways. Despite the general Waldensian commitment to pacifism, many of the Waldensians chose to attempt to defend themselves militarily. They were overwhelmed, however, by the number of their attackers, and their defense, while resulting in the deaths of a few Crusaders, proved to be futile. From 1487 to 1488, more than 150 Waldensians either died in battle or were executed as heretics.[34] In spite of the trials, near the end of the fifteenth century, Waldensians, apparently for the first time, began to form local congregations with located ministers of the Word.

The Waldensians "Join" the Protestant Reformation

By the sixteenth century, most of the Waldensians of France had apparently been dispersed or simply absorbed back into Roman Catholicism.

Likewise, those of Germany and Eastern Europe had also been absorbed into Catholicism or perhaps into the Unity of the Brethren that had arisen in the Czech lands and spread into areas of Poland, Germany, and Austria. This meant that, in general, Waldensians at the beginning of the sixteenth century were confined primarily to the regions of northwestern Italy, southern Italy, and the Provence and Dauphine regions in southeastern France. As a result of the reactionary persecutions that came in the wake of the Protestant Reformation, by the end of the sixteenth century, the Waldensians of southern Italy had also been wiped out.

While the persecution of the Waldensians continued, the sixteenth-century Protestant Reformation exploded onto the European religious scene. In much of Europe, religious dissenters were no longer required to live in secrecy in order to survive. In this new atmosphere, Waldensians were able, in some measure, to come out of hiding, and their leaders, known from the fifteenth century as *barbes* (from a word meaning *uncle*), began to make contact with leaders of the new Protestant movement. For example, William Farel (1489–1565), who later convinced John Calvin to minister in Geneva, was preaching in Waldensian territories in the 1520s, and a Waldensian *barbe* named Martin Gonin met with Farel and helped disseminate Protestant literature among the Waldensians. In about 1530, two *barbes* by the names of George Morel and Pierre Masson met Farel and entered into correspondence with Reformed theologians Johann Oecolampadius (1482–1531) and Martin Bucer (1491–1551), informing them of Waldensian belief and practice and asking for advice, primarily regarding difficult ethical questions.[35]

This contact, however, exposed significant differences in the two movements. The reformers were scandalized by the Waldensians' practices of receiving the sacraments from Catholic priests, celibacy for the *barbes* and some Waldensian "nuns," refusing to take oaths, and practicing their faith in secret to avoid persecutors. The reformers did not understand the Waldensian practice of itinerant preaching but recommended located pastors. Additionally, the Waldensians, who were greatly concerned about proper moral and ethical living, placed little if any emphasis on the reformers' key theological dogma of justification by faith apart from works.[36]

In 1532, in the Piedmont region of Angrogna, leaders of the Swiss Reformation and leaders of the Waldensians held a series of discussions. Later tradition seems to have conflated these meetings into one and (mis)identified the place as the Chanforan valley.[37] A set of propositions from September 12 of that year indicates that a significant segment of the Waldensians agreed to positions that were far more Reformed than the traditional Waldensian positions. For example, they agreed that auricular confession, a long-standing practice of the Waldensians, was not necessary; that marriage should not be forbidden to the *barbes*; and that ministers should not travel from one place to another. Additionally, they accepted a strong affirmation of predestination and the denial of free will. Though not all Waldensians accepted these propositions, it was evident that the Waldensian movement was well on its way to becoming a Protestant church. By the 1550s and 1560s, located pastors had replaced traveling *barbes*. Church buildings had been constructed, ministers were being sent from Calvin's Geneva, and young Waldensians were going to Geneva for ministerial training. Eventually, the Waldensian churches accepted the Geneva Ordinances[38] and came completely into the sphere of the Genevan reform movement. In effect, in their uniting with Protestantism, the Waldensians surrendered many of the basic positions they had held during the Middle Ages.[39]

Because the Waldensian church was an illegal minority church in Catholic-controlled territories, its open identification with Protestantism resulted in renewed persecution. Some of the harshest persecutions faced by the Waldensians came in the sixteenth and seventeenth centuries, with entire villages and communities being wiped out. During this time, many Waldensians again gave up the traditional position of pacifism, and in the Piedmont in 1560–61, they even used military victory to win the right to practice their faith. Nevertheless, the Waldensian church managed to survive, making it the only "heretical" medieval sect that has survived to the present. In the early twenty-first century, some twenty-five thousand Waldensians remained,[40] still considering themselves the first Protestant church.

Teachings and Practices of the Waldensians

When we attempt to generalize the beliefs and practices of the medieval Waldensian movement, we must always keep certain limitations to our knowledge in view. First, we must remember that almost all our information comes from the inquisitorial registers of their enemies, meaning that it is frequently biased and is, therefore, often both confused and inaccurate. Also, we must keep in mind that due to differences in belief and emphases between the Poor of Lyon and the Poor of Lombardy, as the two branches of the movement spread, their differences were also reflected in the respective areas where they took their movements. Additionally, various independent groups may have been identified as Waldensian while maintaining their own unique beliefs and practices. It is also important to be aware that what the preachers believed and taught was not always what the followers themselves believed or practiced. Finally, Waldensian belief and practice evolved over the course of time. Thus, the following is given as a basic overview of general Waldensian belief and practice up to the sixteenth-century unification with the Swiss Reformation, with the disclaimer that it does not necessarily represent every Waldensian group or every chronological period of their existence. Nevertheless, it does highlight characteristics that seem to be most consistently found throughout the history of the movement up until the time of the Protestant Reformation.[41]

Organization and Practice

From the earliest days of the Waldensian movement, the expectation was that everyone in the movement should be able to teach, though with the passing of time, a more formal (and secretive) teaching office was recognized. Also, in some places, such as Italy and Austria, before the pressure of constant persecution, Waldensians had "schools" in which they taught their doctrines. By no later than the early thirteenth century, two levels of membership had developed within the movement. The first tier consisted of the preachers who were constantly on the move spreading the gospel. These were referred to variously as preachers, masters, brethren, pastors, or, from the fifteenth century, *barbes*. The second tier consisted of followers, also known as friends, disciples, or believers, who secretly hosted the preachers, accepted their teachings, and supported them financially and materially. Some sources describe a threefold ministry consisting of a major minister (*majoralis*) or bishop, presbyters or priests, and deacons. Apparently, for much of their medieval existence, many of these masters held annual general meetings or conferences during which they reported on their activities, distributed the alms that had been collected, and made plans for future preaching missions.

Because the biblical text was so important to the Waldensians, they went to great effort to procure translations of Scripture in the vernacular languages, and they spent long hours memorizing enormous portions of the Bible. Apparently, many of their ministers memorized the entire New Testament and large portions of the Old Testament. One critic said of the Waldensians, "I have also seen laymen who . . . could even repeat by heart a great part of the Evangelists . . . and especially all that is said therein of our Lord's teachings and sayings, so that they could repeat them continuously with scarce one wrong word here or there."[42]

Waldensians gave great care to the training of their children in the ways of faith, and, in this way, they passed on the faith, even in the face of persecutors whose aim was to root out the heresy. When a young man was recognized as having the potential to become one of the traveling preachers, he would be mentored by traveling with a master for one to four years. During this time, the young man would learn to read, write, and memorize Scripture. Following this time of apprenticeship, the master would bring him to a council of brethren who would examine him and then ordain him by the laying on of hands. Masters devoted themselves to regular fasting and frequent prayer, especially repetition of the Lord's Prayer, and they were generally expected to be celibate.

In the earliest years of the movement, at least in France, women were included in the itinerant teaching ministry. However, as secrecy became more important, by the fourteenth century, women were excluded from the ranks of the traveling preachers. After all, in medieval Europe, there were any number of reasons for men to travel from place to place, but there were no legitimate reasons for women to do so without raising suspicion.[43]

The Waldensians tended to be generous, often taking collections to support the evangelistic labors of their preachers and to provide for the poor. The monetary support of those followers who earned their living by working in their communities was necessary for the preachers to be able to go about their missionary labors. Of course, there were times when the preachers were accused of accumulating wealth through these generous offerings, and the accusations were likely sometimes to be true.[44] The itinerant preachers made use of a network of hospitality houses along the routes of their preaching tours. These houses were owned by followers, often groups of older celibate women ("nuns" or "sisters"), who provided a place for the preachers to rest in safety, share news about other Waldensian communities, receive funds for their travels, and preach to trusted listeners. In addition, these houses became places of study and prayer for those who would gather even when no preacher was visiting.

Another early development in the movement was the practice by itinerant preachers of hearing the confessions of followers. Typically, followers made confession once or twice a year to masters, who then assigned various penances. This was a dramatic step because it directly challenged the prerogatives of the Roman priests to hear confession and assign penance. In addition, hearing confessions provided an opportunity for additional teaching to the faithful and a sense of identity for the movement.

Worship services were simple and tended to take place at night in the home of a follower or sometimes even outdoors. Usually, only a few people would be present, and the *barbe* or preacher would teach the group, hear confessions, and, perhaps, occasionally celebrate the Eucharist. At times, a meal would be involved, which was introduced by prayer and concluded with singing or blessing.

The Waldensian practice of the Eucharist is interesting, complex, and inconsistent. On the one hand, all the various groupings of the Waldensian movement continued to receive the sacrament, especially at Easter, from the Roman Catholic priests, even though many considered those priests to be unworthy. On the other hand, some Waldensians celebrated their own Eucharists. In some areas, particularly those influenced by the Poor of Lyon, friends shared regular love feasts, while preachers celebrated the Lord's Supper once a year, usually among themselves as a memorial of Christ's death. When celebrating the Eucharist, they received it in both kinds, along with fish. Some groups, influenced by the Poor of Lombardy, seem to have celebrated the Lord's Supper often, and both preachers and followers participated. Many groups celebrated a special meal on Maundy Thursday to commemorate Christ's Last Supper with his disciples.[45]

Although most Waldensians continued to bring their children to the priests for baptism, it appears that some, believing baptism performed by an unworthy priest to be invalid, had their children rebaptized. A few even rejected infant baptism altogether, believing that baptism was appropriate only for those who were capable of making their own confession of faith.

At the beginning of the fifteenth century, an unknown Waldensian wrote a poem called "La Nobla Leyczon" ("The Noble Lesson"), in which he pointed out that the Waldensians were persecuted because they rejected cursing, swearing, lying, adultery, killing, committing fraud, and taking vengeance.[46] This illustrates the reputation Waldensians had, even among their enemies, for their good moral behavior and the purity of their speech during an era of habitual profanity.[47] They were known for being simple in their dress; eschewing extravagance; being content with little; taking their food with moderation; avoiding pubs, dancing, and all vices; and controlling their tempers.[48] In many areas, Waldensians intermarried only among fellow Waldensians.

Waldensian Beliefs

As mentioned above, the Waldensians were theologically orthodox regarding the major doctrines of the church, such as the Trinity, the full divinity and humanity of Christ, and the oneness of the church, to name a few. However, in rejecting the authority of the pope and the Roman Catholic Church, the Waldensians recognized that the Bible, and especially the New Testament, was to be the sole rule of belief and life. At the beginning of the thirteenth century, most Waldensians held what later became known as the normative principle; church traditions or practices that were not prohibited by or otherwise in direct conflict with the Bible could be accepted. Within a short time, however, those from Lombardy reversed their position. They came to advocate what became known as the regulative principle;[49] whatever the Bible did not expressly enjoin was not justified in the church. Further, they argued that Christian teaching was to be limited to those things contained explicitly in Scripture. For the Waldensians, the ancient confessions of faith served only to orient and summarize the teachings of the apostles as the core of the biblical message.[50] This was the reason for the Waldensian rejection of many of the practices of the Roman church. The

Waldensian view was that the various teachings and innovations that the papacy had introduced into the church over the centuries were not signs of progress but, instead, were signs of the fall of the church and denial of the sufficiency of Christ.

One of Valdes's most important disciples and the leading theologian of the early Waldensians, Durand of Osca (Huesca), emphasized that the Waldensian way was based on the authority of the New Testament.[51] As such, Valdes, Durand, and other Waldensians believed that they were advocating a return to the practice of the primitive church. This emphasis on the New Testament did not mean, however, that the movement rejected the Old Testament. In fact, Durand of Osca defended the value of the Old Testament against the heretical Cathars.[52]

Valdes and his followers were particularly influenced by their understanding of Jesus's Sermon on the Mount. As previously mentioned, the common theology of the time made a distinction between the "counsels" and the "commands" of the Gospels and held that while a minority of Christians might attempt to live according to the ideals of Jesus's teachings in the Sermon on the Mount, most Christians were not expected to live according to such a strict ideal. Thus, by the Middle Ages, for many people the observance of the church's rituals often substituted for moral living. The Waldensians rejected this idea. Valdes introduced the idea that all Christians, not only a select few, were expected to live up to ideals of the Sermon on the Mount.[53] He insisted, "We plan to follow the counsels of the Gospels in the same way as their commands."[54]

Waldensians saw Scripture (especially the Sermon on the Mount) as primarily consisting of rules or laws to be followed. In their view, Christ had taken the law of the Old Testament and "made it tougher."[55] This was reflected in the Waldensians' strong emphasis on Christian ethics, particularly in their pacifism, based on Jesus's teaching to love your enemies and do good to those who persecute you, and in their refusal to take oaths. This refusal to take oaths later became one means by which their inquisitors identified them.[56]

Waldensians took the beatitude promising the kingdom of heaven to the "poor in spirit" (Matt. 5:3) to refer to physical poverty, and Valdes believed the teachings of Matthew 6:25–34 about anxiety meant that their preachers should not worry about worldly concerns and family ties.⁵⁷ This is why, for so much of their medieval existence, the itinerate preachers insisted on a life of apostolic poverty, depending on the generosity of their followers for sustenance.

Waldensians, especially the *barbes*, often prayed the Lord's Prayer, especially before meals, and repeated the words as much as ten times, or even eighty to one hundred times, this being their most visible religious act.⁵⁸ One manuscript that contains some of their teachings on the Lord's Prayer interpreted each phrase of the prayer as relating to the avoidance of the seven deadly sins.⁵⁹ "Hallowed be your name" was related to lechery versus chastity. "Your kingdom come" was related to greed as opposed to the gift of spiritual poverty. "Your will be done" was related to the sin of sloth. The request for "daily bread" was related to gluttony. "Forgive our sins/debts" was related to anger. "Lead us not into temptation" was related to pride. Finally, "Deliver us from evil" dealt with various additional sins.

Lombards relied on Matthew 5:31–32 in recognizing only fornication or adultery as grounds for divorce, though, along with those of Lyon, and following the example of Valdes himself, they granted that mutual agreement could also be legitimate grounds.⁶⁰

Valdes had called attention to the importance of the teaching of James 2:14–26 about the connection between faith and works, and this was reflected in Durand of Osca's definition of the church as "where a group of those faithful are gathered who have complete faith and fulfill it with deeds."⁶¹

Roman Church Practices Rejected by Waldensians

Although Waldensians rejected many teachings and practices of the Roman Catholic Church, one of the paradoxes of the movement was that, for the first two or three centuries of their existence, most of them continued to participate in the life and worship of that same Roman Church. That is, they continued going to church, making confession, doing penance, receiving the sacraments, observing fasts and church holy days, and engaging in other similar practices. Although there were significant segments of the movement, such as the Poor of Lombardy, that, at least theoretically, rejected the efficacy of sacraments performed by sinful priests, most did not consistently take such a Donatistic position.[62]

Once their movement was outlawed, however, the Waldensians did come to reject the following teachings and practices of the Roman Catholic Church: the authority of the pope; church councils and synods; the spiritual jurisdiction of the clergy; church tithes and endowments; ecclesiastical courts; pilgrimages; trappings of Catholic worship such as organs, bells, spires, altars, the Latin liturgy, candles, vestments; and "all acts of worship not specifically directed by the Bible."[63] Additionally, they rejected the cult of images; relics; purgatory; prayers for the dead; statues and pictures of Christ, Mary, and the saints; the intercession of saints; indulgences; formal oaths and swearing; and capital punishment. Apparently, some Alpine Waldensians rejected the real presence of Jesus in the Eucharist.[64]

It is, however, important to realize that although the masters may have taught against these things, it is also clear that not all Waldensian followers consistently abstained from certain Catholic practices. For example, the inquisitorial registers indicate that significant numbers of Waldensians did call on the intercession of saints. Whether this was from old habit, persuasion of the efficacy of the practice, or simply for the purpose of blending in with their Catholic neighbors is difficult to determine.[65] Regardless of the reasons, this demonstrates the gap that existed between the official teaching of the ministers and the actual practices of their followers.[66] This same phenomenon is often prevalent in churches today.

As mentioned, one significant weakness of the Waldensians was their ignorance of their own history. For much of their existence, Waldensians suffered from a lack of trained theologians. These deficiencies made their more educated adherents vulnerable to re-Catholization when confronted with actual historical facts that challenged the Waldensians' self-understanding.

Legacy

A major legacy of the Waldensian movement is simply their survival to the present day as both the only medieval "heretical" sect to survive and as the "first" Protestant church. The Waldensians also played a positive, if not always clearly understood, role in the development of both the Taborite movement and the Unity of the Brethren. The Waldensian understanding of the fall of the church as coinciding with the beginning of the partnership of church and state in the time of Constantine was taken up by many later restoration movements, as was their insistence that the teachings of the Sermon on the Mount applied to all Christians, not merely a select few. Finally, the challenge of the question the Waldensians raised as to what extent wealth is compatible with the lifestyle and ministry of followers of Jesus remains as their enduring legacy.

Questions for Thought or Discussion

1. To what extent could the Waldensian movement be considered a restoration movement?

2. Against what were the Waldensians reacting?

3. What in particular were the Waldensians emphasizing in their renewal efforts?

4. What were various strengths or weaknesses of the Waldensians?

5. How were the Waldensians similar to or different from the Franciscans or John Wyclif?

6. What did you find particularly interesting or attractive about the Waldensians?

7. What are the differences between the normative and regulative principles? With which do you most resonate and why? What alternatives other than these two principles might there be?

8. What lessons or applications can you draw from the Waldensians?

NOTES

[1] See, for example, Margaret Deanesly, *A History of the Medieval Church, 590–1500* (London: Routledge, 1969), 128.

[2] For this expression, see Giorgio Bouchard, "An Ancient and Undying Light," *Christian History* 22 (1989): 9.

[3] For the uncertainty concerning his actual name, see Gabriel Audisio, *The Waldensian Dissent: Persecution and Survival, c. 1170–c. 1570*, trans. Claire Davison (Cambridge, UK: Cambridge University Press, 1999), 7–9.

[4] Euan Cameron, *Waldenses: Rejections of Holy Church in Medieval Europe* (Malden, MA: Blackwell, 2000), 11–15; Donald F. Dunbaugh, *The Believers' Church: The History and Character of Radical Protestantism* (Scottdale, PA: Herald Press, 1985), 43; Amedeo Molnár, *Valdenští* (Prague: Kalich, 1991), 15, also published in French as *Les Vaudois au Moyen Age* (Turin: Claudiana, 1974). There is significant uncertainty about the reliability of these legends.

[5] Cameron, *Waldenses*, 33.

[6] Carlos M. N. Eire, *Reformations: The Early Modern World, 1450–1650* (New Haven, CT: Yale University Press, 2016), 48; Gunnar Westin, *The Free Church through the Ages*, trans. Virgil A. Olson (Nashville: Broadman, 1958), 28–29.

[7] Giorgio Tourn, *You Are My Witnesses: The Waldensians across 800 Years* (Turin: Claudiana Editrice, 1989), 15; Dunbaugh, *Believers' Church*, 43; A. Molnár, *Valdenští*, 43.

[8] Cameron, *Waldenses*, 16.

[9] Audisio, *Waldensian Dissent*, 12. It does appear that initially they were given limited permission to preach, but then the permission was revoked, Audisio, 15.

[10] Cameron, *Waldenses*, 18.

[11] The council condemned "those who, behind the mask of piety, take to themselves, though neither authorized nor sent, the right to preach publicly or in private, without the permission of the Holy See or of the Ordinary . . . ." Quoted in Giovanni Gonnet, "The Influence of the Sermon on the Mount upon the Ethics of the Waldensians of the Middle Ages," *Brethren Life and Thought* 35 (1990): 35.

[12] Dunbaugh, *Believers' Church*, 49.

[13] Tourn, *Witnesses*, 24–26.

[14] Jennifer Kolpacoff, "Archiepiscopal Inquisitions in the Middle Rhine: Urban Anticlericalism and Waldensianism in Late Fourteenth-Century Mainz," *Catholic Historical Review* 92, no. 3 (2006): 212.

[15] Amedeo Molnár, *A Challenge to Constantinianism: The Waldensian Theology in Middle Ages* (Turin: World Student Christian Federation, 1976), 14, 24.

[16] Audisio, *Waldensian Dissent*, 101.

[17] Cameron, *Waldenses*, especially 63–206.

[18] There is some question as to whether the Humiliati and the Poor of Lombardy were the same group.

[19] See Audisio, *Waldensian Dissent*, 26–28; and Cameron, *Waldenses*, 43–45, for a summary of this meeting. The text of "A Letter from the Poor Lombards to the Poor of Lyons Who Are in Germany" from 1218, which outlines differences between the groups, can be found in *Christian History* 22 (1989): 33.

[20] These are referred to as *ultramontanes*, meaning "beyond the mountains."

[21] Conrad was an unfortunate inquisitor. He ended up being murdered.

[22] Moneta wrote a great five-volume work against the Waldensians and the Cathars, *Summa adversus Catharos et Valdenses.*

[23] Cameron, *Waldenses*, 120. The "Donation of Constantine" was a document that was included in a larger group of medieval documents known as the *Isidorian Decretals*. It purported to tell of the time when Emperor Constantine endowed the Roman bishop Sylvester with property and authority. It was identified as a forgery by Nicolas of Cusa in 1433 and then was definitely demonstrated to have been a forgery by Lorenzo Valla in 1439-40. Until it was demonstrated to be a forgery, the medieval world believed it to be an accurate historical record.

[24] The degree to which the Waldensians formed an independent church is a matter of debate. See Jarold K. Zeman, "Restitution and Dissent in the Late Medieval Renewal Movements: The Waldensians, the Hussites and the Bohemian Brethren," *Journal of the American Academy of Religion* 44, no. 1 (1976): 13.

[25] For conditions during this time, see Audisio, *Waldensian Dissent*, 35-38; cf. Tourn, *Witnesses*, 41; Murray L. Wagner, *Petr Chelčický: A Radical Separatist in Hussite Bohemia* (Scottdale, PA: Herald Press, 1983), 53.

[26] See Audisio, *Waldensian Dissent*, 88.

[27] On the distinction between *brethren* and *followers*, see below.

[28] This is the first time the name "Peter" is associated with Valdes. On the "Book of the Elect," see Cameron, *Waldenses*, 118-22.

[29] On the Hussites and Taborites, see below, Chapters Three and Four.

[30] Cameron, *Waldenses*, 148. Reiser later referred to himself as a bishop of the faithful.

[31] See below, Chapters Three and Four.

[32] Cameron, *Waldenses*, 147-50; Audisio, *Waldensian Dissent*, 82-84. On the Unity of the Brethren, see below, Chapter Five.

[33] "Declaration of Giovanni Campi and Giovanni Desiderie," reproduced in English in Tourn, *Witnesses*, 64.

[34] Cameron, *Waldenses*, 193-200.

[35] Tourn, *Witnesses*, 65-66; Cameron, *Waldenses*, 212, 233-40; cf. Audisio, *Waldensian Dissent*, 88.

[36] Cameron, *Waldenses*, 237-40.

[37] See the discussion in Cameron, *Waldenses*, 240-53.

[38] Rules drawn up by John Calvin for regulating religious life and social order in Geneva.

[39] "By the 1560s, this particular group of Waldenses had succeeded in preserving their name and identity, while abandoning nearly all their traditional patterns of behavior," Cameron, *Waldenses*, 1.

[40] Michael Homer, "Seeking Primitive Christianity in the Waldensian Valleys: Protestants, Mormons, Adventists, and Jehovah's Witnesses in Italy," *Nova Religio: The Journal of Alternative and Emergent Religions* 9, no. 4 (2006): 23.

[41] I will make limited use of endnotes in the following sections. The general beliefs and practices of the Waldensians are generally well-known. I have gleaned primarily from Cameron, *Waldenses*; Audisio, *Waldensian Dissent*; Durnbaugh, *Believers' Church*; A. Molnár, *Valdenští*; and A. Molnár, *Challenge*.

[42] Durnbaugh, *Believers' Church*, 47.

[43] Cameron, *Waldenses*, 31, 74.

[44] A. Molnár, *Valdenští*, 163.

[45] See, for example, Audisio's discussion, *Waldensian Dissent*, 53-55.

46 Samuel Morland, *The History of the Evangelical Churches of the Valleys of Piemont* (London: Henry Hills, 1658), 114. The entire text of "The Noble Lesson" is found on pages 99–120.

47 Cameron, *Waldenses*, 139.

48 A. Molnár, *Valdenští*, 171.

49 The regulative principle comes to be typical among many restorationist groups.

50 A. Molnár, *Challenge*, 18–19.

51 A. Molnár, *Valdenští*, 42.

52 Unfortunately for the Waldensian movement, at around 1207 or 1208, Durand returned to the Catholic Church, giving up the principle of obedience only to God for the principle of obedience to the church. Durand became involved in a new group of "Poor Catholics" who were allowed to preach. On the reasons for his return, see Adam L. Hoose, "Durán of Huesca (c. 1160–1230): A Waldensian Seeking a Remedy to Heresy," *Journal of Religious History* 38, no. 2 (June 2014): 173–89.

53 Durnbaugh, *Believers' Church*, 43.

54 Gonnet, "Influence of the Sermon on the Mount," 34.

55 Cameron, *Waldenses*, 224.

56 Though the general practice of Waldensians was to refuse to take even civil oaths, some would, on occasion, take civil oaths. Others would dissemble by appearing willing to take an oath without actually taking one. Oaths were an important part of the fabric of medieval society. It was by an oath that vassals demonstrated their loyalty to their lords, and the refusal to do so indicated that one's loyalty was suspect.

57 A. Molnár, *Valdenští*, 61.

58 Cameron, *Waldenses*, 84, 93, 215.

59 Cameron, *Waldenses*, 224. The following description is also taken from Cameron.

60 See A. Molnár, *Valdenští*, 78.

61 Gonnet, "Influence of the Sermon on the Mount," 34–35.

62 Cameron, *Waldenses*, 28.

63 Durnbaugh, *Believers' Church*, 48.

64 In addition to Durnbaugh, *Believers' Church*, 48, for lists of Roman Catholic practices rejected by Waldensians, see Cameron, *Waldenses*, 75, 103, 164, 171; and Howard Kaminsky, *A History of the Hussite Revolution* (Berkeley: University of California Press, 1967), 175–76.

65 Cameron, *Waldenses*, 133; cf. Wagner, *Petr Chelčický*, 53.

66 Audisio, *Waldensian Dissent*, 100–101.

CHAPTER 3

"TRUTH PREVAILS OVER ALL"
The Czech Reformation Part 1

Reform efforts began in the Czech lands in the second half of the fourteenth century. During the period of the Avignon Papacy, the king of the Czechs, Charles IV (1316–78, reigned 1346–78), was elected King of the Romans[1] and Holy Roman Emperor, and he located the capital of the empire in the city of Prague, the population of which was divided between Czechs and Germans. Charles was a deeply religious visionary who launched several significant projects that enhanced the status of his new capital. He had Prague elevated to the status of an archbishopric, founded the New Town of Prague, initiated the construction of several church buildings, including the St. Vitus Cathedral of the Prague Castle and the Charles Bridge, and, in 1348, he established the first university of central Europe and of the empire, now known as Charles University.[2]

During Charles IV's reign, improvements in education led to a more literate society, and the translation of the Bible into the Czech language gave more people access to Scripture and other religious literature.[3] In spite of Charles's religious zeal and the educational improvements, conditions in the Czech church and society were at a low ebb. The Austrian preacher Conrad of Waldhauser (c. 1326–69) began preaching in German about the necessity of reform, and the popular Czech preacher John Milič of Kroměříž (d. 1374), sometimes known as the "Father of the Czech Reformation," preached once a day in Latin, once in German, and three times a day in Czech, thus allowing more people to understand the teachings of Scripture. Milič had been a high-ranking church official, but in line with his own preaching to "give away what you cannot hold to receive what you cannot lose,"[4] he gave up his position to live a life of apostolic poverty and preach against the moral corruptions he saw in society and among the clergy. One of Milič's most impressive achievements was the founding of Jerusalem, a facility for the rehabilitation of former prostitutes and the training of preachers. One of his major emphases was on frequent Communion. Because he witnessed great reforms taking place in Prague, Milič concluded that it was the practice of frequent Communion that was the key to the coming of God's kingdom on earth. Unfortunately, his reforms ran into opposition; his cause was probably not helped by his referring to Charles IV as the Antichrist. The authorities shut down Jerusalem, and Milič was summoned to stand trial for heresy in Avignon, where he died shortly after having been acquitted.[5]

Charles was followed on the Czech throne by his son, Václav IV (1361–1419, reigned 1378–1419), who was known as a drunkard and a womanizer and who gave more attention to hunting and keeping wild animals than he did to administration.[6] During Václav's reign, his realm was ravaged by the plague, which decimated the population and impoverished thousands. Armed bands of highwaymen roamed the countryside, terrorizing anyone who crossed their path and forcing local nobles to take the law into their own hands to provide security for travelers. Václav's relationship with the church was strained, and he even executed the vicar general, John of Nepomuk (1345–93). People feared that the day of judgment was about to dawn.

Preachers such as Matthew of Janov (c. 1350–93/4) and Tomaš of Štítný (1333–1409) continued the message of Conrad of Waldhauser and Milič of Kroměříž in calling for reform. They emphasized preaching in the vernacular, moral reform, frequent Communion, and the centrality of Scripture as the rule of faith and life. In particular, Matthew of Janov compared the church of his day with that of the New Testament church and concluded that the contemporary church, with its multiplicity of human innovations, was different from what it should be. He believed that the Lord's Supper was so important that even the laity should be allowed and encouraged to partake daily. Matthew was a restorationist and argued for "the return by the Church to the teaching and practice of the gospel of Christ and His apostles as exhibited in the primitive Church."[7] He called for renewal based on the authority of Scripture, particularly the Gospels and the New Testament, and he saw the ideal church in the Christian community of apostolic times. Peter Morée suggested that "returning to original Christianity, and therefore to the Bible, was at the heart of the reforms and indeed at the heart of the Reformation in Bohemia."[8]

John Hus and the Hussites

The stage was set for the first national reform movement in Europe that would lead to significant efforts for the restoration of New Testament Christianity. John Hus (c. 1369–1415) became the leading actor on the stage of this drama.[9] He had received his master's degree from the University of Prague in 1396, after which he began teaching at the university as a member of the faculty of arts. At first, Hus was proud of his position as a university professor, especially enjoying wearing the academic costume that went with the position. He was also given to "wasting" time by playing chess. However, sometime prior to his ordination as a priest in 1400, he underwent a significant change that he attributed to the knowledge of Scripture.[10] This change set him on his life's course as a reformer. Hus served as dean of the faculty of arts in 1401 and 1402. Also in 1402, he became the preacher at Bethlehem Chapel, where as many as three thousand people at a time heard, in the Czech language, his calls for reform. In his preaching, he emphasized the authority of the "law of God" (especially the New Testament) for the church and for Christian living. This challenged the idea of the pope's authority over the church. For Hus, Christ, rather than the pope, was the head of the church, and the church itself was composed not just of the clergy but of all the elect. Hus also rejected the primacy of the pope over other bishops, believing that papal primacy had been established by the emperors.[11]

When the writings of John Wyclif arrived at the university in Prague, Hus soon became the most influential leader of those university masters who had read Wyclif's works and were discussing his ideas. In 1409–10, he served as rector of the university while conflict regarding the merit of Wyclif's ideas and other reforms escalated. In spite of fierce opposition from a series of archbishops, Hus was able to preach his reforms for several years because King Václav and Queen Sophie were favorably disposed toward him. Things began to come to a head, however, in 1410–12. First, in July 1410, the archbishop Zbyněk Zajíc excommunicated Hus and those of his followers who continued to propagate Wyclif's views. Hus and his followers ignored the excommunication, which was reissued in February 1411, but again with little effect. Then, in spring 1412, the sale of indulgences began in Prague to raise money for the new Pisan pope, John XXIII,[12] to finance his Crusade against the supporters of his rival, Pope Gregory XII in Rome. Hus spoke out against the indulgences, and disturbances followed. As a result of the disturbances, three young men named Martin, John, and Stašek were treacherously beheaded on July 11, 1412, thus exacerbating the general discontent. Unfortunately for Hus, King Václav stood to profit from the sale of the indulgences, and Hus's opposition cost him the king's favor.[13] On October 18, 1412, a decree of excommunication against Hus was announced in Prague, and the city was placed under the interdict.[14] Hus responded by appealing directly to Jesus Christ and leaving Prague to spare the city. He spent the next two years living in exile in the Czech countryside, and it was during this time that he wrote his most important work, *De ecclesia* (*On the Church*). Composing most of this work verbatim from the writings of Wyclif, Hus held that Christ alone was head of the church; the foundation of the church was Jesus himself, as confessed by Peter, rather than Peter himself (the papacy); and the Roman church was not equivalent to the apostolic church.[15] He suggested, "No human commandment or decree is valid or to be observed except in so far as it is caused by a divine command."[16] Matthew Spinka summarized Hus's views in this work: "The necessary truths of Christianity are contained in Scripture. Whatever is beyond or contrary to it is to be rejected."[17] Many of Hus's assertions in this work would be used against him after he was taken into custody in Constance, Germany.

Hus was summoned to the Council of Constance in 1414, and Sigismund (1368–1437), King of the Romans,[18] verbally granted him a safe-conduct to attend, though Hus did not receive the written document until after his arrival in Constance. In spite of the safe-conduct, shortly after his arrival in Constance, Hus was arrested on November 28, 1414, by order of Pope John XXIII.[19] Although Sigismund made a show of protesting that his safe-conduct had not been honored, the general feeling at the time was that a safe-conduct should never have been promised to a heretic and was not necessary to honor.[20]

Hus hoped to be able to present his views to the council, convinced that the council would agree with him. Instead of being permitted the discussion he had expected, however, Hus was subjected to the process of an inquisition. The council charged him with spreading the teachings of Wyclif and simply commanded him to recant positions, many of which he had never held. Those positions he did hold he refused to recant unless convinced by Scripture that he was in error. Believing to the end that ultimately truth would prevail,[21] Hus was condemned with no legitimate opportunity to defend himself and was finally burned at the stake on July 6, 1415. According to legend, at some point prior to his condemnation, Hus was supposed to have said, "They may kill a goose, but a hundred years from now a swan will arise which they will not be able to kill."[22]

Because of its later significance, one more item needs to be mentioned. Hus had departed for Constance in October 1414. By late October or early November, Hus's close coworker, Jakoubek of Stříbro (1372–1429), began offering Communion in both kinds (*sub utraque specie*) to the laity in Prague.[23] Initially, Hus had been cautious about Communion in both kinds, fearing that his position would be compromised by its introduction. After his arrival in Constance, however, Hus approved and encouraged the practice. The chalice, signifying Communion in both kinds, was to become a major symbol for Hus's followers, who came to be known as Hussites.

The Hussite Movement Grows

Hus's death did not put an end to the reform movement. Many Czechs viewed Hus as a martyr and not only vowed to continue his reforms but were also willing to go beyond his suggestions. Following Hus's death, leadership of the movement fell to Jakoubek of Stříbro, "the most consistent exponent of restorationism"[24] among the reforming circle in Prague. Like Hus, Jakoubek had received his Master of Arts degree (1397) from the university in Prague. He taught as a member of the philosophical faculty, was ordained to the priesthood in 1402, and ultimately followed Hus as the preacher at Bethlehem Chapel. Jakoubek, who was known even by his enemies for his holiness and humility, was, nevertheless, much more radical than Hus, believing "that the reform of the church was possible only by a radical return to the practices of the primitive church."[25] As mentioned above, Jakoubek, desiring a "restoration of the primitive Church order,"[26] was perhaps the first to advocate Communion in both kinds, a practice that signified the Hussite recognition that, in the eyes of God, all Christians were equal regardless of whether they were from the clergy or the laity.[27] Though Hus had approved Communion in both kinds before his death, it was Jakoubek and his followers who were determined to carry it out, arguing that Communion in both kinds had been established by Christ and had been the practice of the primitive church.[28] Hussites, with the chalice as their symbol and "Truth prevails over all"[29] as their motto, took control of the churches and began offering the cup to the laity. As time went on, several priests who refused to serve Communion in both kinds were removed from their churches.

Jakoubek's basic hermeneutical principle was to keep those practices in the worship that did not hinder the law of Christ; otherwise, they "should be pruned away." He believed, however, that it was safer to follow only what Jesus and the primitive church had done.[30] After Hus's death, Jakoubek realized that his role was now to attempt to keep the movement together. Although he heavily influenced the doctrine of the radical branch of Hussites, later known as the Taborites, and although he approved many of the practices and positions that the Taborites later affirmed, now that he found himself as the leader of the movement, he became much more cautious than he had been during Hus's lifetime. In order to avoid alienating the more moderate Hussites, Jakoubek was forced to modify some of his views, causing the more radical Hussites to claim that Jakoubek refused to follow his true beliefs to their logical conclusions. Ultimately, he was forced to disassociate himself from the Taborites.

Other teachers were arriving in Prague and spreading the fires of radical reform. Chief among these was Nicholas of Dresden (d. 1417) and his group of disciples in the dormitory called the Black Rose. Nicholas's commitment to biblical authority was reflected in his motto "*Verbum Dei non est alligatum*" ("The word of God is not bound," from 2 Tim. 2:9 ESV).[31] He initially worked with Jakoubek but ultimately became more radical in the reforms he advocated. Nicholas asserted that the church fathers were to be believed only insofar as they agreed with the Bible and, more particularly, with the New Testament. He was also influenced by the Waldensians, adopting from them, for example, the rejection of purgatory and prayers for the dead. He argued, "For who does not know that the most secure way to life is to live as Christ and his apostles taught?"[32] The Taborites later adopted and advocated these same positions.

King Václav IV decided in 1419, under pressure from his brother Sigismund and Pope Martin V, to restore the priests who were loyal to Rome to the positions from which they had been removed. Although this move had the effect of limiting the chalice for the laity, the masters in the university and the Czech nobility put up little, if any, resistance. Other, more radical reformers, however, did not remain silent, and the tension between the groups led to unrest and frequent disturbances. These disturbances were soon to explode into full-blown revolution.

The Taborite Restoration Movement

By spring 1419 and on into 1420, large groups of pilgrims had begun gathering on mountaintops in the Czech countryside for religious purposes, particularly for receiving Communion in both kinds, since they were no longer able to do so in many of the church buildings. To be sure, there were social and political aspects to these gatherings, but at their core, they were religious in nature. In addition to Communion, there was preaching, singing of hymns, and the sharing of food; the common sharing of food prepared the way for the later practice of contributing to the common chests that would be managed by the priests. The first such meeting took place on Easter Sunday, April 16, 1419, on a mountain (or hilltop) that the pilgrims named Tabor in honor of the mountain where, according to tradition, Jesus had been transfigured and where he issued his Great Commission.

The radicals continued their gatherings on other mountains and also gave these other mountains biblical names, such as Horeb or Mount Olivet. The greatest of the mountaintop gatherings was on Saturday, July 22, 1419, when tens of thousands of pilgrims again assembled on Mount Tabor. The people, who were committed to pacifism, dedicated themselves to the things that led to the salvation of the soul, while the priests assumed three duties. Some priests divided the people into groups and took turns preaching all day to them. Others listened to confessions, and still others served Communion in both kinds, even to children.[33] The priests at these gatherings proclaimed several revolutionary principles: (1) Worldly wealth and power of the clergy should be abolished. (2) Mandatory tithing, which the preachers claimed was according to the Jewish or Constantinian practice, should be abolished and replaced by voluntary contributions to provide for the physical needs of the priests. (3) Priests should voluntarily surrender their civil jurisdiction over lands and buildings. (4) The evangelical law of Christ (i.e., the New Testament) was sufficient for the ordering of the church, without the rituals of the Old Testament and human innovations. (5) The faithful should avoid the evils of the clergy of the Antichrist, and they should only obey the True Shepherd.[34] Ultimately, what they desired was a restoration of the primitive church.

The radicals in Prague were aware of what was happening on the mountains and perhaps even joined some of the gatherings. The unrest and dissatisfaction of the radicals culminated in Prague's Church of Saint Mary of the Snows on Sunday, July 30, 1419, when John Želivský (1380–1422) preached a fiery sermon about God's vengeance from Ezekiel 6:3–5. Following his sermon, Želivský led his emotionally charged listeners to the New Town Hall, where the mob stormed the building and threw the magistrates out the windows. The mob waiting below murdered those who survived the fall. Revolution was underway. At the time of the defenestration, King Václav was at his Nový Hradek castle just south of Prague. Upon hearing the news of events in Prague, he fell into a depression, followed by some sort of seizure or heart attack, and a few days later, on August 16, he died.

The anarchy that followed led to an unstable and dangerous situation that found three major groups vying for political and religious control of the Czech lands: (1) Loyal Roman Catholics wanted to eliminate Communion in both kinds, and they demanded that Václav's brother, Sigismund, be recognized as the lawful king. (2) Moderate or conservative Hussites, primarily from the university (the Prague masters), simply wanted the church and Sigismund to acknowledge the legitimacy of the Czech reforms, particularly Communion in both kinds. This group came to be known as the Utraquists or Calixtines,[35] and was ultimately led by the future Utraquist archbishop, John Rokycana. (3) Radical Hussites insisted on a total reform of the church and were willing to make a clean break with the Roman Catholic Church if that became necessary. Additionally, they absolutely rejected Sigismund as their king.[36] Taking the name of Taborites, the radicals fortified the town of Sezimovo Ústí and renamed it Tabor, where they organized themselves into a new religious, political, and military society with the aim of restoring the purity of the primitive church.

Nicholas Biskupec of Pelhřimov (1385[?]–1460[?]), who was to become their one and only bishop, believed that the restoration for which Tabor was striving was simply following the example of Nehemiah's restoration in Old Testament times.[37] The Taborites demanded a rejection of all ceremonies and rituals invented by humans and insisted that they wished to simply follow the commands of Christ and the practice of the primitive church. Specifically, the Taborites defined the primitive church as the church "whose rectors were the apostles,"[38] that is, the church about which they read in the New Testament.

On the other hand, the more moderate Utraquists saw no need to eliminate those practices that were not expressly forbidden in Scripture and that did not go against Scripture. The difference between the Taborite approach of eliminating everything not expressly authorized by Scripture and the moderate approach of retaining those things not expressly forbidden was one of the major factors that led to the fatal divisions between the various Hussite reformers.[39]

To stamp out the alleged Hussite heresy, from 1420 to 1431, the Roman Catholic Church organized a total of five unsuccessful Crusades against the Czechs. The impending Crusades led to a significant theological crisis for the Hussites, particularly for the pacifist Taborites. Were Christians allowed to take up arms, and if so, under what conditions? After much debate, the conclusion of the university masters was that, under certain circumstances, it was permissible for Christians to fight in defense of the law of God.[40] The first two Crusades against the Hussites took place from 1420 to 1422, and their general effect was to unite the various Hussite factions against their common enemy. The great one-eyed Taborite general John Žižka (d. 1424), who could never be defeated on the battlefield, led the Hussite field armies to several spectacular victories. So successful were their armies that "for fifteen years the Taborites maintained the most feared and successful army in medieval Europe."[41] Thus, the original Taborite ideal of pacifism fell by the wayside. As we have already seen with the Waldensians, theoretical pacifism is easier to maintain in times of peace than actual pacifism is in times of imminent danger.

About the same time as the Crusades, violent persecution against the Hussites broke out, and many Taborites responded with violence, accompanied by great and unrealistic chiliastic expectations of the coming judgment of God and the establishment of his kingdom physically in the realm of the Czech kingdom.[42] The people who wished to escape God's coming wrath were urged to flee the cities and villages and to gather in five special cities where they could escape the coming doom. Many of these expectations were based on outlandish interpretations of Old Testament texts. Petr Chelčický, a committed pacifist who separated from the Taborites when they surrendered their pacifist ideals, described what happened this way: "Then the Devil came to them clothed in other garb, in the prophets and the Old Testament, and from these they sought to confect an imminent Day of Judgement, . . . and so they committed many killings and impoverished many people."[43] According to Howard Kaminsky, "the congregations degenerated morally to the point where their reaction to persecution, in the winter of 1419–20, was not the Christian suffering of the New Testament but the self-conscious violence of the Old."[44]

The high-pitched fanaticism did not last long among the majority of Taborites, and as the excitement and expectation began to wane, it became necessary to organize the Taborite religious community on a more permanent and stable basis. This led the Taborites in September 1420 to select Nicholas Biskupec of Pelhřimov as their bishop. The significance of this lay in the fact that by appointing its own bishop, Tabor declared its independence from the papal hierarchy, and, for all practical purposes, formed its own church without regard to the tradition of apostolic succession. Shortly after his ordination, Biskupec took up residence at the Taborite town of Písek, which became his primary seat of operation. As bishop or senior of the Taborites, Biskupec had several responsibilities. He was in charge of regulating the preaching that went on among the Taborites, and he also had charge of the distribution of the money that was collected into the common chest.[45] It is probable that Biskupec was a leading figure in the translation of the so-called Taborite Bible, and he certainly would have been a leader in the development of the Taborite liturgy. What was perhaps his major responsibility was that of producing written defenses of Tabor's theological positions.

The early days of the Taborite movement were marked by a religious, social, and political equality that few had previously experienced. The pooling of resources reduced the distinctions between rich and poor and contributed to a sense of solidarity.[46] The Taborites laid great emphasis on "the law of God" and expected everyone to know Scripture. The emphasis on knowing Scripture was so great that, roughly thirty years later, an observer claimed that, among the Taborites, one could hardly find even a woman who could not demonstrate familiarity with the Old and New Testaments.[47] This may have been hyperbolic, but the point is that Taborites had the reputation of knowing Scripture. People were allowed to engage in religious activities with a freedom they had never before known.

Not everything, however, was ideal. For example, in spite of the fact that the Taborite priests had taught that the peasants no longer had to pay rents in an effort to end economic exploitation, by October 1420, the Taborite leaders were collecting rents from their own people.[48] In addition, a constant point of contention between the Taborites and the Utraquists was the manner in which they understood the presence of Jesus in the Eucharist. While the Utraquists generally accepted the doctrines of transubstantiation or consubstantiation,[49] the Taborites held the view that Jesus was "really, truly, virtually, spiritually, and sacramentally present in the Eucharist," but not substantially or corporeally present in his human form in the sacrament.[50] A few months after his ordination, Biskupec, along with John of Jičín, wrote to the leaders in Prague warning them of

Pikart extremists led by Martin Huska in and around Tabor. Pikarts were a chiliastic sect that had broken from the Taborites and denied any presence of Jesus at all in the Eucharist, holding that it was a mere memorial. Additionally, they held that, for the believer, the body and blood of Jesus could be taken "sacramentally" in any normal food. Reports suggested that even more extreme Pikarts became Adamites who went about naked and engaged in various forms of sexual immorality. This was all too much to tolerate, so Taborite forces led by John Žižka eradicated the Pikarts and Adamites. Unfortunately for the Taborites, the fanaticism that had arisen in Tabor from the chiliastic expectations and the Pikart/Adamite extremes gave the Taborites a reputation that they could never shake.

Questions for Thought or Discussion

1. Would you consider John Hus to have been more of a reformer or a restorationist? Why?
2. What were the major wings of the Hussites, and how did they differ?
3. To what extent, if any, could the various Hussite movements be considered restoration movements?
4. Against what were the Hussites reacting, and what were they emphasizing in their renewal efforts?
5. What were various strengths or weaknesses of the Hussite movements?
6. How were the various Hussite groups similar to or different from the previous movements discussed in this book?
7. What did you find particularly interesting or attractive about the Hussite movements?
8. What lessons or applications can you draw from the Hussite movements?

NOTES

[1] The title "King of the Romans" was basically a synonym of "King of the Germans" within the territories of the Holy Roman Empire. The King of the Romans would normally be crowned later as Holy Roman Emperor. Thus, the King of the Romans might be referred to as "emperor" even before his official coronation.

[2] For historical information regarding the Czech Reformation/Revolution in English, I draw primarily from Howard Kaminsky, *A History of the Hussite Revolution* (Berkeley: University of California Press, 1967); Thomas A. Fudge, *The Magnificent Ride: The First Reformation in Hussite Bohemia* (Brookfield, VT: Ashgate, 1998); and František M. Bartoš, *The Hussite Revolution*, ed. John M. Klassen (New York: Columbia University Press, 1986). I also draw from Czech works, primarily František Šmahel, *Husitská revoluce*, 4 vols. (Prague: Univerzita Karlova, 1995–96). Craig D. Atwood, *The Theology of the Czech Brethren from Hus to Comenius* (University Park, PA: Pennsylvania State University Press, 2009), is also useful, though his lack of facility in the Czech language is a limitation.

[3] František Šmahel notes, "From the long-term perspective of the Czech reformation and also of the biblicism of the laity, the first edition of the translation of the Old and New Testaments into Czech had an absolutely extraordinary significance," *Husitská revoluce*, 1.240 (translation mine, as is the case whenever citing Czech authors).

[4] On Milič, see Peter C. A. Morée, *Preaching in Fourteenth-Century Bohemia* (Slavkov, Czech Republic: Evangelické manufakturní alternativní nakladatelství, 1999). The quotation is from 140.

[5] Some have seen in Milič's teachings the roots of the later Four Articles of Prague. See Fudge, *Magnificent Ride*, 48–51.

[6] Matthew Spinka, *John Hus: A Biography* (Princeton, NJ: Princeton University Press, 1968), 9.

[7] Spinka, *John Hus*, 19.

[8] Morée (summarizing František Bartoš), *Preaching in Fourteenth-Century Bohemia*, 240. The term *Bohemia* refers to the Czech lands.

[9] For biographical information on Hus, I draw primarily from Spinka, *John Hus*; and František Šmahel, *Jan Hus: život a dílo* (Prague: Argo, 2013).

[10] Spinka, *John Hus*, 45–46.

[11] Šmahel, *Jan Hus*, 210.

[12] In 1409, the Council of Pisa met to resolve the Great Western Papal Schism. It deposed the two papal claimants and appointed a new pope. The two deposed popes refused to recognize the authority of the council, with the result that there were now three papal claimants: an Avignon pope, a Roman pope, and a Pisan pope.

[13] Spinka, *John Hus*, 134, 151, 158, 161.

[14] The interdict banned priests from performing duties such as baptisms, marriages, the Mass, and other rituals.

[15] John Hus, *De Ecclesia: The Church*, trans. David Schley Schaff (1915), 27–30, 56–66, 73–78, 133, accessed July 15, 2020, https://en.wikisource.org/wiki/De_Ecclesia._The_Church.

[16] Hus, *De Ecclesia*, 227.

[17] Spinka, *John Hus*, 186.

[18] Sigismund was Václav's brother. Sigismund's official reigns are a bit complicated. He was king of Hungary from 1387, king of the Romans [Germans] from 1410 or 1411, though not crowned until 1414, king of the Czechs from 1419, though not acknowledged by the Czechs until 1436, king of Italy from 1431, and officially Holy Roman Emperor from 1433. As king of the Romans, he was something like the Holy Roman Emperor-elect, so he was sometimes referred to as the emperor long before it was official.

[19] Spinka, *John Hus*, 235.

[20] Šmahel, *Jan Hus*, 210; Murray L. Wagner, *Petr Chelčický: A Radical Separatist in Hussite Bohemia* (Scottdale, PA: Herald Press, 1983), 32.

[21] Less than a month before his death, Hus had written, "It is better to die well than to live wickedly. One should not sin in order to avoid the punishment of death. Truth conquers all things," Spinka, *John Hus*, 178. The last phrase may also be translated, "Truth prevails over all." See Note 29 below.

[22] This statement was cited at Martin Luther's funeral. John D. Woodbridge and Frank A. James III, *Church History*, vol. 2: *From Pre-Reformation to the Present Day* (Grand Rapids: Zondervan, 2013), 50. The Council of Constance ended the papal schism by deposing John XXIII and Benedict XIII while accepting the resignation of Gregory XII and appointing Martin V as pope. A great irony of the Council of Constance was that while it condemned Hus in large measure for rejecting the supreme authority of the pope, it was the same council that itself rejected the supreme authority of the three papal claimants and deposed John XXIII, on whose authority Hus was arrested!

[23] Kaminsky, *History*, 108. See his fuller discussion on the dating of the beginnings of Communion in both kinds, 107–28.

[24] Spinka, *John Hus*, 80.

[25] Spinka, *John Hus*, 90.

[26] Spinka, *John Hus*, 256.

[27] Fudge, *Magnificent Ride*, 162.

[28] See Amedeo Molnár, Noemi Rejchrtová, and Luděk Rejchrtový, eds., *Slovem obnovená: čtení o reformaci* (Prague: Kalich, 1977), 29.

[29] In Latin, "*Super omnia autem vincit veritas*," and in Czech, "*Pravda vítězí nade vším.*" This had been a phrase of Hus's and can also be translated as "Truth conquers all." A shorter form, "Truth prevails," is included on the presidential standard of the Czech Republic. The phrase is taken from the Apocrypha, 1 Esdras (3 Esdras in the Vulgate) 3:12; cf. 4:35, 38, 41.

[30] Kaminsky, *History*, 191, 194.

[31] Giovanni Gonnet, "The Influence of the Sermon on the Mount upon the Ethics of the Waldensians of the Middle Ages," *Brethren Life and Thought* 35 (1990): 37.

[32] Kaminsky, *History*, 214.

[33] Vavřinec z Březové, *Husitská kronika, Píseň o vítězství u Domažlic*, trans. František Heřmanský (Prague: Svoboda, 1979), 107.

[34] According to Nicholas Biskupec in his *Chronicon causam sacerdotum Taboriensium*. Taken from the Czech translation in Bohuslav Havránek, Josef Hrabák, and Jiří Daňhelka, eds., *Výbor z české literatury doby husitské* II (Prague: Československá akademie věd, 1964), 260. Kaminsky, *History*, 287, adds infant Communion to the list of what the priests taught.

[35] *Utraquist* from the Latin for *both kinds* and *Calixtine* from the Latin for *chalice*.

[36] Allen Diles, "A Comparison of Nicholas of Pelhřimov and the Taborite Restoration with Alexander Campbell and the American Restoration Movement," *Restoration Quarterly* 44, no. 4 (2002): 244.

[37] Biskupec, *Chronicon*, 258.

[38] See Kaminsky, *History*, 490n166, where it is noted that Nicholas Biskupec once referred to the "*ecclesie primitive, cuius rectores erant et sunt apostoli*" ("the primitive church, whose rectors were the apostles").

[39] Thus, the Taborites followed the regulative principle, and the moderates accepted the normative principle.

[40] Kaminsky, *History*, 325–26. Conditions included a just cause, legitimate authorization, and proper intentions.

[41] Atwood, *Theology of the Czech Brethren*, 114.

[42] *Chiliasm* is a synonym for millennialism and is the idea that Jesus will return to reign physically on earth for either a literal or figurative one thousand years.

[43] Cited in Howard Kaminsky, "Chiliasm and the Hussite Revolution," *Church History* 26, no. 1 (1957): 51; and Kaminsky, *History*, 321.

[44] Kaminsky, *History*, 322.

[45] Kaminsky, *History*, 385–90. On the Taborite community of goods, see also Thomas Fudge, "Neither Mine Nor Thine: Communist Experiments in Hussite Bohemia," *Canadian Journal of History* 33, no. 1 (April 1998): 25–47.

[46] There were, however, accusations that some of the priests were helping themselves to the contents of the chests, Kaminsky, *History*, 331–32.

[47] Howard Kaminsky, "Pius Aeneas Among the Taborites," *Church History* 28 (1959): 290; cf. Thomas A. Fudge, "The 'Law of God': Reform and Religious Practice in Late Medieval Bohemia," *The Bohemian Reformation and Religious Practice* 1 (1996): 68.

[48] Kaminsky, *History*, 386.

[49] While the Roman Catholic doctrine of transubstantiation holds that the bread and wine change into the body and blood of Jesus, consubstantiation is the doctrine that although the bread and wine are not changed, the body and blood of Jesus are nevertheless present in or with the bread and wine.

[50] Atwood, *Theology of the Czech Brethren*, 122.

CHAPTER 4

"JESUS CHRIST, THE BEST LAWGIVER"
The Czech Reformation Part 2

In spite of significant differences, by 1420, both moderate and radical Hussite groups were able to agree on four demands called the Four Articles of Prague: (1) Communion in both kinds, (2) free preaching of the Word of God and of his every truth by the priests, (3) divesting the church of its wealth and influence in politics, and (4) purgation of and cessation from mortal or public sins.[1]

For the radicals, however, the Four Articles were their minimum expectations for beginning the renewal of the church. As previously mentioned, the Taborites intended to eliminate all Roman innovations, which they defined as everything that was not expressly authorized by the New Testament. This included practices directly related to worship itself (such as the Latin liturgy, clerical vestments, rituals associated with the Mass, the doctrine of transubstantiation, and organs and other musical instruments), as well as items related to other aspects of Christian piety (the use of candles, holy water, the sign of the cross, prescribed church fasts, images and statues, relics, belief in purgatory, prayers for the dead, praying to Mary and for the invocation and intercession of the saints, mandatory tithing, and auricular confession to the priests). From the Taborite perspective, not only were these doctrines and practices not authorized by Scripture, but they also distracted people from what was truly spiritual and contributed to superstition and idolatry. On the other hand, the moderate Hussites viewed the Four Articles as the extent of their demands and insisted on retaining the usages of the Roman Church so long as they were not detrimental to the faith or prohibited by the "law of God." Thus, they insisted on maintaining belief in purgatory, Masses and prayers for the dead, intercession of the saints, auricular confession and penance, holy water, images, church fasts, and other ceremonies, customs, and rites.[2]

Conflicts between Utraquists and Taborites

The differences between the Hussite factions were always simmering below the surface, and when not being threatened by Crusaders, they often erupted. In May and June 1423, the Prague Utraquist and Taborite forces almost came to blows over the issue of vestments and liturgy. Instead of fighting, however, they agreed to meet twice at Konopiště Castle to try to resolve their differences by means of theological disputation. The practice of theological disputation among the Hussites played an important role and was seen as a battle for the discovery of truth, ultimately based on the authority of the "Law of God."[3] It was obvious from the beginning of the Konopiště discussions that the real problem was not the vestments themselves, but the question of authority. As spokesman of the Taborites, Nicholas Biskupec proclaimed, "The Taborites believe every truth promulgated as worthy of belief by the Lord Jesus Christ, by the holy prophets, and by the apostles; nor do they refuse to include here the statements of other saints in which Christ speaks and which are truly founded in the aforementioned truth."[4]

For Tabor, this formulation meant that Scripture was to be the deciding authority, but the Prague masters were willing to accept the authority of church fathers as well. The Taborites appeared to be conciliatory, coming to agreement with the Prague masters on several points. The solution reached was that each party would select someone to administer the elements of the Eucharist according to the practice of the other side. The

Taborites selected Prokop Holý (later also known as Prokop the Great)[5] to administer the elements while wearing vestments, but unfortunately, the Utraquists reneged on their part, and the bad feelings continued to fester. Additionally, during the discussions, the uncompromisingly conservative John Příbram (d. 1448) unleashed an attack on Biskupec for his "heretical" opinions concerning the Eucharist.[6]

Meeting at a synod in Klatovy in November 1424, the Taborites produced a comprehensive summary of their theological positions in which they made it clear that they were separating from the Roman church in rituals, teachings about the sacraments, and essential articles of faith.[7] Later that month, the Taborites met in Prague with the masters, but no agreement was reached.

In the meantime, John Žižka became disenchanted with Tabor and separated from it, though he and the Taborites remained allies. After his death from the plague in 1424, his followers began calling themselves the Orphans. Thus, three distinct Hussite reform groups existed in uneasy tension: (1) moderate Prague Utraquists or Calixtines, led by the university masters; (2) Taborites; (3) and Orphans, previously known as Orebites from Mount Horeb, who were generally aligned with Tabor but often played a middle role between Tabor and Prague. Command of the field armies was taken up by the Taborite priest Prokop Holý.

The tension between the factions reached a boiling point, and actual war broke out in 1425 between the Taborite and Orphan brotherhoods on one side and the Prague Utraquist forces supporting Sigismund Korybut (1395–1435), a Lithuanian prince who hoped to become the king of the Czech lands, on the other. Peace was restored with the treaty of Vršovice that called for another diet at which both parties were to try to come to agreement. This meeting took place in January 1426 and again concluded with no agreement.

In spite of being unable to reach political and theological agreement, the various Hussite reform factions were again forced to unite by the third Crusade that was launched against them later in 1426. The Hussites won a spectacular victory over the Crusaders near Ústí nad Labem, but following the battle, they were again plagued by their own disagreements. These disagreements culminated a year later in the arrest and banishment of Korybut, just as the fourth Crusade against the Hussites was getting underway. In the wake of Korybut's fall, many of the most conservative masters, including John Příbram, left Prague, and this helped strengthen the ever-fragile relationship between Prague and Tabor. They again joined forces and drove back the Crusaders.

Another important theological disputation took place in 1429 between Peter Payne (1380–1455), an Englishman who had taken up the cause of the Hussites, and Příbram (who had returned to Prague) regarding the Eucharist and transubstantiation. A panel of theologians, including Biskupec and John Rokycana, was set up to oversee the disputation. It was during the course of these discussions that Rokycana came to be the recognized head of the Prague clergy and assumed his position as theological leader of the Utraquists, a position that he held for the rest of his life. Although Biskupec agreed with Payne's rejection of transubstantiation, the two were in the minority, and no agreement between the sides was reached. Příbram responded by attacking the Taborites in a tract titled "The Lives of the Taborite Priests."[8] A Taborite synod responded in January 1430 with a condemnation of Příbram's attack and a statement of the Taborite positions. The synod affirmed the Taborite order of worship as consistent with that of the early church, asserting that Tabor would not restore ceremonies that had been previously eliminated, and it affirmed its basic agreement with the teachings of Jakoubek of Stříbro. The synod clearly rejected Příbram's doctrine of transubstantiation.[9]

In addition to the theological wrangling that was going on in 1429–30, the Hussites were also waging a tremendous offensive campaign into the territories of their enemies. This campaign, known as the Magnificent Rides, won substantial victories for the Hussites and provided them, and particularly the Taborites, with an opportunity to advocate their theological cause abroad.[10] The Hussites produced several manifestos that defended their positions, explained the Four Articles, and issued a challenge for theological disputation. These manifestos enjoyed wide circulation outside the Czech lands.[11]

From late December 1430 through February 1431, Prokop Holý and his captains appointed a committee to maintain good relationships among the various Hussite factions. The committee appointed a delegation to attend a disputation in Krakow, Poland, to consider the conditions under which the Hussites might attend the Council of Basel that had been convened in 1431 to resolve issues related to papal supremacy and the Hussite heresy. Before the Hussites could appear at Basel, however, it was necessary to negotiate the terms under which the proceedings would be governed. Before these terms could be negotiated with the Roman Catholic representatives, the Hussites had to negotiate their own position among themselves. The intra-Hussite meeting took place in the Carolinum in Prague in April 1431. At this meeting, John Rokycana accused the Taborites of, among other things, rejecting prescribed fasts, allowing their priests to be involved in civil affairs, refusing to pray for the souls of the dead or for the intercession of Mary and the saints, rejecting several of the sacraments, and despising rituals associated with the Mass.[12]

Nicholas Biskupec responded with his *Confession and Defense of Tabor*,[13] which is the most complete account of the mature Taborite faith. It is a thoroughly restorationist document in which Biskupec clearly identifies that the difference between the Taborites and the Utraquists revolved around the question of authority. On the one hand, the Utraquists found authority for the ordering of the church not only in Scripture, but also in the tradition of the church, particularly in the ecumenical councils and the writings of Ambrose, Augustine, Jerome, and Gregory the Great. On the other hand, the Taborites insisted that authority was to be found only in the law of God and the way of life of Christ, the apostles, and the primitive church—in other words, in the teachings of Scripture, particularly in the New Testament. The councils and church fathers were to be followed only to the extent that their teachings were based on God's law.[14]

Biskupec began the *Confession* with eight suppositions upon which all the Taborite arguments were based, in which he laid out the Taborite basis for authority. He argued that, because Christ alone was the best lawgiver and because everything related to faith should be measured by Christ, the safest approach for life, faith, and morals was to imitate Christ. He also made a clear distinction between the Old Testament and the "law of the Gospel," which, for Biskupec, was practically equivalent to the New Testament. He argued that the law of the Gospel excelled above the Old Testament and was sufficient for the ordering of the church. Therefore, since Christ had "ordained that the church in the age of grace should be free regarding" various "signs," the church had no need for all the ceremonies of the Old Testament nor for the multiplicity of ceremonies that the Roman church had added to the liturgy. Additionally, the teachings of those who followed the apostles were not to be received as proof of binding church doctrine, and Christians were to accept them only to the degree that they agreed with the teachings of the law of Christ.[15]

In the rest of the *Confession and Defense*, Biskupec answered Rokycana's charges and explained the Taborite positions regarding such issues as the sacraments and the Mass, the doctrine of purgatory, the invocation of the saints, and the simplification of the liturgy. Because of the Taborites' firm commitment, which Biskupec repeated time and again, to base their practice on the teachings of Jesus, the apostles, and the primitive church, they retained only baptism and the Eucharist as sacraments commanded by Christ. Additionally, although they accepted some of the practices associated with the other Roman Catholic sacraments, they rejected much of the sacramental meaning and ritual that had been added to them. For the same reason, they rejected the doctrine of purgatory and the invocation of the saints, and they greatly simplified the liturgy of the church. Near the conclusion of the *Confession and Defense*, Biskupec expressed his hope that his readers might be encouraged to desire the order of the primitive church.[16]

At the same time the disputation was being held in Prague, imperial forces were preparing the fifth and final Crusade against the Hussites. The decisive battle, fought near Domažlice on August 14, 1431, resulted in the overwhelming defeat of the Crusaders. One result of this battle was that the Council of Basel passed a resolution to grant the Hussites a fair hearing.

The next step was to arrange for a meeting with delegates from Basel, which was set for May 1432 in the western Czech town of Cheb. It is clear from the negotiations that took place at Cheb and later at Basel that the Taborites had been the dominant party at the Carolinum discussions in April 1431. The major difficulty at the Cheb meeting involved the question of final authority. The Hussites, whose leaders included John Rokycana, Peter Payne, and Nicholas Biskupec, insisted on the authority of Scripture and the law of God, and the Roman side resisted this concession. The Hussites refused to back down and finally forced the Roman side to agree to the famous seventh article of the Cheb agreement, stating that in the Basel disputations, the final authority would be neither the council nor church tradition, but rather "the law of God and the practice of Christ, of the apostles and the primitive Church, together with the Councils and doctors who are truly founded on this practice."[17] This formulation was primarily Taborite and indicates the influence the Taborites held among the Hussites at this point. The Cheb agreement represented the first and only time in history that representatives of the Roman Church acknowledged an authority higher than the pope and the church councils.[18] While this was a substantial victory for the Hussites, it was far more a victory for Tabor than for the Prague masters who, generally speaking, were more willing to accept the teachings of the church fathers as authoritative. As it turned out, it was also an ephemeral victory.

From January to April 1433, the Hussite theologians presented their case to the Council of Basel. The council, however, had no intention of negotiating sincerely with the Hussites and certainly had no intention of surrendering supreme authority to Scripture as had been agreed at Cheb. Instead, the council took advantage of the differences between the various Hussite positions by secretly negotiating with the moderate Utraquists. The Hussites left Basel in April, accompanied by delegates of the council who were to go to Prague for the next round of negotiations with the Czech diet.

At the diet in Prague, the representatives of the council proposed that the Hussites submit to the council and surrender the gains of Cheb. The diet rejected this proposal, but that was not the end of the matter. By eventually promising to accept Communion in both kinds, provided the Hussites submitted to the Roman Church on all other matters, the Roman negotiators were able to gain the support of the Prague moderates against the Taborites, whom they knew would never agree to such a stipulation.[19]

The Battle of Lipany and Its Aftermath

The Utraquists were exhausted from the violence and devastation of war, and the concession of the cup for the laity satisfied their major demand. The Taborites were not willing to give up on the other three Articles of Prague, and this difference between the sides eventually led to the Battle of Lipany on May 30, 1434. The Prague Utraquists, who had joined forces with some Roman Catholic troops, defeated the Taborites. Prokop Holý was killed, and the invincible military power of Tabor was forever crushed. Without denying the serious political issues at stake on the religious front, the irony is that it was Tabor's insistence on three articles that the Prague masters themselves had supported and defended for more than a decade, rather than issues of real disagreement, such as vestments, the Eucharist and other sacraments, and teachings about purgatory, that led to the fatal military confrontation.

After the Battle of Lipany, the brotherhoods of Tabor and the Orphans were officially dissolved, and at the Prague diet of June and July, a truce was declared between the Roman Catholics and the Utraquists. The defeat at Lipany did not mean, however, the end of Tabor as a religious force, and Tabor continued for some time to have an influential role in addressing the problems of state administration and worship. Martin Wernisch claims that the defeat benefited Tabor because its leaders were now able to concentrate on propagating their ideals without violence.[20] In spite of their official dissolution, the Taborite John Roháč (d. 1437) called an assembly of the Taborite and Orphan brotherhoods that gathered in Tabor on December 21, 1434, to decide on the common platform they intended to defend in upcoming negotiations. Additionally, they issued a manifesto in which the members of the brotherhoods pledged to observe the Four Articles. Definite decisions regarding the differences between the Taborites and the Prague masters continued to be delayed until Peter Payne was finally entrusted with the position of making a final judgment on four of the main theological differences between the two groups. This he delayed doing until finally being forced to rule against Tabor after the return of Sigismund in 1436.[21]

The year 1435 saw more fighting, more negotiations, and more intrigue as the Taborite and Orphan brotherhoods strove to reestablish themselves, the supporters of Communion in one kind strove to bring the Utraquists into submission, and Sigismund, who had been crowned emperor in 1433, strove to attain the Czech crown. Additionally, John Rokycana was elected as archbishop of the Czech church, an event that was not received kindly and was never confirmed by the Roman authorities.

Finally, on July 5, 1436, the peace of Jihlava[22] was arranged, with the Utraquists promising to live in peace and unity with the Roman church in return for the council's agreement to order all Christian rulers to live in peace with the Czechs and Moravians and not regard them as heretics. The Roman bishops were also ordered to ordain Utraquist priests and not to prevent Communion in both kinds. While the Jihlava agreement provided a measure of religious freedom and tolerance, it did not provide acceptance of the Taborite concept of reform. Additionally, the agreement was never approved by the pope.

The Jihlava agreement did, however, clear the way for Sigismund to be recognized as king of the Czech lands, and his coronation took place on August 14, 1436. He immediately began to reveal his treachery by placing people loyal to him in positions of power and ignoring his agreements and obligations. He also forced Peter Payne to issue his decision against Tabor. Tabor refused to accept the decision because, according to Nicholas Biskupec, it violated the condition of arbitration that the decision would be in accordance with Scripture.[23] Refusing to recognize both the agreements at Jihlava and Payne's arbitration decision, Tabor continued to oppose Sigismund, and the city of Hradec Králové revolted. In order to isolate Hradec Králové, Sigismund, in negotiations with Bedřich of Strážnice, granted a measure of political and religious freedom to Tabor.[24] In spite of gaining some freedom, Tabor and its priests were no longer players on the international stage. Instead, they now negotiated only for their own survival. How far the power and influence of Tabor had fallen is illustrated by the fact that at the final disputations in Basel in August 1437, the Hussite cause that had once been defended by three theologians with Taborite sympathies was now defended by John Příbram, one of the most conservative of all Utraquist theologians and one of Tabor's bitterest enemies.

By 1437, the only remaining point of armed resistance was John Roháč's castle, Sion (Zion). After a siege of about four months, Sion fell on September 6. Roháč was brutally tortured, and he and some forty other men of the Sion garrison were executed in Prague. Sigismund lived only a short time to celebrate his final victory. Three months later, he died.

Another diet met in Prague in early 1440 and issued the letter of peace establishing the agreements of Jihlava as law and providing conditions favorable to the Utraquists. Because there was no king, the country governed itself, for all intents and purposes, as a republic for the next ten years.

During this time, the Taborites continued to struggle for recognition of their positions, but it was a losing cause. The Taborites vainly continued their attempt to assert the principle of the seventh article of the Cheb agreement as the basis for doctrine. During the 1440s, several synods and disputations were held to debate the religious differences between Tabor and the Utraquist church as represented by John Rokycana and John Příbram. The final great disputation between Tabor and Prague was held in Kutná Hora from July 7–12, 1443, but the Taborites did not budge in their positions. Finally, on January 31, 1444, the Prague synod officially condemned Tabor, stating that the faith of John Rokycana and John Příbram was "safer, better, and more certain" than that of the priest Nicholas Biskupec and his colleagues.[25] The faith of Rokycana became the law of the land, and Tabor became an illegal sect. It was just a matter of time until it was definitively vanquished.

In the early 1450s, the Utraquist George of Poděbrady (1420–71) came to power and immediately turned his attention to the subjugation of Tabor. On September 1, 1452, Tabor surrendered, and its remaining priests, including Nicholas Biskupec, were taken into custody. Biskupec was imprisoned and never heard from again. Thus ended the Taborite restoration.

Practices and Theological Positions of Tabor

The Taborites were determined to reconstitute the primitive church in their own time and place, and they consistently insisted on Scripture ("the law of God") as the primary authority for life and faith. Although they knew and used the Old Testament extensively, they recognized the New Testament, particularly after the chiliastic phase had passed, as the primary source of instruction for the church in the "age of grace." They respected the writings of early Christian teachers, but they subjected that teaching to the scrutiny of the New Testament. In terms of traditional Christian orthodoxy, the Taborites were in no way heretical. They accepted the deity of Jesus, the work of the Holy Spirit, the Trinity of one God in three persons, and the doctrines embodied in the historic creeds of Christendom. Their heresy lay in their rejection of the authority of the Roman Catholic Church and the human traditions and innovations that the Catholic Church had introduced.

The Taborites saw themselves as a brotherhood and referred to one another as brothers and sisters. At first, with their priests in charge of the common chest, they practiced the community of goods, though, with the passing of time, this became unsustainable. Chiliastic hopes at the beginning faded, and although the Taborites were originally committed to pacifism, once they were attacked, they practiced warfare both to defend and propagate their beliefs. To be sure, not all of the priests, such as Nicholas Biskupec, were necessarily comfortable with the practice and extent of the warfare, but they were powerless to prevent it.[26] On the other hand, other priests encouraged warfare, accompanied the troops into battle, and one of them, Prokop Holý, was a successful military leader. Because of their rejection of religious ostentation and what they perceived as idolatry, the Taborites also engaged in large-scale destruction of church buildings, monasteries, organs, and religious images and statues, though they claimed that they were using the treasures they acquired from this destruction for the poor.

Though they did not eliminate it completely, the Taborites minimized the distinction between clergy and laity, symbolized particularly in their insistence on Communion in both kinds and in the rejection of clerical vestments and auricular confession.[27] Still, they retained their bishop, whom they preferred to refer to as senior, and they retained their priests, who administered the religious activities and teaching of the community. On the other hand, they also had secular leaders who governed Tabor and the cities affiliated with it.

Taborites drastically simplified the liturgy of the church and eliminated "human innovations" and anything that did not contribute to the purpose of worship. They conducted worship services in the vernacular rather than in Latin and compared singing in Latin to the howling and barking of dogs, since it was incomprehensible to the common person.[28] They were willing to worship almost anywhere, including in homes and in open fields, either under a tent or under the sky. In Tabor itself, they built a simple wooden building for worship services.[29] Although Taborite worship was simple and emphasized the rational, it was also joyful. Taborites conceived of their worship as being true to the primitive pattern of the first Christians; it consisted in the reading of Scripture, preaching, praying, and the singing of spiritual songs. The main focus of the assembly was on the Lord's Supper, which was normally preceded by the congregational recitation of the Lord's Prayer.[30]

The Taborites considered singing to be the only music that was appropriate in the church, and it was to be joyful and encouraging, even during funerals. Words were important in religious music, not the melody, and Taborite songs were usually paraphrases of biblical texts. The Taborites viewed organs and other musical instruments as toys that made a mockery and vanity of worship and were only for the entertainment of the "saucy ears of vain and worldly people." Organs were for "religious donkeys" who rejoiced from music without understanding the sense of the words. They simply did not belong in church.[31] Additionally, Taborites rejected singing in parts during worship because they considered it a mark of vanity. Hussite singing, both Taborite and Utraquist, led to the Czechs to be known as a musical nation.[32]

For the Taborites, receiving the Lord's Supper in both kinds was not just following the biblical pattern. As spiritual food, based on their interpretation of John 6:53–58, it was normally necessary for salvation.[33] Following the pattern of Matthew of Janov, they practiced frequent Communion—usually daily. Interestingly, because the Lord's Supper was to be a communal event, the priests offered it only once each day, and everyone who intended to partake was expected to be present. There were no provisions for private or individual Communion, which in their view would have been an oxymoron.[34] As mentioned above, the Taborites rejected the doctrine of transubstantiation, but they did emphasize the presence of Christ sacramentally in the Lord's Supper, while the bread and wine remained bread and wine. The emphasis of the eucharistic service was on the aspect of communing with or receiving Christ.[35] This differed from the Roman and Utraquist emphasis on the service as a sacrifice. Following the logic that Communion is for all those in the church and that the church is made up of all those who have been baptized, the Taborites practiced infant Communion.[36]

Taborites understood that baptism also was a sacrament instituted by Christ and normally necessary for salvation. They continued the normal medieval practice of infant baptism, but they scandalized their opponents by their willingness to baptize without using consecrated water and by baptizing instead in lakes, streams, rivers, and ponds.[37] There is some indication that at times they may have practiced immersion instead of sprinkling or pouring, though they rejected triple immersion. As a matter of principle, they advocated imitating the primitive practice in all they did. They knew that immersion was the practice of the primitive church, and Nicholas Biskupec referred to baptism as the "immersion of the whole body."[38] At Tabor itself, they baptized in the pond Jordán, which still exists and was clearly a place with sufficient water for immersion. For the Taborites, baptism represented spiritual birth and was for the purpose of cleansing the soul from sin. Interestingly, they acknowledged that baptism was for those who believe, something the later Anabaptists never tired of pointing out that infants could not do.[39]

As mentioned, the Taborites considered only the Eucharist and baptism as sacraments commanded by Christ for the salvation of souls. Instead of confirmation, they practiced the laying on of hands. In place of penance with private auricular confession to a priest, they recommended inner repentance and private confession to any believer, as well as public confession before the brothers and sisters with congregational prayer for repentant sinners. Instead of extreme unction prior to death, they advocated prayers and anointing with oil for the healing of the sick who requested it. Though they recognized ordination and marriage as useful biblical rituals, they divested the ceremonies of the rites common to the Roman Catholic sacraments.[40]

Although in the beginning, those who gathered on the mountaintops were in some ways freeing themselves from the established order of society, by the time Tabor established itself as a town, the Taborites themselves were required to establish their own civil order, founded upon what they conceived of as the "law of God." Additionally, this was a civil order they hoped to impose on all of their countrymen. Thus, their restoration moved beyond simply a restoration of the primitive church to include the dream of a social and political reconstitution of all society as well.[41]

Legacy

We can identify the legacy of the Taborite movement in several areas, most of which are interrelated. First, and most obvious, was the renewal of the practice of Communion in both kinds for the laity, a practice they shared with the Utraquists. Second was their efforts to minimize the differences between clergy and laity. Third was their radical simplification of worship and religious practice. Fourth was their reduction, for all practical purposes, of the number of sacraments from seven to two, retaining only baptism and the Eucharist. Each of these first four practices anticipated understandings and practices that were to be implemented roughly one hundred years later during the sixteenth-century Protestant Reformation. Fifth was the founding of the *Unitas Fratrum* (Unity of the Brethren). Five years after the Taborites were finally eliminated as a religious force with the fall of Tabor in 1452, a man known as Brother Gregory, who had been influenced by Petr Chelčický, founded the Unity of the Brethren. It was this group through which the ideals of the Taborites survived into the future.

Questions for Thought or Discussion

1. To what extent could the Taborite movement be considered a restoration movement?

2. Against what were the Taborites reacting?

3. What in particular were the Taborites emphasizing in their renewal efforts?

4. What were various strengths or weaknesses of the Taborite movement?

5. How were the Taborites similar to or different from the previous movements discussed in this book?

6. What did you find particularly interesting or attractive about the Taborite movement?

7. What lessons or applications can you draw from the Taborite movement?

NOTES

[1] Mortal or public sins included such things as murder, theft, fornication, gluttony, usury, and perjury among the laity and, among the clergy, simony, fornication and concubinage, the buying and selling of indulgences, and demanding payment for religious services. As stated in the previous chapter, for historical information regarding the Czech Reformation/Revolution in English, I draw primarily from Kaminsky, *A History of the Hussite Revolution*; Fudge, *The Magnificent Ride*; and Bartoš, *The Hussite Revolution*. I also draw from Czech works, primarily Šmahel, *Husitská revoluce*. Atwood, *The Theology of the Czech Brethren*, is also useful, though his lack of facility in the Czech language is a limitation. Lists of the Four Articles can be found in several places with variations in the wording. See, for example, Kaminksy, *History*, 369; Fudge, *Magnificent Ride*, 98; Atwood, *Theology of the Czech Brethren*, 94.

[2] Kaminsky, *History*, 260–62.

[3] On the role of Hussite disputations, see Amedeo Molnár, "Zur hermeneutischen Problematik des Glaubensdisputs in Hussitentum," *Communio Viatorum* 29 (1986): 1–14.

[4] Kaminsky, *History*, 467. This is almost the same formulation that was later incorporated into the seventh article of the famous Cheb agreement of 1432. See below.

[5] In Czech, the word *holý* means *bald* or *shaven*, so Prokop the Bald.

[6] Bohuslav Havránek, Josef Hrabák, and Jiří Daňhelka, eds., *Výbor z české literatury doby husitské*, vol. 2 (Prague: Československá akademie věd, 1964), 263; Bartoš, *Hussite Revolution*, 2.

[7] For a discussion of Klatovy and its articles, see Kaminsky, *History*, 500–516.

[8] *Život kněží táborských*, found in Josef Macek, *Ktož jsú Boží bojovníci: čtení o Táboře v husitském revolučním hnutí* (Prague: Melantrich, 1951), 262–309. Jaroslav Boubín has issued a newer edition as *Život kněží táborských* (Příbram, Czech Republic: Podbrdsko—Fontes 1, 2000).

[9] Bartoš, *Hussite Revolution*, 46–47.

[10] Amedeo Molnár, "Táborský boj duchovní," *Theologická příloha Křesťanské revue* 1 (1958): 7.

[11] Several of the manifestos are published in Amedeo Molnár, *Husitské manifesty* (Prague: Odeon, 1980), 128–70.

[12] Found in Amedeo Molnár, introduction to Nicholas Biskupec, *Mikuláš z Pelhřimova: Vyznání a obrana Táborů*, ed. Amedeo Molnár and František M. Dobiáš (Prague: Československá akademie věd, 1972), 21–25; cf. R. Allen Diles, "The *Confessio Taboritarum* of Nicholas Biskupec of Pehhrimov: His Eight Suppositions and His Approach to the Old Testament," *Communio Viatorum* 56, no. 2 (2014): 122.

[13] Latin: Nicholas Biskupec, *Confessio Taboritarum*, ed. Amedeo Molnár and Romolo Cegna (Rome: Istituto Storico Italiano Per Il Medio Evo, 1983); Czech Translation: Biskupec, *Vyznání*.

[14] Diles, "*Confessio Taboritarum*," 128–29.

[15] A full English translation of the eight suppositions can be found in Diles, "*Confessio Taboritarum*," 124–26; cf. my earlier condensed translation in "A Comparison of Nicholas of Pelhřimov and the Taborite Restoration with Alexander Campbell and the American Restoration Movement," *Restoration Quarterly* 44, no. 4 (2002): 249–50.

[16] Biskupec, *Confessio*, 338; *Vyznání*, 271.

[17] Bartoš, *Hussite Revolution*, 80.

[18] Fudge, *Magnificent Ride*, 110; A. Molnár, "Táborský boj," 8.

[19] Fudge, *Magnificent Ride*, 113–14; Bartoš, *Hussite Revolution*, 102–10.

[20] Martin Wernish, *Husitství: Raně Reformační Příběh* (Brno, Czech Republic: Pontes Pragensis, 2003), 106.

[21] The four issues were the number of sacraments, the invocation of saints, the use of vestments, and the existence of purgatory; see William R. Cook, "John Wyclif and Hussite Theology," *Church History* 42 (1973): 348.

[22] This agreement was based on terms accepted by the Utraquists and the Council of Basel, known both as the Prague Compacts and as the Basel Compacts. Some literature also uses the term *Jihlava Compacts*.

[23] Cook, "John Wyclif," 348.

[24] A brief overview of the role of Bedřich of Strážnice can be found in Robert Kalivoda, "Über den Aufmarsch der Reformation und über den Ausgang des Tábor," *Communio Viatorum* 30 (1987): 143–56. Kalivoda notes that after Lipany, Nicholas Biskupec was the primary intellectual representative of Tabor, while Bedřich of Strážnice was the primary political representative—he calls him the "only Taborite victor of Lipany" (der einzige taboritische "Sieger" von Lipany), 149–51.

[25] Šmahel, *Husitská revoluce*, 4: 83.

[26] Nicholas himself was never entirely comfortable with the use of force in defense of the faith, believing that the safest way was to fight spiritually rather than with physical swords, and he was particularly appalled at many of the abuses involved in warfare. Unlike the case with other Taborite priests, we never read of Nicholas joining the field army in battle. Nicholas felt that just as God disallowed the warlike David from building the temple in favor of the peaceful Solomon, it would be impossible for cruel and warlike people to renew or restore the church. See my discussion in Robert Allen Diles, "The Old Testament and Restoration: A Comparison of the Approach to and Use of the Old Testament in Restoration Movements of Fifteenth-Century Tabor and Nineteenth-Century North America, As Seen in the *Confessio Taboritarum* of Nicholas Biskupec of Pelhřimov and in Selected Works of Alexander Campbell" (ThD diss., Charles University, 2005), 68–69.

[27] Biskupec, *Confessio*, 80–83, 96–100; *Vyznání*, 81–82, 93–96.

[28] Zdeněk Nejedlý, *Dějiny husitského zpěvů—kniha čtvrtá, TábořI* (Prague: Československá akademie věd, 1955), 194.

[29] Howard Kaminsky, "Pius Aeneas Among the Taborites," *Church History* 28 (1959): 289.

[30] See Kaminsky, *History*, 445–46 for a description of the Taborite liturgy.

[31] Nejedlý, *Dějiny husitského zpěvů*, 40–42.

[32] Nejedlý, *Dějiny husitského zpěvů*, 80.

[33] Biskupec, *Confessio*, 78; *Vyznání*, 79.

[34] Nejedlý, *Dějiny husitského zpěvů*, 212–13.

[35] Nejedlý, *Dějiny husitského zpěvů*, 213.

[36] Atwood, *Theology of the Czech Brethren*, 83. It should be noted that the Utraquists also practiced infant Communion.

[37] Kaminsky, *History*, 339.

[38] Biskupec, *Confessio*, 177; *Vyznání*, 154.

[39] Biskupec, *Confessio*, 72; *Vyznání*, 75.

[40] Biskupec, *Confessio*, 71–88; *Vyznání*, 74–86. See discussion in Atwood, *Theology of the Czech Brethren*, 121–29.

[41] See Kaminsky, *History*, 384–433.

CHAPTER 5

"Faith, Love, and Hope"

The Unity of the Brethren (*Unitas Fratrum*)

Petr Chelčický (c. 1390–1460) had been associated with the Taborites in the early days of the radical Hussite movement, but when the Taborites abandoned their pacifist position, he abandoned Tabor.¹ Chelčický moved to southern Bohemia, where he continued to teach and write, gathering around himself a small group of disciples. He was highly respected, and both moderate Utraquist and radical Taborite Hussites continued to consult with him and seek his advice. His formal education was limited, neither reading nor writing in Latin, but he was well-read and produced several works in Czech. Jarold K. Zeman says of Chelčický that "he may well be called the forgotten prophet of separatism and restitutionism".² Chelčický felt that the church of his day had lost its way, believing that "poison [had] been poured into the Holy Church" when Constantine had "pushed himself into the Christian community along with his pagan lordship."³ He made a clear distinction between the church and society, and he argued in his most famous work, *The Net of Faith*, that two great whales, Constantine (representing the emperor) and Pope Sylvester (representing the papacy), had, by their alliance, torn the net of the church.⁴ Chelčický revealed his restorationist perspective in the following statements:

> Thus we of the latter day are like after the burning out of a house which has fallen down making a pile of ruins; here and there we see by some signs that there stood a chamber before—but everything fell onto the foundation (which, buried,) is grown over by a forest where animals graze and dwell. Who will then find the buried foundation of the burned house that is in ruins and which is deeply covered (with debris) and the top of which has long since been overgrown by defiant weeds?
>
> The whole matter of finding the true foundation is made all the more difficult because these defiant weeds which have sprung upon it are called the true foundation by many; they, pulling to themselves the growth on top of the house ruins, declare, "This is the foundation and the way, all should follow it. . . ."
>
> There are many who would like to dig in order to find the original foundation, in the like manner as Nehemiah, Zerubbabel, and the prophets have done. . . . And they had a great difficulty in rebuilding the city and the Temple on the charred ruins. Now there are also spiritual ruins long ago covered up (by weeds); these, too, shall be mended and rebuilt, and for this no one can give a true foundation save Jesus Christ from whom many have run away to other gods, building themselves new foundations, denying and covering up Jesus Christ, the Son of God, by a (layer of) falsehood.⁵

Chelčický continued:

> Through [the apostles'] teaching they have established a perfect community of faith and life; this people has remained an example to all future faithful Christians, so that all believers can look back to these first Christians and discover in them the evident fruit of apostolic labor. . . . The future generations can safely emulate their work and expect eternal life.⁶

Given his emphasis on Jesus and the teachings of the apostles, it is no surprise that, like Nicholas Biskupec, Chelčický also gave greater weight to the New Testament, believing the Old Testament to be inferior and incomplete. For Chelčický, the Old Testament was to be interpreted in light of the New.[7]

The Unity of the Brethren

Following the Taborites' 1434 defeat at the Battle of Lipany, Chelčický's restorationist ideals were carried on by a group of young disciples who had been advised by John Rokycana to read Chelčický's works, many of which he had in his possession.[8] This group, led by Rokycana's nephew, Gregory (d. 1474), was seeking a purer church, and after reading some of Chelčický's writings, group members met with him in person. According to Peter Brock, Gregory and his followers would come to accept all of Chelčický's political, social, and theological doctrines.[9] As a result of their readings and discussions with Chelčický, Brother Gregory's group established a religious community at the Bohemian town of Kunvald, about one hundred miles east of Prague. Referring to one another simply as brethren of the Law of Christ, the group established a community in 1457 or 1458, and at a synod in Rychnov in 1464, they more formally established themselves as the *Unitas Fratrum* (Unity of the Brethren).[10]

Initially, they set up their new society, or assembly, emphasizing Scripture, the Four Articles of Prague, and moral living. They were committed not only to biblical doctrine, but also to "the practical application of biblical teaching."[11] They advocated pacifism and stressed the importance of receiving the Lord's Supper in both kinds. Additionally, they simplified church ritual related to the celebration of the Lord's Supper by meeting in homes and other available structures, dispensing with vestments, and using ordinary bread (rather than unleavened wafers) served in ordinary vessels (rather than gold or silver vessels), and they rejected "sacramentals" such as holy water and oil.[12] Though the Brethren initially did not see themselves as a new church, according to Daniel Crews, they "hoped to be an example to the rest of the church for thoroughgoing renewal."[13] They were looking for "devout Christians who had preserved the faith and order of the primitive church,"[14] and they attracted members from former Taborites, Waldensians, and other "radical" groups.[15] The Unity Statutes of 1464 emphasized the importance of being sound in faith, united in love, and certain in hope, a triad that represented for the Unity the essentials of Christian faith. The Statutes also stressed obedience, discipline, hospitality, proper relationships, accountability, and Christian simplicity.[16]

Because the Unity was excluded from the provisions of the Jihlava peace agreement, the Brethren were technically an illegal group and could be subject to persecution at any time. The first wave of persecution broke in 1461.[17] Following the martyrdom of Brother Jacob Chulava at the hands of the Roman Catholic authorities in 1467, and realizing they were, in effect, on their own religiously, the Brethren formally established their own ministry, thus intentionally separating themselves from both the Czech Utraquist church and Rome. Gregory referred to the Constantinian fall of the church to justify this step.[18] Anticipating Luther's concept of the priesthood of all believers, they selected twenty elders, all laypersons, and then, following the example of the New Testament church's selection of Matthias (Acts 1:21–26), from those twenty, they selected three ministers by lot. Apparently, this was followed by the rebaptism of their members.[19] A short time later, one of the three, Matthias of Kunwald (d. 1500), was ordained as their first bishop, or senior. Matthias then appointed an Inner Council made up of priests and laypersons. According to Crews, "Its members consciously established for themselves their own priestly order with the assurance that the origin of the Unity was undeniably founded on the pattern of the apostolic church and the revelation of the will of God." Although Brother Gregory held no official position in the movement, he continued, as "patriarch," to exert influence until his death in 1474.[20]

Due to the level of commitment that was demanded, becoming a member of the Unity was not easy. The Unity followed Petr Chelčický and Brother Gregory in its distrust of urban centers, commerce, and participation in civil affairs. Thus, members of the early Unity were generally expected to eschew wealth, making their living from agriculture and simple crafts, and those from the cities who joined were expected to move to the country. Even nobles were expected to surrender their titles, feudal rights, and magisterial duties. The Unity emphasized the Sermon on the Mount and maintained a strict doctrine of pacifism. Members were forbidden to swear oaths, which eliminated the possibility of their holding government office or becoming guild masters.[21]

One interesting feature of the early Unity was that, although they retained simplified forms of the traditional seven sacraments of Roman Catholicism, they practiced the rebaptism of converts to their movement and, for a time, baptized only adults, thus anticipating a practice of the later Anabaptist movement.[22] Later, however, the Unity accepted the practice of baptizing those infants born to members. The practice of rebaptizing within the Unity was likely rooted in a Donatist-like rejection of the efficacy of the sacraments of a corrupted church.[23]

The Unity stressed simplicity in its worship assemblies and retained few medieval liturgical forms. The Brethren gathered for their assemblies on Sundays, major feast days, and sometimes on weekdays as well. Before the Unity was able to build its own meeting places, the assemblies were usually in homes, since the Brethren were not allowed to use Roman Catholic or Utraquist church buildings. In addition to preaching, activities included prayer, the reading of Scriptures in the Czech language (with a characteristic restorationist emphasis on the New Testament over the Old), and a cappella singing. The singing could be so enthusiastic that sometimes outsiders complained that it was too loud. Communion in both kinds, accompanied by singing, was received "whenever needed" and generally came to be celebrated four times a year.[24]

As the Unity moved into its second generation of leadership, it faced its greatest internal challenge. Many, led by younger men with more formal education than the first generation leaders, began to feel that the strict separation from the world, particularly the expectations of leaving urban centers and requiring nobles to give up their rights, was going beyond the demands of the gospel and stunting the potential growth of the movement. This group became known as the "Major Party" or "New Brethren." Theologically, they felt that the more conservative members of the movement placed too much emphasis on the necessity of good works and Christian morals, perhaps to the detriment of a doctrine of grace. The "Minor Party" or "Old Brethren" continued to insist on the ideals and the practices of the movement from the time of Brother Gregory. By the late 1490s, the crisis had led to actual schism.[25]

Following a period of prayer and fasting, the Inner Council held a synod in the town of Brandýs in 1490 to deal with the pressing issues. Most of the issues concerned the relationship between members of the Unity and the demands of the secular powers: To what extent were members of the Unity permitted to exercise secular power under a governing authority, and were there no circumstances under which a person might legitimately swear an oath?[26] These were important questions because, following Peter Chelčický and Brother Gregory, the Unity had traditionally held the position that the Brethren were to remain entirely separated from the government apparatus, and because of Jesus's teachings in the Sermon on the Mount, under no circumstances were they to make oaths. The synod reached a unanimous decision that, while providing some guidance, ultimately left the decisions regarding these questions as a matter of each individuals' conscience—in certain circumstances, one could choose or choose not to participate in secular power, and one could choose or choose not to swear. No one should judge those who reached differing conclusions. It decreed, in part, "We cannot give uniform instruction and teaching as to how one should conduct oneself, on account of the divergence of cause, place, time, and persons." Clearly, the Unity was abandoning some of the foundational principles of Chelčický and Brother Gregory.[27]

Although the decision at Brandýs had been unanimous, two leaders of the Minor Party, Jacob and Amos, continued to agitate against the new positions, and they found sympathy with the bishop Matthias. What amounted to a coup in the Inner Council took place, and those who had favored the Brandýs decision resigned. Matthias then replaced them with "good old Brethren." In response, the Major Party sent four brothers to the East (Russia, Constantinople, the Balkans, Palestine, and Egypt) to seek out the "church of the apostles," but they returned, disappointed in their search.[28]

Questions regarding the relationship between faith and works also continued to be a source of contention, with the Old Brethren holding to a much greater degree of separation from the world and the New Brethren cautioning that this might be placing unnecessary burdens on people. They suggested that those from the Minor Party advocated a "works righteousness" that could lead to hypocrisy, pride, and self-righteousness. The Minor party responded that, without genuine righteousness, faith was dead, and that the "grace party" was too worldly.[29]

Those of the Old Brethren remained in control of the Inner Council until another synod in Rychnov in 1494 basically reaffirmed the previous decisions of Brandýs. Matthias surrendered his leadership (or was removed), and the Major Party was restored to power.[30] Jacob and Amos continued to resist what they perceived as a betrayal of the Unity's principles, and over the next few years, several more synods were held, but each time the synods "consistently ruled in favor of greater freedom and toleration."[31] Finally, in 1500, Amos formed a separate community of the Old Brethren, with its own priesthood, but by the mid-sixteenth century, the Minor Party had died out.[32] The victory of the Major Party allowed the Unity to expand into the cities, where it experienced greater numerical growth among the educated, wealthy, and ruling classes. By allowing participation in government service, the taking of oaths, and even some military service (thus, turning from absolute pacifism), the Unity was on its way to a greater measure of cultural accommodation.[33] Nevertheless, according to Craig Atwood, "Although the new Unity emphasized grace and freedom more than the old Brethren, it remained separatist, persecuted, and morally rigorous."[34]

The greatest theologian of the Major Party was Luke of Prague (c. 1458–1528).[35] Luke had received his bachelor's degree in Prague (1482) after which, having been influenced by the writings of Chelčický, he joined the Unity of the Brethren. He was ordained as one of the bishops of the Unity in 1500, then as senior bishop in 1517, and he was a leading influence in the movement's acceptance of the progressive views of the Major Party. Believing that the Unity had become too restrictive, he advocated the normative principle of biblical interpretation, reintroducing parts of the Roman liturgy and rejecting from Roman practice only what was contrary to the gospel but retaining from it what was good and useful.[36]

Theologically, Luke made distinctions between those things that were considered essential for salvation, things that ministered to salvation, and those things that were incidental.[37] According to Luke, the essentials were made up of two categories: the work of God and the human response. The work of God included the grace of the Father, the merit of Christ, and the gifts of the Spirit. The human response consisted of the Unity's triad of faith, love, and hope.[38] The ministerial things, such as the Word of God, discipline (the keys), the sacraments, and the church, were the divine means by which people knew and received the essentials. The incidental things were the ceremonies and traditions of the church. Luke also made distinctions between the terms *church*, which he used to refer to the one worldwide church, *unity*, which he used to refer to each part, or denomination, of the worldwide church (Roman Catholic, Utraquist, and Brethren), and *community*, which he used for each local congregation of the Brethren but which he never used for the Roman Catholic or Utraquist congregations.[39]

As mentioned, because the provisions of the peace of Jihlava of 1436 (and of another agreement in 1485) had applied only to Roman Catholics and Utraquists, the Unity of the Brethren was not a legal religious entity, so throughout its history, it faced much persecution. Brother Gregory himself had been tortured on the rack, and others were martyred. Several times, members of the Unity were exiled from their homeland, though exile was not always consistently enforced by the nobles on whose lands they lived. Less than a decade before the onset of the Protestant Reformation, the Mandate of St. James, issued in 1508, banned all activities of the illegal Unity. Persecution intensified, and more Brethren were imprisoned and martyred. The Unity came to believe that persecution was a mark of the true church.[40]

The Protestant Reformation and the Unity of the Brethren

With the coming of the sixteenth-century Protestant Reformation, a new era of hope dawned upon the Unity of the Brethren, and they began to make overtures, first toward the Lutherans and then toward the Reformed (Calvinist) Protestants.[41] Several of their future ministers even went to the university in Wittenberg to study; later, many were trained in Geneva. The coexistence of the Unity with Protestantism (Lutherans, Utraquists, and Reformed), however, was always uneasy. Leaders of the Unity were especially uneasy with the apparent antinomianism of the Lutherans and with some of John Calvin's speculations on predestination. They were also uneasy with Ulrich Zwingli's more symbolic view of the Lord's Supper, insisting instead on Christ's presence "sacramentally, spiritually, powerfully, and truthfully in the bread and wine."[42] Another area of concern was that, more so than the Protestants, the Unity continued to stress the connection between salvation by faith on the one hand and works as fruits of faith on the other. Of course, the Unity always resisted the Protestants' cooperation with civil authorities in church matters.[43] Additionally, in spite of early overtures, relations with the Utraquists went from bad to worse, before finally improving as the sixteenth century progressed.

As the Unity sought alliances with Protestantism, it gave up some of its older practices, such as rebaptizing converts and using plain bread for the Lord's Supper instead of unleavened wafers.[44] As was typical of Protestants (and like the Taborites before them), it was at this time that the Unity reduced the number of sacraments from seven to two—baptism and the Eucharist.[45] In 1535, the Unity developed and addressed its new Confession, containing a preface by none other than Martin Luther, to both the Holy Roman Emperor Charles V and Charles's Spanish-born younger brother, the Czech king Ferdinand I. This Confession of 1535, which is comparable to standard sixteenth-century Protestant confessions, became the basic statement of faith for the Unity of the Brethren until the end of its existence.[46]

In spite of their hopes, the coming of the Reformation did not end persecution of the Brethren in their Czech homeland. A critical point came in the aftermath of the first Schmalkaldic War (1546–47) in Germany. King Ferdinand had called for the Czech nobles to muster troops for his effort to put down the Lutheran rebellion in Germany. Nobles who belonged to the Unity refused to join Ferdinand's forces, and this gave him the excuse he was looking for to suppress the Unity upon his triumphant return. He revived the Mandate of St. James, and churches were closed or destroyed, while many Brethren were imprisoned. During this persecution, Bishop John Augusta (d. 1572), a disciple of Luke of Prague, was imprisoned and tortured repeatedly for sixteen years (1548–64) but steadfastly refused to deny or compromise his faith.[47] In conjunction with Augusta's imprisonment, the Brethren were given six weeks to renounce their faith or leave the country. Many found refuge in more tolerant Moravia, and many others moved to Poland, where new Unity congregations were established. The other surviving bishop, Mach Sionský, was leading a group of refugees in East Prussia, but after only a short time, he died, leaving the Unity with only one bishop, and he was in prison with little contact with the outside world.[48] Eventually, Augusta was released, but persecutions continued.

As persecution continued, so did efforts by the Unity to forge closer ties with both Utraquists and Lutherans. They reached a high point of cooperation in 1575 when the nobility (rather than the clergy) of the three groups produced the Bohemian Confession, which went beyond the 1485 agreement by recognizing the legitimacy not only of Catholics and Utraquists, but also of Czech Lutherans and the Unity of the Brethren. King Maximillian II (1527-76), however, refused to allow the Confession to be printed and reissued the Mandate of St. James, outlawing the Unity. Fortunately for the Unity, many of the Utraquist nobles continued to honor the terms of the Bohemian Confession and tolerated the Brethren who lived in their territories.[49]

Ironically, about the same time that Utraquists, Czech Lutherans, and the Unity were coming to agreement on the Bohemian Confession, German Lutherans were becoming more exclusive. This development, along with increasing personal contacts with Calvinists, led the Unity to turn its orientation toward the Reformed. By the seventeenth century, the Unity was strongly aligned with the Reformed, though it continued to be a voluntary church representing a "third way" within Protestantism.[50]

One of the most important contributions of the Unity came in the period 1579-94, during which the Brethren published a complete Czech translation of the Bible, known today as the Kralice Bible.[51] The Kralice Bible was the fruit of labors begun much earlier by Bishop John Blahoslav (1523-71), a leading voice within the Unity in advocating for greater education for its clergy. He had himself completed an important translation of the New Testament as early as 1564 and was also important to the Unity for his work in producing hymns and hymnals.[52]

By 1600, the Unity had about 150 congregations in Bohemia and Moravia and another 40 congregations in Poland, and its members made up perhaps as much as 5-10 percent of the Czech population.[53] Finally, in 1609, facing external threats and internal pressure, Emperor Rudolf II (1552-1612) issued the "Letter of Majesty," granting religious liberty to all who accepted the Bohemian Confession of 1575. For the first time in its history, the Unity of the Brethren was legally recognized. Its legal status did not last long.

Facing threats from the new king, Ferdinand II, Protestant nobles confronted Catholic officials on May 23, 1618, and, not satisfied by their responses, they threw two officials and their secretary from a window of the Prague Castle.[54] The officials survived the fall, apparently by landing in a heap of trash or manure, but the damage was done. This defenestration precipitated the armed conflict that was to become the Thirty Years' War. The Czech nobles, including some of the Unity, rebelled and elected a Calvinist, Frederick of the Palatinate, who was one of the electors of the Holy Roman Empire, as their new king. Ferdinand gathered his army of imperial troops, who were joined by allies from the German Catholic League, and, just outside the city of Prague, his forces, under the command of Johann Tilly, routed the Protestants in the Battle of White Mountain on November 8, 1620. Frederick fled the country and left the Protestants to fend for themselves. On June 21, 1621, twenty-seven Protestant leaders, including seven nobles of the Unity, were executed, most by beheading.[55] Forcible re-Catholization was imposed on the Czech lands and Moravia. Authorities gave people the choice to convert to Roman Catholicism, emigrate, or face prosecution (imprisonment and/or death). Many "converted," and many others went into exile.

After several years of hiding, in 1628, a Unity priest named John Amos Comenius (Komenský, 1592–1670) led a band of the Brethren to Poland.[56] As the refugees crossed the border, they prayed that God would preserve a "hidden seed" that might someday renew the Unity. In exile, Comenius became an important leader among the Brethren; in 1632, in Leszno (or Lissa), Poland, he was ordained as a co-bishop or co-senior, and then, in 1648, as sole bishop or senior of the Czech and Moravian branch of the Brethren.[57] Over the years, he traveled throughout Europe and was a prodigious writer, both on spiritual and educational matters, among other subjects. In fact, he was recognized as one of the world's leading educational theorists. As an example of the international esteem in which Comenius was held, according to the American Puritan Cotton Mather, Comenius was invited to become the first president of Harvard University.[58]

In 1668, near the end of his life, Comenius wrote his famous work *Unum Necessarium* (*The One Thing Needful*), in which he adapted what has become a famous phrase: "The prime law of Christian concord is threefold: in absolutely necessary things to maintain unity, in less necessary things . . . liberty, in all things, toward all, love."[59] Comenius advocated for unity among all Christians, suggesting that they surrender their man-made names and simply be identified as Christians. He refused to become bogged down in the pressing theological issues of the day. For example, regarding predestination, he believed that Scriptures could be found to support both sides of the debate, so he concluded that both views must contain a measure of truth. Additionally, he questioned those who debated about the Lord's Supper: "Why do ye wish to discuss that about which the Scriptures are silent?" He also pointed out that the Lord's Supper had been ordained as a means of uniting Christians rather than for the purpose of dividing them.[60] Perhaps most touching is his plea for unity in his work *The Last Will and Testament of the Dying Mother, the Unity of Brethren*. This work was written in 1650 after the Peace of Westphalia had set the terms for the conclusion of the Thirty Years' War, thus assuring that the Unity would not be allowed to return to their homeland. The dying mother is the Unity itself:

> To all Christian unities I bequeath a yearning for the unity of thoughts and reconciliation and unity in faith and love leading to the Unity of spirit. Oh if only that spirit . . . could come to all of you, so that you would long with all your heart, as much as I was longing, for the true unity in Christendom with all those confessing the name of Christ in truth! Oh, if only God would give you to find the foundations of all things essential, things of service, and accidental . . . so that all of you would know what is necessary to enthuse about and what not. . . .
>
> Oh, if only all of you longed for true participation in the Mercy of God, for true participation in the merits of the Christ, for true participation in the sweet inner gifts of the Holy Spirit, which you can achieve through the true faith, true love and true hope in God, which is the foundation of Christianity! These you

can then achieve by the services ordained by God for service to us: Word, Keys, and Sacraments, whose power is most certainly proved by the inner power of the Spirit, when they are being used simply and honestly, humbly and in faith as if given by God, without the human-invented beauty of rites.

Oh, if only you would . . . hit at least sometimes something which would make happy the heart of Our Compassionate One, who prayed for all of us [that we might be one], so that all of you who claim allegiance to the house of the Church were only one house of God, well ordered and joined together, and only in that house the one family of God, under the unanimous order of God in concord, loving and helping one another, standing as one body, although consisting of many members . . . , so that one day the Christian Church and angels can sing: "how good and delightful it is when brothers dwell in unity!" (Ps. 133:1).[61]

Comenius worked tirelessly for the return of the Unity to its homeland. Unfortunately, he put too much stock in failed prophesies about the Brethren's return, and this damaged his reputation.[62] He died on November 15, 1670, at the age of seventy-eight, having spent his last forty-two years in exile. Comenius is recognized as the last bishop of the Czech Unity of the Brethren, and with his passing, the Czech Unity of the Brethren also passed from the scene.[63]

Teachings and Practices of the Unity of the Brethren

The *Ratio Disciplinae*, composed in the seventeenth century, described the Unity of the Brethren in the final decades prior to its ultimate demise.[64] In this document, the Brethren described their movement's aim from the beginning as "to restore the purity of doctrine and simplicity of Christian life," and they proposed to organize themselves "after the model of the apostolic and primitive church" so far as conditions during persecution allowed.[65]

The Unity divided its membership into three groups: the beginners (children and adult converts who were learning the rubrics of the faith), the proficient (those who had been well-taught and conformed to the teachings of the church), and the perfect (those who were mature enough to lead and teach others). The normal organizational structure of the Unity of the Brethren was for two to six bishops, called *antistites* in the *Ratio Disciplinae*, and often referred to as seniors, to be elected by the clergy and to serve as the primary leaders over the whole church. Though the Unity exhibited a preference for apostolic succession, it was not absolutely bound to it for the selection of its bishops. An Inner Council made up of clergy and laypersons would hold regular synods for making important decisions and would operate in conjunction with the bishops, one of whom would be elected president of the Inner Council. Each congregation was led by its own minister or priest, typically referred to as a spiritual administrator.[66] The administrators were assisted by what they called civil elders (lay elders), who were themselves chosen by the congregation. The Unity also had female elders for work with women. *Almoners* and *aediles* were in charge of receiving and distributing contributions from the members. Additionally, deacons, who were awaiting their own ordination, assisted the ministers. The Unity believed that this organization was based on the teaching of Scripture, and the *Ratio Disciplinae* contained many passages in support of it. Interestingly, the Unity expressed a preference for clerical celibacy, even during the Reformation period. Like other Protestants, however, they did not require it.[67]

As previously mentioned, the Unity made an important distinction between essential things, ministerial (or auxiliary) things, and incidental (or accidental) things. The essentials were things necessary for salvation and consisted of both the work of God (grace, the merit of Christ, and the work of the Holy Spirit in redemption and sanctification) and the human response (faith, love, and hope). The ministerial things, such as the Word of God, discipline (the keys), the sacraments, and the church, were the divine means by which people knew and received the essentials. They were things "the Holy Spirit uses as a tool for imparting the essential things" and were "completely dependent on the essentials."[68] The incidental things were the ceremonies and external rites, such as forms of liturgy and church government, which needed to be exercised according to Christian liberty and prudence and which could differ according to circumstances.[69] The Unity claimed that the ways in which it practiced the accidentals were drawn from Scripture and "the example of the primitive church."[70] In a note on this point, Comenius added, "No one can doubt that apostolic traditions are the purest fountains and the customs of the primitive church the nearest streams from them. No one, therefore, ought to doubt that those things which have crept in since the Apostles should be reduced to these rules and that the better things are nearer the fountains."[71]

As its name implied, throughout its existence the Unity sought unity and dialogue with other Christians and frequently made overtures to Utraquists, Lutherans, and the Reformed in efforts to find common ground. Additionally, the Brethren were willing to approach the Roman Catholics, Eastern Orthodox, and even Waldensians and Anabaptists. According to Craig Atwood, "The Unity understood that it could affirm another community of faith as Christian without sacrificing its own independent status."[72] They believed that, although in God's eyes, there was only one true church, no individual earthly church or denomination could claim to be that one. Nevertheless, it was their goal to restore the ideals of that church as much as possible, particularly in faith, practice, and life.[73]

Until they accommodated themselves to the Protestant Reformation, the Unity retained the seven sacraments of the Roman Catholics and Utraquists, but they simplified the rituals and did not see them as possessing any sort of mysterious power in the sense that many people understood them.[74] The Confession of 1535 stated that the sacraments were necessary for salvation but went on to note that for those who were unable to avail themselves of the sacraments, faith in Christ was sufficient for salvation.[75] The early practice of the movement was to abandon infant baptism, and until they began to curry the favor of the Lutherans and the Reformed, the Brethren required the rebaptism of those who came to them from other churches.[76] By the time of the Confession of 1535, they accepted infant baptism and rejected the practice of rebaptism.[77] In spite of their rapprochement with Protestantism and their acceptance of infant baptism, however, the Unity never accepted the Protestant alliance of church and state. Atwood claimed, "The Brethren were the most radical of the Hussites in their complete rejection of a state church."[78] This, as we shall see, anticipated the stance of the sixteenth-century Anabaptists.

Regarding the Lord's Supper, the Brethren tended to be somewhat ambiguous in their statements. They clearly rejected both transubstantiation and consubstantiation and the idea of the Lord's Supper as being no more than a symbolic memorial;[79] instead, they followed the Taborite teaching that Christ was present "sacramentally, spiritually, powerfully, and truthfully in the bread and wine."[80] They accepted that the bread "is the true body of Christ" and "the chalice is his true blood," but they refused to speculate as to the way in which this was true, insisting "that no one should add to, mix in with, or take away anything of one's own from these words of Christ."[81] They received the Supper in both kinds, usually kneeling, not because they believed kneeling to be necessary, but because they had been compelled by their persecutors to give up the practice of standing.[82]

While the Confession of 1535 recognized the authority of Scripture over all other authorities and gave clear preference to the New Testament, it also accepted the normative principle that only those traditions that are "not opposed to piety" or that "obscure the glory of Christ . . . and lead astray" were to be eliminated.[83] A specific tradition the Unity retained was the celebration of saints' days by gathering to worship God and remember the example of the saints, even singing songs about them. However, they were clear on two points. First, all believers are saints in the biblical sense, and second, neither the saints nor their images are to be worshiped.[84]

Even before their association with the Protestants, the Unity rejected the doctrine of purgatory, and they reaffirmed this in the Confession of 1535.[85] While Luther influenced Protestantism to give significant attention to the writings of Paul and particularly to the doctrine of justification by faith, from the beginning and throughout its history, the Unity placed a heavy emphasis on the Gospels and particularly on the Sermon on the Mount as the ethical guide for Christian living.[86] In fact, their emphasis was always more on Christian living (orthopraxy) than on doctrinal precision (orthodoxy).[87] Given this emphasis on Christian living, it is not surprising that the Unity always expected strict discipline among its members and practiced excommunication of those who refused to repent of sinful behavior.[88]

Whereas a tendency of some restorationist groups is, like the Old Brethren, to become stuck in the traditions of the past, as a whole, the Unity showed a remarkable ability to adapt to new situations without surrendering its quest for God's truth. This ethos was captured in a 1531

Brethren proclamation that its priests "should feel free to use contemporary conditions as an aid in seeking out the precious truth of people's salvation and not be hindered in the quest for truth by their predecessors."[89]

Legacy

The following points may be suggested as the legacy of the Unity of the Brethren: (1) Some members of the Unity in the Czech and Moravian lands, while outwardly professing Roman Catholicism, kept the faith alive secretly. Some of those eventually immigrated to Texas and, in 1903, formed a modern Unity of the Brethren church. (2) Unity writings influenced Philip Jacob Spener and August Hermann Francke, leaders of seventeenth- and eighteenth-century German Pietism.[90] Pietism then influenced Nicholas Ludwig von Zinzendorf and contributed to his openness to the refugees who formed the Renewed Unity of the Brethren (the Moravian Brethren), the direct spiritual descendants of the Unity of the Brethren. (3) Several churches of the modern Czech Republic have proclaimed themselves to be heirs of the Brethren's spiritual heritage. These include the Evangelical Church of the Czech Brethren, the Church of the Brethren, the Unity of the Brethren, and the Baptist Union.[91] (4) The Kralice Bible became the Bible of choice of the Czech people until the late twentieth century. It has been as important to the Czech people in terms of both its religious and linguistic influences as the King James Version has been in the English-speaking world and Luther's translation in the German-speaking world. (5) The Unity's refusal to consider itself the only true church and its emphasis on unity among believers, regardless of confessional loyalty, anticipated modern ecumenical efforts and unity movements. (6) Although the Unity of the Brethren has been considered by some to be "the oldest among all the Reformed churches,"[92] others have identified a different family tree. The Unity always adhered to the principle that faith and religious conviction could not be coerced. Although it came to practice infant baptism for the children of its members, from its inception, it valued the ideal of a church to which people chose to belong. Thus, rather than the first of the Reformed churches, Jarold K. Zeman stated, "In the history of restitutionism, *Unitas Fratrum* must rightfully be designated as the first believers' church and the first free church."[93]

Questions for Thought or Discussion

1. To what extent could the Unity of the Brethren be considered a restoration movement?
2. Against what was the Unity reacting?
3. What in particular were the Brethren emphasizing in their renewal efforts?
4. What were various strengths or weaknesses of the Unity?
5. How was the Unity of the Brethren similar to or different from the previous movements discussed in this book?
6. What did you find particularly interesting or attractive about the Unity of the Brethren?
7. What is the proper relationship between orthodoxy and orthopraxy?
8. What lessons or applications can you draw from the Unity of the Brethren?

NOTES

[1] On Chelčický, see Murray L. Wagner, *Petr Chelčický: A Radical Separatist in Hussite Bohemia* (Scottdale, PA: Herald Press, 1983). I also draw from Jaroslav Boubín, *Petr Chelčický: Myslitel a Reformátor* (Prague: Vyšehrad, 2005). For Chelčický's relationship with and break from Tabor, see Wagner, *Petr Chelčický*, 55–64.

[2] Jarold K. Zeman, "Restitution and Dissent in the Late Medieval Renewal Movements: The Waldensians, the Hussites and the Bohemian Brethren," *Journal of the American Academy of Religion* 44, no. 1 (March 1, 1976): 20.

[3] Petr Chelčický, *Replika proti Rokycanovi*, quoted in Howard Kaminsky, *A History of the Hussite Revolution* (Berkeley: University of California Press, 1967), 392.

[4] Petr Chelčický, *Net of Faith*, in Enrico C. S. Molnár, "A Study of Peter Chelčický's Life and a Translation from Czech of Part One of His Net of Faith" (master's thesis, Pacific School of Religion, 1947, transcribed, formatted, and edited by www.nonresistance.org, Oberlin, Ohio, 2006), 73, accessed March 12, 2020, https://archive.org/details/TheNetOfFaith/mode/2up.

[5] Chelčický, *Net of Faith*, 49.

[6] Chelčický, *Net of Faith*, 58.

[7] Craig D. Atwood, *The Theology of the Czech Brethren from Hus to Comenius* (University Park, PA: Pennsylvania State University Press, 2009), 135; Boubín, *Petr Chelčický*, 132.

⁸ For the history of the Unity of the Brethren, I rely primarily on Peter Brock, *The Political and Social Doctrines of the Unity of Czech Brethren in the Fifteenth and Early Sixteenth Centuries* (London: Mouton & Co., 1957); C. Daniel Crews, *Faith, Love, Hope: A History of the Unitas Fratrum* (Winston-Salem, NC: Moravian Archives, 2008); and Atwood, *Theology of the Czech Brethren*.

⁹ Brock, *Political and Social Doctrines*, 40–41.

¹⁰ Sometimes also referred to as the Bohemian Brethren or the Czech Brethren; for the 1458 date, Atwood, *Theology of the Czech Brethren*, 156.

¹¹ Ian M. Randall, "A Missional Spirituality: Moravian Brethren and Eighteenth-Century English Evangelicalism," *Transformation* 23, no. 4 (2006): 206–7.

¹² Crews, *Faith, Love, Hope*, 99, 103; Atwood, *Theology of the Czech Brethren*, 159.

¹³ Crews, *Faith, Love, Hope*, 102.

¹⁴ Crews, *Faith, Love, Hope*, 108.

¹⁵ Atwood, *Theology of the Czech Brethren*, 157; Brock, *Political and Social Doctrines*, 76.

¹⁶ *Unity Statutes of 1464*, Moravian Archives, accessed March 12, 2020, https://www.moravianarchives.org/wp-content/uploads/2012/01/Unity-Statutes-of-1464.pdf.

¹⁷ Brock, *Political and Social Doctrines*, 77.

¹⁸ Atwood, *Theology of the Czech Brethren*, 169.

¹⁹ Crews, *Faith, Love, Hope*, 110.

²⁰ On the beginnings of the movement and their selection of elders, see Atwood, *Theology of the Czech Brethren*, 152–72; and Crews, *Faith, Love, Hope*, 108–12. The quotation is from Crews, 112; cf. E. Molnár, "Study of Peter Chelčický's Life," 19–20.

²¹ Brock, *Political and Social Doctrines*, 98–99; Crews, *Faith, Love, Hope*, 129–30; Atwood, *Theology of the Czech Brethren*, 159–60, 183.

²² Petr Chelčický had questioned the practice of infant baptism, though there is no evidence that he argued for rebaptism, Wagner, *Petr Chelčický*, 53; Boubín, *Petr Chelčický*, 98–99, 102.

²³ See Crews, *Faith, Love, Hope*, 110, 127; Zeman, "Restitution and Dissent," 23. On their view of the sacraments, see Atwood, *Theology of the Czech Brethren*, 177–82.

²⁴ On the Unity's worship assemblies, see Crews, *Faith, Love, Hope*, 125–26, 128, 246n, 255, 278, and 320; see also the *Ratio Disciplinae*, translated by Benjamin Seifferth as *Church Constitution of the Bohemian and Moravian Brethren* (London: W. Mallalieu and Co., 1866), 35–36.

²⁵ On the conflict between the two factions, see Brock, *Political and Social Doctrines*, 103–81; Atwood, *Theology of the Czech Brethren*, 189–206; Crews, *Faith, Love, Hope*, 133–41.

²⁶ Brock, *Political and Social Doctrines*, 124; Atwood, *Theology of the Czech Brethren*, 195.

²⁷ Atwood, *Theology of the Czech Brethren*, 196–97; Brock, *Political and Social Doctrines*, 127–30. The quotation of the decree is from 128. So, for example, a Christian might use secular power to resist violence or injustice instead of passively allowing it.

²⁸ Brock, *Political and Social Doctrines*, 137; Atwood, *Theology of the Czech Brethren*, 198–99.

²⁹ Atwood, *Theology of the Czech Brethren*, 200–201.

³⁰ Atwood, *Theology of the Czech Brethren*, 204–5.

³¹ Atwood, *Theology of the Czech Brethren*, 206.

[32] Many joined the sixteenth-century Hutterite movement and other Anabaptists, Atwood, *Theology of the Czech Brethren*, 191, 206. On Anabaptists and the Hutterites, see Chapters Seven and Eight below.

[33] See Zeman, "Restitution and Dissent," 23-24.

[34] Atwood, *Theology of the Czech Brethren*, 216.

[35] On Luke, see Atwood, *Theology of the Czech Brethren*, 189-240. Atwood suggests that "under Luke the Unity brought together in a creative synthesis the three streams of Hussitism—the Utraquists, the Taborites, and Chelčický—to form a strong and stable community of faith," 216.

[36] See Crews, *Faith, Love, Hope*, 144.

[37] Luke was not the first of the Brethren to make the first two distinctions; he may have been responsible for articulating the third. On Luke's understanding of the essentials, ministerials, and incidentals, see Atwood, *Theology of the Czech Brethren*, 217-39.

[38] Zeman, "Restitution and Dissent," 24.

[39] Zeman, "Restitution and Dissent," 24.

[40] Atwood, *Theology of the Czech Brethren*, 281.

[41] The branch of Protestantism that originated in Switzerland under the influence of Ulrich Zwingli and John Calvin is referred to as the Reformed.

[42] Atwood, *Theolog of the Czech Brethren y*, 253.

[43] On these concerns, see Crews, *Faith, Love, Hope*, 166-69, 205, 278-79.

[44] Atwood, *Theology of the Czech Brethren*, 257-58.

[45] Crews, *Faith, Love, Hope*, 170, 189.

[46] Crews, *Faith, Love, Hope*, 192-93.

[47] Crews describes some of the torture: "He was first stretched out and burned with candles. Then hot pitch was applied to his body, set on fire, and ripped off with pincers, taking portions of skin with it. Later he was stretched on a rack suspended by a hook and weighted down with stones. This did not stop until he was half dead," *Faith, Love, Hope*, 212.

[48] Crews, *Faith, Love, Hope*, 217-19, 238.

[49] Atwood, *Theology of the Czech Brethren*, 319-20.

[50] Atwood, *Theology of the Czech Brethren*, 295-326, 331.

[51] On this translation, see Crews, *Faith, Love, Hope*, 281-83; and Milan Salajka and Jiří Svoboda, eds., *Czech Ecumenical Fellowship* (Brno, Czech Republic: TISK, 1981), 159-76.

[52] On Blahoslav, see Atwood, *Theology of the Czech Brethren*, 309-15.

[53] Crews, *Faith, Love, Hope*, 290; Jaroslav Pánek, *Comenius, Teacher of Nations* (Prague: Orbis, 1991), 11.

[54] Often referred to as the defenestration of Prague, this was the third such action. The first was July 30, 1419; the second was September 24, 1483; and the third was May 23, 1618.

[55] Crews suggests that one of the condemned men was pardoned on the scaffold, *Faith, Love, Hope*, 345.

[56] For biographical information on Comenius, see Matthew Spinka, *John Amos Comenius: That Incomparable Moravian* (Chicago: University of Chicago Press, 1943); Pánek, *Comenius*; Jan Kumpera, *Jan Amos Komenský: Poutník na Rozhraní Věků* (Ostrava, Czech Republic: Nakladatelství Svoboda, 1992).

[57] Spinka, *John Amos Comenius*, 55, 113; Atwood, *Theology of the Czech Brethren*, 353, 358.

[58] Spinka, *John Amos Comenius*, 84-86. Although it seems certain that Comenius was involved in discussions related to Harvard, there is some uncertainty as to whether he

was actually offered the presidency. See Kumpera, *Jan Amos Komenský*, 88; and Atwood, *Theology of the Czech Brethren*, 356.

[59] John Amos Comenius, *Unum Necessarium: The One Thing Necessary*, trans. Vernon H. Nelson (Winston Salem, NC: Moravian Archives, 2008), 67, accessed July 28, 2020, https://www.moravianarchives.org/images/pdfs/Unum%20Necessarium.pdf; cf. "*In necessariis unitas, in dubiis libertas, in omnibus autem caritas.*" The phrase was apparently originally coined by the German Lutheran theologian Peter Meiderlin (Rupertus Meldenius). The famous Puritan Richard Baxter (1616–91) used almost the same motto: "Unity in things necessary, and Liberty in things unnecessary, and Charity in all." In a slightly different form, this phrase became a characteristic motto of the US Stone-Campbell Movement: "In faith, unity; in opinions, liberty; in all things, charity." For an interesting discussion of the background and use of this "Peace Saying," see Hans Rollmann, "In Essentials Unity: The Pre-History of a Restoration Movement Slogan," *Restoration Quarterly* 39, no. 3 (1997): 129–39.

[60] Eve Chybova Bock, "Seeking a Better Way," *Christian History* 13 (1987): 8.

[61] John Amos Comenius, *The Last Will and Testament of the Dying Mother, the Unity of Brethren*, Article 18, accessed March 11, 2020, https://en.wikisource.org/wiki/Translation:The_Last_Will_and_Testament_of_the_Dying_Mother_The_Unity_of_Brethern.

[62] Atwood, *Theology of the Czech Brethren*, 361–62.

[63] A Polish branch, however, survived until its last bishop died in 1841, Atwood, *Theology of the Czech Brethren*, 363.

[64] The *Ratio Disciplinae* was originally written in 1609, revised in 1616, published in 1632 or 1633, and included comments from Comenius in 1660.

[65] *Ratio Disciplinae*, 10.

[66] Though the Brethren were wary about the use of the term *priest*, in Article 9 of the *1535 Confession*, 19, they used Hebrews 5:1 to give a biblical basis to the idea of priests in the church. The Confession was translated by Daniel C. Crews, accessed March 12, 2020, http://moravianarchives.org/wp-content/uploads/2012/01/Confession-1535.pdf.

[67] Article 9 of *1535 Confession*, 20. Descriptions of the Unity organization taken primarily from *Ratio Disciplinae*, 13–20. See also Crews, *Faith, Love, Hope*, 125, 311–15; and Atwood, *Theology of the Czech Brethren*, 163–67.

[68] Atwood, *Theology of the Czech Brethren*, 223.

[69] *Ratio Disciplinae*, 11–12; cf. Crews, *Faith, Love, Hope*, 310; Zeman, "Restitution and Dissent," 24; Article 15 of *1535 Confession*, 31.

[70] *Ratio Disciplinae*, 12.

[71] *Ratio Disciplinae*, 55n3.

[72] Atwood, *Theology of the Czech Brethren*, 296.

[73] Crews, *Faith, Love, Hope*, 124, 126; cf. articles 8 and 15 of *1535 Confession*, 17, 31.

[74] Crews, *Faith, Love, Hope*, 126–29.

[75] Article 11 of *1535 Confession*, 22.

[76] See Crews, *Faith, Love, Hope*, 110, 121. "The Czech Brethren could completely convince [Luther] of their agreement with him only by 'renouncing the building of an elective community which one joins by personal commitment,' which meant the end of the practice of adult baptism," Giovanni Gonnet, "The Influence of the Sermon on the Mount upon the Ethics of the Waldensians of the Middle Ages," *Brethren Life and Thought* 35 (1990): 38–39.

[77] The Brethren were caught in the same inconsistency as Luther in arguing that faith was necessary for the efficacy of the sacraments, while also insisting on the baptism of

infants who could have no faith of their own. They cited Genesis 17 and Mark 10:13–14 as the biblical basis for infant baptism, *Ratio Disciplinae*, 32–33.

[78] Atwood, *Theology of the Czech Brethren*, 226.

[79] On these views, see Chapter Six below.

[80] Atwood, *Theology of the Czech Brethren*, 122, 253.

[81] Article 13 of *1535 Confession*, 25.

[82] *Ratio Disciplinae*, 36. It is interesting that in the *Confession of 1535*, Article 13, on the Lord's Supper ends with the type forming the words of the text into the shape of a chalice, 27.

[83] See articles 1–2, 15 of *1535 Confession*, 6–7, 29.

[84] Article 17 of *1535 Confession*, 33–35.

[85] Article 20 of *1535 Confession*, 38; cf. Crews, *Faith, Love, Hope*, 128.

[86] Amedeo Molnár, Noemi Rejchrtová, and Luděk Rejchrtový, eds., *Slovem obnovená: čtení o reformaci* (Prague: Kalich, 1977), 154.

[87] Atwood, *Theology of the Czech Brethren*, 4, 295, 331, 349, 352.

[88] *Unity Statutes of 1464*, 3–4; Article 8 of *1535 Confession*, 17–18; *Ratio Disciplinae*, 51–53.

[89] Atwood, *Theology of the Czech Brethren*, 240.

[90] Crews, *Faith, Love, Hope*, 378; Pánek, *Comenius*, 69.

[91] See Salajka and Svoboda, *Czech Ecumenical Fellowship*, 12, 48, 56–64, 75.

[92] Salajka and Svoboda, *Czech Ecumenical Fellowship*, 56.

[93] Zeman, "Restitution and Dissent," 23. Similarly, Atwood suggests, "The Unity can legitimately be considered the first voluntary church in Western history," *Theology of the Czech Brethren*, 2.

CHAPTER 6

"FOR THE GREATER GLORY OF GOD"

The Protestant and Catholic Reformations of the Sixteenth Century

By the sixteenth century, reform of the church in Europe could no longer be delayed.[1] In addition to the attempts of conciliarism and the Hussites, other movements had arisen. The *Devotio Moderna* or Modern Devotion was a movement dating from the fourteenth century emphasizing spiritual renewal through practices of personal piety.[2] Inspired by the *Devotio Moderna*, the Brethren of the Common Life called laypersons to band together in communities of religious commitment, but without taking monastic vows. What is referred to as Renaissance humanism, with its motto of *ad fontes* (back to the sources), had exploded onto the scene in Italy and beyond. Writers such as Erasmus of Rotterdam (1466–1536), who was himself a product of both humanism and the Brethren of the Common Life, published scathing critiques of the church. Erasmus had also given the scholarly world a published edition of the Greek New Testament, thus opening new possibilities for biblical study. When Johann Tetzel (1465–1519) set up shop to sell indulgences outside Wittenberg, Germany, this set the stage for the match that would light the fuse of what is commonly known today as the Protestant Reformation.[3] In opposition to Tetzel's sale of indulgences, the German Augustinian priest Martin Luther (1483–1546) nailed his "Ninety-Five Theses on Indulgences" to the door of the All Saints' Church in Wittenberg and set in motion events that in many ways were the culmination of the reform efforts of John Wyclif, John Hus and the Hussite movement, and others. Thus, the traditional date of that event, October 31, 1517, is generally considered the birthday of the Protestant Reformation.[4]

Given the general accessibility of materials related to the sixteenth-century Reformations, this chapter will merely note highlights that are important for providing the context for the other movements covered by this volume.

Martin Luther and the Reformation in Germany

Martin Luther[5] had been a monk and priest at the Augustinian monastery in Erfurt, Germany, but moved from there to the new university in Wittenberg where he received his doctorate in 1512 and at which he became a professor of theology the following year. Luther had struggled mightily with consciousness of his own sinfulness and his concept of the righteousness of God that demanded the punishment of the sinner. Sometime between 1515 and 1519, during the course of his biblical studies and teaching at Wittenberg, however, he discovered the concept now known commonly as justification by faith alone (*sola fide*), based on Romans 1:17. No longer did he understand the righteousness of God as that quality of God that demanded the punishment of the sinner, but instead, he now understood it as a gift that God freely bestowed on the believer.[6] This understanding of the role of faith in the justification of the sinner put Luther theologically at odds with the teachings of the Roman Catholic Church, especially with the system of sacraments by which a person, in effect, gained merit before God. In Luther's understanding, no person could do anything by which he or she might gain merit before God. For Luther, salvation, and even faith itself, was entirely due to the grace of God (*sola gratia*).

When Tetzel began selling indulgences in the vicinity of Wittenberg, Luther was scandalized by the idea that one might pay money in order to have time in purgatory reduced. He was following the normal procedure for obtaining discussion or debate on an issue by nailing his "Ninety-Five Theses on Indulgences" to the door of the church in Wittenberg. Although Luther was merely asking for an academic debate on the question of indulgences, his document created a sensation; in a short time, the theses had been translated, copied, and distributed across Germany and other parts of Europe, and the Reformation was born.

Many people agreed with the obscure German theologian's critique of the church's use of indulgences, and now they were willing to say so. The Roman Catholic Church's hesitant and uncertain response to Martin Luther gave time to allow him to gain such a following that by the time Pope Leo X realized the danger, it was too late to deal summarily with Luther as the church had done one hundred years before with John Hus. By the time Luther was finally granted a disputation in May 1518, he was challenging the church's whole understanding of what was involved in human salvation.

Luther then appeared at another disputation in Leipzig in July 1519 when Johann Eck (1486–1543) egged him on step by step until Luther declared that some of John Hus's views were "Christian and evangelical," that both popes and general councils of the church could err, and that only the Scriptures were authoritative (*sola scriptura*). A short time later, Luther went on to write, "I have taught and held all the teaching of John Huss [sic], but thus far did not know it. . . . In short we are all Hussites and did not know it."[7] Luther maintained that he would concede that he was in error only if convinced that his positions were contrary to the Bible and sound reason. He had broken with the authority of the Roman Catholic Church.

In 1520, Luther published three works that in many ways articulated the basics of his positions. In his *Address to the Christian Nobility of the German Nation*, Luther advocated the doctrine of the priesthood of all believers, arguing that, by virtue of their baptism, all Christians were priests and were therefore authorized, when needed, to perform the duties of priests, particularly hearing the confession of the sinner. It was important for Luther that he win over local authorities for the reforms because he wanted the reforms to be carried out in an orderly fashion and with the consent of the government. Luther justified the magistrates' involvement in church reform through his doctrine of the priesthood of all believers

(1 Pet. 2:5–9). Because all Christians were priests, and although clergy (ministers) were necessary for the sake of good order, when the clergy did not fulfill its role, the magistrates were the logical agents to step in and implement the needed reforms.[8] In the *Babylonian Captivity of the Church*, Luther attacked the sacramental system of Roman Catholicism, reducing the sacraments from seven to two, retaining only baptism and the Eucharist. He also retained a place for confession, though he no longer considered it a sacrament instituted by Christ.[9] Finally, in his *Freedom of the Christian*, Luther argued that because Christians were justified by God's grace through faith, they were free from many of the laws the church had imposed.[10]

Pope Leo X excommunicated Luther in January 1521, and when, in April of the same year, he famously refused to recant his positions before Emperor Charles V (1500–58; reigned 1519–56) at the Diet of Worms, the emperor pronounced Luther an outlaw and declared his intention to proceed against him. By the time Charles issued the Edict of Worms against Luther, however, Luther already had a significant following, and reforms were being enacted throughout Germany. Some of the significant changes that were introduced included the following: Communion in both kinds was made available, and sacrificial language was eliminated from the Mass; the doctrine of transubstantiation was rejected;[11] monks and clergy married (including Luther in 1525); preaching in the vernacular was implemented; and congregational singing was encouraged. One of Luther's most important contributions to the reform of the church was his translation of the New Testament into German, which he completed while in hiding in the Wartburg castle. Although Luther desired to purge the church of the corruptions and innovations of Rome, he also was willing to preserve much of post-apostolic practice. He advocated the normative principle, believing that what the Scriptures did not forbid was allowable so long as it did not distract people from the gospel. Thus, for example, he favored the continued use of candles, crucifixes, and pictures.

In 1529, the German diet met at Speyer with a Catholic majority and decreed that the 1521 Edict of Worms condemning Luther was to be enforced and that Lutherans were to have no liberty of worship in Catholic territories. Catholics, however, were to have liberty of worship in Lutheran territories. This caused the Lutheran representatives to enter a formal protest against the decision of the diet, and this protest was the origin of the term *Protestant*.

Though Luther never intended to start a new church, his followers took his name, and the church in much of Germany became known as the Lutheran church. Eventually, the Schmalkaldic Wars broke out between the Roman Catholics and Lutherans in the German territories. The warfare concluded on September 25, 1555, with the treaty known as the Peace of Augsburg, the provisions of which allowed each prince to determine the kind of religion that would prevail in his territories.[12]

Zwingli and Calvin and the Reformation in Switzerland

In the meantime, reform had also begun in Switzerland. The leading figures of this story were Ulrich Zwingli (1484–1531) and John Calvin (1509–64). At the age of twenty-two, Zwingli was ordained in Constance and became a parish priest in Glarus, near his hometown of Wildhaus.[13] Although he did not have much formal theological training, Zwingli read widely and studied diligently, making himself a competent self-educated theologian. The ideas of the Christian humanists such as Erasmus particularly influenced him, and he was especially attracted to the ideal of going back to original sources (*ad fontes*); he wanted to know what the church was like in the beginning. Therefore, Zwingli studied the Greek New Testament and the church fathers and came to know them well. One of the most important aspects of Erasmus's influence on Zwingli was the concept of a sharp distinction between the creaturely and the divine (or the worldly and the spiritual), which should not be mixed and implied that the physical could not mediate the spiritual. Zwingli was also heavily influenced by Augustine, giving him, along with the biblical writings of John, credit for teaching him the real meaning of the gospel.[14]

In 1516, Zwingli moved to the parish of Einsiedeln, an important pilgrimage center, where he became a popular preacher. At Einsiedeln, Zwingli was in a position to observe the superstition and excesses associated with the veneration of images, relics, and saints. This disturbed him such that he began to speak out against the abuses. It was at Einsiedeln where Zwingli also began voicing opposition to the practice of selling indulgences.

When, in 1519, Zwingli became the pastor of the Great Minster Church in Zurich, he began a program of preaching through the New Testament, beginning with the Gospel of Matthew, followed by the book of Acts and then the epistles of Paul. Over the course of six years, Zwingli preached through the entire New Testament. Of this program of preaching, he reflected somewhat audaciously: "Thus I planted. Matthew, Luke, Paul, and Peter watered, but God in a wonderful manner gave the increase."[15] His study of the New Testament had convinced him that many of the practices of the church as he knew it were not consistent with the practices of the early church as revealed in the texts of the Scriptures he was preaching.

Reform in Zurich began as early as 1521, but 1522 was crucial for the reform movement. By that year, Zwingli was suggesting that Scripture was the sole authority for church practice and Christian living. A corollary of this principle was that church practices that could not be supported by Scripture were to be eliminated. People began to take things into their own hands at the beginning of the Lenten fast of 1522. On the evening of Ash Wednesday (March 9, 1522), a dozen or so people gathered at the home of a local printer and cut two sausages into pieces, which they then distributed among themselves in order to demonstrate they were not bound by the church rules for fasting. Although Zwingli was present, he did not eat. He did, however, come out in support of those who did. When others began breaking the fast, the city council intervened and, although the offenders were acquitted, the council ruled that people should continue to observe the fasts for the time being for the sake of good order. The city council's ruling was significant because, at this point, the civil authorities effectively took control of the Zurich churches;[16] for all practical purposes, they ignored the authority of the bishop of Constance and established the precedent that city magistrates rather than church officials would determine church practice.

The following year, in 1523, two important disputations were held, first in January and then in October, with Zwingli declared the victor in both. At the January disputation, Zwingli presented sixty-seven articles or conclusions that summarized his preaching. He asserted, for example, the authority of the gospel over all other teachings, that salvation was in Christ alone through faith, that the Mass was not a sacrifice, and that clerical celibacy was not biblical. He went on to affirm the authority of the Christian civil powers, and he called into question the sacrament of penance and the doctrine of purgatory.[17] Because no one had effectively refuted Zwingli, the city council ruled that from that time forward, all preaching in Zurich would be only that which could be proved by the gospel and the Scriptures. Zwingli introduced a new German liturgy, reformers began to remove images of the saints from the churches, and there were calls for changes in the celebration of the Mass. Once more, the city magistrates were taking upon themselves the authority for making decisions regarding the reform of the church.

Like Luther, Zwingli insisted that Scripture was the sole authority for church practice and Christian living (*sola scriptura*). Zwingli's approach, however, followed the regulative principle that only what the Bible expressly commanded or authorized was allowable and that all practices that could not be supported by Scripture were to be eliminated.[18] The regulative principle thus became the prevailing view of those in the Reformed tradition that originated in the Swiss Reformation, in contrast to those in the Lutheran tradition who accepted the normative principle that whatever was not expressly forbidden was permissible. Based on this regulative principle, Zwingli attacked such practices as the veneration of saints, the civil obligation of tithing, monastic vows, clerical celibacy, the intercession of the saints, images, vestments, the sacrificial character of the Mass, and the rituals associated with various church festivals. As a result, worship and ritual in Reformed churches tended to be plainer and simpler than worship in Lutheran churches. Throughout 1524, the city council permitted various reforms, but it was not until the Easter season of 1525 that the Mass was abolished and the first Reformed Communion, in both kinds, was celebrated in Zurich.

Zwingli had the most radical view of the sacraments among the main leaders of the Reformation, wishing that the word *sacrament* had not even been used.[19] For Zwingli, a key verse in his understanding was John 6:63: "It is the Spirit who gives life; the flesh provides no benefit" (NASB). In his view, because sacraments are material/fleshly symbols only, they cannot by themselves mediate anything spiritual. He wrote, "There can be no doubt that only the spirit can give life to the soul. For how could the physical flesh either nourish or give life to the soul?"[20] Since human nature was freed from the power of sin by Christ, Zwingli concluded that the sacraments simply demonstrate to the church that one is a follower of Christ.[21]

Zwingli's view of the Eucharist can be called the symbolic interpretation.[22] Although Zwingli recognized that by faith Christ was present to believers during the Eucharist, he strongly objected to the idea that Christ's physical body was present in the elements themselves, since it was actually in heaven in the presence of the Father. He asked rhetorically, "What is darkness if not the delusion that the bread is flesh and the wine blood, and that we partake of the flesh and blood really or essentially?"[23] For Zwingli, the Eucharist was a memorial or commemoration that stimulated the hearts of believers to remember Christ's death with thanksgiving or gratitude. The elements of bread and wine were symbols to call the mind to faith.[24] He wrote:

> In the same way he himself instituted a remembrance of that deliverance by which he redeemed the whole world, that we might never forget that for our sakes he exposed his body to the ignominy of death, and not merely that we might not forget it in our hearts, but that we might publicly attest it with praise and thanksgiving, joining together for the greater magnifying and proclaiming of the matter in the eating and drinking of the sacrament of his sacred passion, which is a representation of Christ's giving of his body and shedding of his blood for our sakes.[25]

Their different understandings of the Lord's Supper was the main disagreement between Luther and Zwingli and prevented the unification of the Lutheran and Reformed movements at the Marburg Colloquy of 1529.[26] Nevertheless, this symbolic understanding of the Lord's Supper has left its mark on many religious bodies to this day. Additionally, Zwingli's practice of celebrating the Lord's Supper four times a year (Christmas, Easter, Pentecost, and autumn) has also greatly influenced many Protestant groups.

Similarly, Zwingli's understanding of baptism was that because it was external and physical, it could not effect anything spiritual. Certainly, it could play no role in forgiveness of sins. Zwingli went so far as to claim that all the teachers since the time of the apostles had been in error in ascribing forgiveness to baptism![27] For Zwingli, baptism was not a means of grace, but it was a symbol or sign that the baptized person belongs to God. As with the Lord's Supper, Zwingli's symbolic understanding of baptism has left its mark on many modern Protestant denominations.

In May 1526, Zwingli was condemned and officially excommunicated from the Roman Catholic Church. Religious warfare broke out between the Reformed and the Roman Catholics in Switzerland in 1531, and on October 11, Zwingli fell in battle at Kappel. In response, the city of Zurich called a young Heinrich Bullinger (1504-75) to be Zwingli's successor. Throughout this period, Bullinger provided leadership among the Reformed as he corresponded and debated with a number of individuals, including a Frenchman in Geneva by the name of John Calvin.

Calvin broke from the Roman church sometime between 1530 and 1534, and because of his Reformed views, he had been forced to flee from France.[28] As he passed through Geneva in 1536, William Farel (1489-1565), who was leading the reform there, persuaded Calvin to stay in Geneva to assist the reform movement in that city.[29] Calvin believed that he could organize the reform of the church in Geneva according to the practices of the early church as he discerned them in the New Testament and early church history. Many of his efforts were unpopular and he, along with Farel, was expelled from the city in 1538. After Calvin gained a strong reputation as a leading reformer in Strasbourg, however, the Genevan magistrates invited him back in 1541. He would spend the rest of his life organizing and leading the Reformation in Geneva, from whence he also shaped Reformed Protestantism throughout Europe.

Like Zwingli, Calvin followed the regulative principle, believing that in areas of church organization and worship only what was authorized by the Bible was allowable; otherwise, it was prohibited. He wrote, "On no pretext is it lawful to attempt anything but what [God] permits."[30] Because Calvin was trying to be guided by the Bible in his efforts to reform both the church and society, and since the New Testament does not provide guidance for the organization of society as a whole, he was forced to rely heavily on the Old Testament for regulating civil society.[31] Working with the city council of Geneva, Calvin formed Geneva into what many saw as the model of a Reformed Christian community. Due to the theocratic nature of Geneva's reform, however, many others saw it as an oppressive society controlled by one man's interpretations of God's will.

A particular view of the sovereignty of God was the basis of Calvin's theology. Because Calvin believed that anything that might happen outside the will of God would invalidate God's sovereignty, he argued that "it is clear that all events take place by [God's] sovereign appointment."[32] Naturally, therefore, Calvin held to a strong view of predestination. Because human beings were totally incapable of anything good in and of themselves, salvation was entirely dependent on God's sovereign election. Indeed, according to Calvin, God has chosen from all eternity not only who will be saved, but also who will be damned.[33] Calvin affirmed, "[God] gives to some what he denies to others."[34] In fact, some were created for the purpose of being condemned. This extreme view is known as the doctrine of double predestination. Calvin's followers developed a five-point summary of Calvin's teaching on this subject that is known in English by the acronym TULIP: total depravity, unconditional election (predestination), limited atonement, irresistible grace, and perseverance of the saints (once saved, always saved). This theological perspective has been influential in churches that have inherited the Reformed perspective.

In addition to Calvin's efforts to organize Geneva itself, he was also active in working toward unity among Protestants, particularly between the Lutherans of Germany and the Reformed of Switzerland. For example, he tried unsuccessfully to find an understanding of the Lord's Supper that would be acceptable to both Lutherans and Zwinglians.[35] Following Augustine of Hippo, however, he did not believe in unity that was not faithful to the truth of Scripture, asserting, "Apart from the Lord's Word there is not an agreement of believers but a faction of wicked men."[36]

Both the Lutheran and Reformed strands of the Protestant Reformation saw themselves as reforming the church to bring it into conformity with their perceptions of the primitive church. In many ways, their focus was primarily doctrinal, not in terms of rethinking the great doctrines of historical Christian orthodoxy, but in terms of God's plan or order of salvation. Because they rejected the Roman Catholic view that there was something human beings could contribute to their own salvation by work or merit, they reacted against the Roman Catholic system of sacraments, flatly rejecting most of them as sacraments, and from a Roman Catholic perspective, they devalued the two sacraments, baptism and Eucharist, that they retained. As we have seen, Zwingli in particular rejected the historical position of the church from the time of the apostles that baptism was connected with forgiveness of sins.

Organizationally, the Lutheran and Reformed movements were intimately connected with the local governmental magistrates. Thus, they are termed *magisterial reformers*.[37] Although the reformers rejected the organizational hierarchy of the Roman Catholic Church, none of them rejected the close relationship between the church and the civil authorities. Like Roman Catholics, they took for granted that church and state were inseparable. They assumed that the only way for the church to be properly reformed and governed was for the civil magistrates to cooperate and, in many cases, to set the pace.[38] Zwingli and Calvin envisioned Zurich and Geneva, respectively, as taking the form of a theocracy in which church and civil affairs were to be coregulated. For example, in Geneva, the consistory, which was the primary organ for the exercise of church discipline in Geneva, was made up of both pastors and elders. The elders were political appointees chosen by the magistrates, and the pastors were all employees of the municipal government![39] Another aspect of the Protestant organization was that, in general, in Reformed and Lutheran churches, pastors replaced the Roman bishops, and the strong personal authority of the early leaders in each city or region replaced the authority of the pope.

In addition to doctrinal reform, leaders such as Zwingli, and especially Calvin, were interested in holy living among Christians. Although Luther was concerned that Christians live like they ought, his emphasis on justification by grace through faith and his distinction between law and gospel gave the impression to many that Lutherans were not particularly concerned about how Christians actually lived.[40] Be that as it may, because the magisterial reformers continued to believe that society and the church were coterminous, they were forced, just as Roman Catholics, to include in their churches many who were not necessarily committed to discipleship.

Finally, although the reformers were anxious to spread their teachings throughout Europe, for a variety of reasons, it was much later before

Protestant churches participated in missions to the outside world in any significant way.

The Reformation Comes to Britain: Anglican England and Presbyterian Scotland

Not long after the sixteenth-century Reformation began on the European continent, Protestant ideas found support in England. Lollards, with their emphasis on Bible reading, were still active, Lutheran ideas had reached England by 1520 and were spreading at both Cambridge and Oxford, various efforts were underway to make the Bible available in the English language, and there was a growing sense of anticlericalism.[41] Nevertheless, the key to the Reformation taking hold in England was the king's break with the papacy. Although Pope Leo X had previously given King Henry VIII of England (1491–1547; reigned from 1509) the title "Defender of the Faith," by 1529, Henry himself was at odds with the Roman Catholic Church over his wish to have his marriage to Catherine of Aragon annulled so he could marry Ann Boleyn. Because of Pope Clement VII's refusal to grant an annulment, Henry began applying pressure on the English clergy such that, in 1531, they recognized the King as the protector and even supreme head of the church "as far as the law of Christ allows." In 1534, the English Parliament passed the Act of Supremacy, recognizing the king as the absolute head of the church in England. Additionally, Henry forced the closure of the monasteries in England and confiscated their properties for the crown. Thus was born, largely out of personal and political reasons,[42] the Church of England, also known as the Anglican Church.

Although King Henry was officially head of the newly formed Church of England, his theological orientation was still basically Roman Catholic. Although several theologians and members of the clergy favored large-scale reform, Lutheran and Reformed practice and theology made little impression in the Anglican Church until after the death of Henry and the ascension to the throne of his nine-year-old son, Edward VI (1537–53; reigned from 1547). Edward had been raised as a Protestant, and the advisors of the young king steered him to follow a Protestant course for the Church of England. The cautious but reform-minded Thomas Cranmer (1489–1556) had been Archbishop of Canterbury since the reign of Henry, but now he was free to implement changes that reflected a Protestant orientation in the church's liturgy. Within a few short years, a new official liturgy was provided in English (the *Prayer Books* of 1549 and 1552), the Latin Mass was abolished, Communion in both kinds was introduced, reformers began to eliminate images, and clergy were permitted to marry.[43]

The Reformation in England suffered a temporary setback with the early death of Edward in 1553 and the succession to the English throne of his half-sister, Mary, who attempted unsuccessfully to forcibly restore Roman Catholicism. During her reign, nearly three hundred people, including Thomas Cranmer, were burned as Protestant heretics, but Mary was unable to stem the tide of the advance of Protestantism. When Mary died childless in 1558, her half-sister, Elizabeth, came to the throne, and the future of Protestantism in England was ultimately secured.[44] In 1571, Parliament approved the Thirty-Nine Articles of Religion as the official statement of Anglican doctrine. The Anglican Church was to become an interesting hybrid that retained features of Roman Catholicism, such as a highly ritualized liturgy and episcopal polity,[45] but it also incorporated features of Lutheran and especially Reformed Protestantism.

We cannot leave our discussion of the Reformation in England without a word about the Puritan movement. Although Protestantism had been securely established in England during the reign of Elizabeth, many Protestants were not satisfied by the pace of reform and by the vestiges of Catholicism that were remaining. The Puritan movement, as its name implies, was a movement that attempted to bring a purer form of (Calvinistic) Christianity to the Church of England and to the lives of individual Christians. In general, the Puritans adhered to the regulative principle that what Scripture did not authorize was prohibited.[46] Although a large number of Puritans hoped to work within and reform the existing Church of England, others were more willing to separate. For example, Robert Browne (1550–1633), whose followers became known as Brownists, established a nonconformist congregation in Norwich in 1580. He rejected state control and advocated a free church with congregational polity.[47]

Often the terms *Independents* and *Separatists* are used interchangeably when discussing the Puritan movement, but a distinction can be made. Generally speaking, Independents were Puritans who wanted to remain within the Anglican Church but wished to replace the episcopal polity of the Church of England with a congregational polity. Basing their conclusions on what they saw as the church government described in the New Testament, advocates of congregational polity felt that each congregation should be free to choose its own pastor, determine its own policies, and, in general, manage its own affairs instead of having decisions passed down from some higher authority such as bishops. Separatists also advocated congregational polity, but, unlike the Independents, they were not willing to remain within the Church of England. Rather, they separated and went about establishing their own autonomous congregations. Members of these congregations often bound themselves by a church covenant to Christ and one another. An important Separatist was John Smyth (1554–1612), who fled to Holland and, desiring to restore the church he read about in the book of Acts, became convinced of the necessity of believers' baptism and, in 1609, started the first English Baptist church.[48]

When the English Civil War broke out in 1642, most Puritans sided with the Presbyterian- and Independent-oriented Parliament against Catholic-leaning King Charles I. Oliver Cromwell, who was an Independent, led the forces of Parliament to victory, setting up the Commonwealth (1650–60). It was also Puritans who produced the Westminster Confession of Faith of 1646. The result of all this was that Puritans, though still a minority overall, came to exert significant power. Both Independents and Separatists eventually formed Congregationalist churches, many of which were established in North America.

England was not the only part of Britain where the Reformation had taken hold. By the 1520s, supporters of Luther's views had already been propagating their ideas in Scotland.[49] The reform-minded priest John Knox (1513–72) had participated in 1546–47 in an unsuccessful Protestant rebellion at St. Andrews Castle and had been condemned to a French prison ship as a galley slave. After his release, he ministered for a time in England before making his way to Geneva, where he came under the influence and training of John Calvin. Meanwhile, in 1557, Scottish Protestant nobles had formed a league or covenant for the purpose of defending the Word of God and making Protestantism the religion of Scotland. The role of the covenant was to become important in Scottish Protestantism. When

Knox finally returned to Scotland to stay in 1559, he almost immediately became the leader of the Reformation there. It was largely the Reformed theology of Calvin that Knox brought with him and that became the basic theology of Scottish Presbyterianism. In 1560, the Scottish Parliament officially repudiated the authority of the pope and abolished the Mass, while accepting a confession of faith drafted by Knox.

The Kirk of Scotland adopted a presbyterian polity by which congregations called their own ministers/presbyters. These presbyters would themselves form presbyteries, synods, and assemblies for the governing of the church. There was much more local control under the presbyterian polity than under the episcopal polity established in England, and in years to come, several English monarchs would attempt to impose episcopal polity on the Scottish Kirk. These policies would lead to great bitterness, and often violence, as the Scots attempted to defend their church.

The Catholic Reformation

Before we leave our discussion of the sixteenth-century Reformations, it is necessary also to consider the movement for renewal within the Roman Catholic Church that took place in response to the Protestant Reformations.[50] Clearly, efforts were underway to bring about reform within the Catholic Church prior to the posting of Luther's "Ninety-Five Theses," so not every reform impulse in sixteenth-century Roman Catholicism should be seen as a response to Protestantism. Nevertheless, the power of the Protestant Reformations gave momentum to these impulses within the Roman Catholic fold that earlier efforts, such as conciliarism, had failed to produce. Pope Paul III (1534–49) was committed to reform and appointed a commission to explore what needed to be done. Although he established the Inquisition in Italy in 1542, Paul initially had been willing to try to find some common ground with the Protestants. Several colloquies, however, failed to achieve unity.

One mark of sixteenth-century Catholic renewal was the rise of new religious orders and an emphasis on lay spirituality. Several new monastic orders, such as the Jesuits, Capuchins, Theatines, and the Ursuline order of nuns, were founded.[51] Perhaps more important, though, than the new monastic orders was the new emphasis on lay involvement in confraternities. These were voluntary associations for spiritual devotion and charitable activities, and they could consist of thousands of members.[52]

A figure who greatly influenced personal spirituality and was involved in the founding of perhaps the most significant of the new orders during this period was Ignatius of Loyola (1491–1556).[53] Ignatius was a Spanish soldier who, in 1521, suffered a severe injury when a cannonball broke his leg. He almost died in surgery and his leg was improperly set, resulting in its having to be rebroken and reset. Because part of the bone was protruding, it had to be sawn off, and the leg had to be stretched by weights to regain its proper length. During his long period of convalescence, he read a great deal of devotional literature and went through a spiritual conversion. After his recovery, he devoted himself to severe ascetic discipline and had several ecstatic visions, but ultimately, he could find no lasting peace and even considered suicide. Eventually, he came through his crisis and began writing his *Spiritual Exercises*, a handbook on spiritual discipline. He resolved to make a pilgrimage to Jerusalem, but after arriving in the Holy Land, the Franciscans forced him to return to Europe.[54]

Upon his return to Spain, Ignatius studied for some time at Alcalá and eventually made his way to Paris, where, in 1534, six men, including Francis Xavier (1506–52), joined him in a new brotherhood dedicated to the conversion of Muslims. In 1538, the group offered themselves directly to Pope Paul III to be sent anywhere the pope desired. In Rome in the spring of 1539, they formed themselves into the "Company of Jesus," receiving official recognition in 1540 as the Society of Jesus, or Jesuits, for the purpose of the "propagation of the faith." This purpose was later expanded to the "propagation and defense" of the faith. Ignatius himself was named as the first Superior General, and the order grew rapidly with a complex hierarchy, based on military organization and absolute obedience to one's superiors in the order. Whereas Luther finally found peace in his understanding of faith and the grace of God, Ignatius found it in unquestioning submission and obedience.[55]

An example of a more mystical spirituality during this time was the Carmelite Teresa of Avila (1515–82). After becoming a nun, Teresa suffered an illness during which she saw visions of Christ. Perhaps her best-known vision was that of seeing the Lord piercing her heart with a golden spear pointed with fire. After her recovery, she believed that she was called to reform her order. She founded the convent of Discalced (barefoot) Nuns of the Primitive Rule of Saint Joseph in 1562, and she influenced John of the Cross (1542–91) in the foundation of a monastery for men. Through her autobiographical and devotional writings, she became highly influential.[56]

Another emphasis of sixteenth-century Roman Catholic renewal was in the area of education. An important figure in setting the stage for educational reform predated the Protestant Reformations. Cardinal Francisco Ximenes de Cisneros (1436–1517), the confessor to Queen Isabella and primate of Spain (from 1495), had already prepared some of the groundwork for reform within the Roman Catholic Church in Spain. His accomplishments included enforcing the vows of poverty on monks and friars; leading educational reforms for children; creating a strong university at Alcalá for training the clergy; producing a Hebrew, Latin, and Greek Bible called the *Complutensian Polyglot*; and granting funding to hospitals and other causes. His efforts greatly strengthened the Roman Catholic Church in Spain and insulated it from the coming of Protestantism.

One of the decisions of the sixteenth-century Council of Trent was the requirement for any bishop in a diocese that did not have a university to establish a seminary or university for the training of young men for the clergy. In addition to the establishment of universities and the training of clergy, the Catholic Church gave new emphasis to lay education, primarily in the form of catechisms, devotional literature, and schools for children. Ultimately, the Jesuits became the leading order engaged in the higher education of Catholics, founding many colleges in Catholic-held lands. By the 1560s, Jesuits had charge of about 150 colleges, and this number had increased to 370 by 1615.[57] They were also successful in the theological controversies with Protestantism, and they played a significant role in converting several Protestant areas back to Roman Catholicism.

An aspect of the renewal of Roman Catholicism that must not be overlooked was the aggressive work of missions to all parts of the globe. The fifteenth and sixteenth centuries were times of great maritime exploration for Roman Catholic countries, and missionaries accompanied explorers and traders wherever they went. Just as with education, the Jesuits were in the forefront in spreading the Roman Catholic faith to mission fields throughout the world. One of Ignatius's principles that later became a motto of the Jesuit order was *"ad maiorem Dei gloriam inque hominum salutem"* ("for the greater glory of God and the salvation of man"), and mission work was a natural outgrowth of this ideal.[58]

The most important official response of the Catholic Reformation to the Protestants was the Council of Trent (1545–63), but not only was the council a reaction against Protestantism, it was also concerned positively with renewal.[59] Although there were significant difficulties in bringing a council together, Pope Paul III and others realized that if meaningful responses to the challenges of the Reformation and reform of the church were to take place, a council of the church would have to meet. The Council of Trent met in sessions that convened intermittently over a period of almost twenty years and involved basically three phases: 1545–47, 1551–52, and 1561–63. It had three primary objectives: Resolve the Protestant problem, clarify points of doctrine and ritual, and eliminate corruption and abuses.[60] The council confirmed many important doctrines of the Roman Catholic faith against Protestant teaching and practice. For example, in place of "faith alone," Trent affirmed that hope and love were also necessary for justification. Although Protestants had reduced the number of sacraments, Trent confirmed that Christ had instituted the seven traditional sacraments, which were therefore necessary for salvation. Against the Protestant concept of *sola scriptura*, the council insisted that tradition was to be held equally with Scripture and that the Roman Catholic Church was the sole interpreter of Scripture. Jerome's Latin Vulgate, including the Apocrypha, was defined as the official Scripture of the church. The Mass, which was to be conducted in Latin, was indeed a sacrifice, and the council officially affirmed transubstantiation and Communion in one kind, while condemning Protestant positions and practices. Calvinistic double predestination was rejected. It was clear from these decisions that rapprochement with the Protestants would not take place.

In addition to these doctrinal affirmations, Trent also took practical measures for the reform of the church. Bishops were encouraged to function more pastorally for their flocks. Bishops and other clergy were expected to place greater emphasis on preaching, and the requirement for bishops to establish educational institutions for the training of young men for the clergy has already been mentioned. Given that it was the sale of indulgences in Wittenberg that lit the fuse of the Protestant Reformation, one of the great ironies of the sixteenth century was that the Council of Trent abolished the office of the indulgence seller.

The Council of Trent represented the culmination of the sixteenth-century Catholic Reformation. It established reform in both morals and the organization of the church, and it also confirmed and defined the positions of the Roman Catholic Church in relation to the chief positions of Protestantism. Its effects would be felt for years to come. Trent was so significant that it was another three hundred years before another general council of the church was held, and it solidified Roman Catholic doctrine until the Vatican II Council of 1962–65, almost exactly four hundred years later.

Carlos M. N. Eire has observed: "The difference between this and preceding ages was one of perception, not necessarily of increased corruption: during the course of the fifteenth century the abuses and failings of the church became more conspicuous, more openly discussed, and more deeply resented by a wider spectrum of people."[61] Though they took drastically different shapes, the Protestant and Catholic Reformations were both responses to this perception. Although the events of the sixteenth century laid the foundations for freedom of conscience and toleration in religious matters, they also shattered the visible unity of the Western church that had persisted for centuries.

Questions for Thought or Discussion

1. To what extent, if any, did the various reformations of this chapter attempt restoration?

2. Against what were these reformations reacting?

3. What in particular were the various reformations emphasizing in their renewal efforts?

4. What do you see as strengths or weaknesses of each of these attempts at reformation?

5. In what ways were these reformations similar to or different from one another?

6. What did you find particularly interesting or attractive about each of the reformations?

7. What lessons or applications can you draw from these efforts?

NOTES

[1] Outstanding recent treatments of the Reformation era include Carlos M. N. Eire, *Reformations: The Early Modern World, 1450–1650* (New Haven, CT: Yale University Press, 2016); and Carter Lindberg, *The European Reformations*, 2nd ed. (Malden, MA: Wiley-Blackwell, 2010). Still accessible and less technical is Owen Chadwick, *The Reformation* (New York: Penguin, 1985).

[2] *Devotio Moderna*'s best known expression has been *The Imitation of Christ* by Thomas a Kempis (1380–1471).

[3] The indulgences were intended to finance both the work on St. Peter's Basilica in Rome and the repayment of Archbishop Albert of Mainz's debts that he had incurred through the purchase of his archbishopric.

[4] It is problematic to think in terms of a single "Protestant Reformation," as I implicitly acknowledge both in the title and in the remainder of the chapter. Previous chapters highlight that one could argue that the "Reformation" itself began long before the sixteenth century. Even in the sixteenth century, there were multiple "reformations." But it was not until the sixteenth century that the Roman Catholic monopoly on religious power in Western Europe was truly broken.

[5] For biographical information on Luther, I draw primarily from Roland H. Bainton, *Here I Stand: A Life of Luther* (New York: New American Library, 1950); and Derek Wilson, *Luther, Out of the Storm* (Minneapolis: Fortress Press, 2007).

[6] "For I hated that word 'righteousness of God,' which, according to the use and custom of all the teachers, I had been taught to understand philosophically regarding the formal or active righteousness, as they called it, with which God is righteous and punishes the unrighteous sinner. Though I lived as a monk without reproach, I felt that I was a sinner before God with an extremely disturbed conscience. I could not believe that he was placated by my satisfaction. I did not love, yes, I hated the righteous God who punishes sinners, and secretly, if not blasphemously, certainly murmuring greatly, I was angry with God. . . . Thus I raged with a fierce and troubled conscience. . . . [Meditating on Romans 1:17], I began to understand that the righteousness of God is that by which the righteous lives by a gift of God, namely by faith. And this is the meaning: the righteousness of God is revealed by the gospel, namely, the passive righteousness with which merciful God justifies us by faith, as it is written, 'He who through faith is righteous shall live.' Here I felt that I was altogether born again and had entered paradise itself through open gates. There a totally other face of the entire Scripture showed itself to me," Martin Luther, "Preface to the Complete Edition of Luther's Latin Writings,"

in *Luther's Works: American Edition*, ed. Jaroslav Pelikan and Helmut T. Lehman (Philadelphia: Muhlenberg Press, 1960), 34: 336-37.

[7] Luther, *Luther's Works*, 48: 153.

[8] Luther, *Luther's Works*, 44: 123-217. For example, "We are all consecrated priests through baptism, as St. Peter says in I Peter 2:9," 127; "This is why in cases of necessity anyone can baptize and give absolution," 128; "Therefore, when necessity demands it, and the pope is an offense to Christendom, the first man who is able should, as a true member of the whole body, do what he can to bring about a truly free council. No one can do this so well as the temporal authorities," 137; and "For this reason the Christian nobility should set itself against the pope as against a common enemy and destroyer of Christendom for the salvation of the poor souls who perish because of this tyranny," 158.

[9] Luther, *Luther's Works*, 36: 11-126. For example, "To begin with, I must deny that there are seven sacraments, and for the present maintain that there are but three: baptism, penance, and the bread," 18; and "Nevertheless, it has seemed proper to restrict the name of sacrament to those promises which have signs attached to them.... Hence there are, strictly speaking, but two sacraments in the church of God—baptism and the bread.... The sacrament of penance, which I added to these two, lacks the divinely instituted visible sign, and is, as I have said, nothing but a way and a return to baptism," 124.

[10] Luther, *Luther's Works*, 31: 333-77. For example, "For the person is justified and saved, not by works or laws, but by the Word of God, that is, by the promise of his grace, and by faith, that the glory may remain God's, who saved us not by works of righteousness which we have done, but by virtue of his mercy by the word of his grace when we believed," 362-63; and "Anyone knowing this could easily and without danger find his way through those numberless mandates and precepts of pope, bishops, monasteries, churches, princes, and magistrates upon which some ignorant pastors insist as if they were necessary to righteousness and salvation, calling them 'precepts of the church,' although they are nothing of the kind," 370.

[11] Luther's view has often been called *consubstantiation*. This is the understanding that the bread and wine are not changed into the body and blood of Jesus, but that the true human bodily presence of Jesus is "in, within, or under" the elements of bread and wine. Instead of using the term *consubstantiation*, Lutherans tend to prefer the term *sacramental union*. See discussion of the Lutheran understanding in David P. Scaer, "Lutheran View, Finding the Right Word," in *Understanding Four Views on the Lord's Supper*, ed. John H. Armstrong (Grand Rapids: Zondervan, 2007), 87-101.

[12] *Cuius regio, eius religio*—Whose the region, his the religion.

[13] For biographical information on Zwingli, I draw primarily from Ulrich Gäbler, *Huldrych Zwingli, His Life and Work*, trans. Ruth C. L. Gritsch (Philadelphia: Fortress Press, 1986).

[14] Gäbler, *Huldrych Zwingli*, 48.

[15] Translated in Hans Hillerbrand, ed., *The Reformation: A Narrative History Related by Contemporary Observers and Participants* (Grand Rapids: Baker, 1989), 119.

[16] Eire, *Reformations*, 228-29.

[17] Zwingli's "Sixty-Seven Articles" can be found in Denis R. Janz, ed., *A Reformation Reader: Primary Texts with Introductions*, 2nd ed. (Minneapolis: Fortress Press, 2008), 189-93.

[18] For example, after quoting from Deuteronomy 2:1-2 and 12:32, Zwingli wrote, "Faithfulness demands ... that we shall add nothing to what we have learned from [God], and take away nothing. For they that add accuse God of lack of wisdom," and "If,

then, that worship . . . is vain which proceeds from human invention or law, solid and true surely is that religion . . . which is guided by the word of God alone," Ulrich Zwingli, *Commentary on True and False Religion*, ed. Samuel Macauley Jackson and Clarence Nevin Heller (Eugene, OR: Wipf and Stock, 2015), 93, 95. The regulative principle, as understood by the Reformed tradition, is summarized in the *Westminster Confession of Faith* 21.1: "The acceptable way of worshipping the true God is instituted by Himself, and so limited by His own revealed will, that He may not be worshipped according to the imaginations and devices of men, or the suggestions of Satan, under any visible representation, or any other way not prescribed in the holy Scripture."

[19] John A. Maxfield, "Luther, Zwingli, and Calvin on the Significance of Christ's Death," *Concordia Theological Quarterly* 75 (2011): 99.

[20] Huldrych Zwingli, "On the Lord's Supper," in *Zwingli and Bullinger*, vol. 24 of *The Library of Christian Classics*, ed. G. W. Bromiley (Louisville, KY: Westminster John Knox, 2006), 206.

[21] Maxfield, "Luther, Zwingli, and Calvin," 100.

[22] Explained in Zwingli, "On the Lord's Supper."

[23] Zwingli, "On the Lord's Supper," 186.

[24] Zwingli, "On the Lord's Supper," 199, 225, 226.

[25] Zwingli, "On the Lord's Supper," 234.

[26] Several accounts of the Marburg Colloquy are found in Luther, *Luther's Works*, 38: 15–89. "Zwingli spoke several times about the sacramental presence of Christ's body as signifying that his body is in the Supper in a representative way," 48. Zwingli repeatedly cited John 6:63 to support his position, 20, 54–55, 64, 65, 74. On the other hand, "Before the colloquy began, and as he was about to debate with Zwingli and Oecolampadius, Luther had written on his table, 'This is my body,' in order that he might not allow himself to be diverted from these words," 52. Later, "Luther removed the velvet cloth and showed him the passage, 'This is my body,' which he had written for himself on the table with chalk," 67.

[27] Zwingli wrote, "In this matter of baptism—if I may be pardoned for saying it—I can only conclude that all the doctors have been in error from the time of the apostles. . . . [F]or all the doctors have ascribed to the water a power which it does not have and the holy apostles did not teach. They have also misunderstood the saying of Christ about water and the Holy Ghost in John 3," Zwingli, "Of Baptism," 130.

[28] For biographical information on Calvin, I draw primarily from Bruce Gordon, *Calvin* (New Haven, CT: Yale University Press, 2009).

[29] In that same year, Calvin, who was only twenty-six years old, had issued the first edition of his important *Institutes of the Christian Religion*. The final edition was published in 1559. See John Calvin, *Institutes of the Christian Religion*, trans. Henry Beveridge (Peabody, MA: Hendrickson, 2008).

[30] Calvin, *Institutes*, 3.19.13.

[31] On the magisterial reformers' desire "to establish 'godly' magistrates who would govern according to the biblical law, especially the Old Testament," See Craig D. Atwood, *The Theology of the Czech Brethren from Hus to Comenius* (University Park, PA: Pennsylvania State University Press, 2009), 307.

[32] Calvin, *Institutes*, 3.23.6.

[33] Calvin, *Institutes*, 3.21.5, 7.

[34] Calvin, *Institutes*, 3.21.1.

35 Calvin's view can be called the *pneumatic* or *spiritual presence* view. For a discussion of his view, see I. John Hesselink, "Reformed View, The Real Presence of Christ," in Armstrong, *Understanding Four Views* (Grand Rapids: Zondervan, 2007), 59–67.

36 Calvin, *Institutes*, 4.2.5.

37 All the "classical" reformers such as Luther, Zwingli, Calvin, Melanchthon, Beza, Bucer, Bullinger, and Knox were magisterial reformers.

38 Again: "The practical goal followed by all the great Reformers has always been to convince the holders of governmental authority to take in hand the reform of the church," Amedeo Molnár, in Giovanni Gonnet, "The Influence of the Sermon on the Mount upon the Ethics of the Waldensians of the Middle Ages," *Brethren Life and Thought* 35 (1990): 38.

39 Lindberg, *European Reformations*, 247–48.

40 For example, this was a concern of the Unity of the Brethren, discussed in Chapter Five above, and it was a concern of many Anabaptists and Pietists, discussed in Chapters Seven, Eight, and Nine below.

41 Lindberg, *European Reformations*, 294–301.

42 Lindberg, *European Reformations*, 301.

43 Lindberg, *European Reformations*, 307; Eire, *Reformations*, 329; Chadwick, *Reformation*, 117–18.

44 Under Elizabeth, nearly two hundred Roman Catholics were executed, but Elizabeth was politically astute enough to have them executed for treason rather than as religious heretics, Eire, *Reformations*, 353.

45 Episcopal polity is a top-down form of church organization in which the church as a whole is governed by bishops. The bishops select which individual bishop will administer each diocese of the church, and church members have no control of who their bishop will be.

46 Lindberg, *European Reformations*, 313.

47 Eire, *Reformations*, 345.

48 Smyth later joined the Mennonites. It was also a group of Separatist Puritans who came to the New World on the *Mayflower*.

49 Patrick Hamilton became the first reformer to be martyred in Scotland. He was burned at St. Andrews in 1528.

50 Terminology is tricky here. Since the nineteenth century, it was common for Protestants to refer to the Catholic response to the Reformations as the "Counter-Reformation." More recently, the trend has been to refer to the "Catholic Reformation" or "Catholic Reform," and still other scholars reject all of these terms, preferring instead to refer to "Early Modern Catholicism" or "Roman" Catholicism (suggesting that only after the Council of Trent is it proper to think in terms of "Roman" Catholicism). See discussion in Lindberg, *European Reformations*, 10–11.

51 More than thirty new orders were founded in the sixteenth and seventeenth centuries, Eire, *Reformations*, 424.

52 Eire, *Reformations*, 409.

53 On Ignatius, see Eire, *Reformations*, 442–65.

54 The Franciscans were concerned about the number of ransoms they had to raise to obtain the release of kidnapped pilgrims and did not wish Ignatius to be added to that number.

[55] See Chadwick, *Reformation*, 257; Lindberg, *European Reformations*, 335; cf. Tim Dowley, ed., *Introduction to the History of Christianity*, 2nd ed. (Minneapolis: Fortress Press, 2013), 346.

[56] Teresa was canonized in 1622, proclaimed copatron saint of Spain, and named a Doctor of the Church in 1969, the first woman to receive that honor.

[57] Eire, *Reformations*, 452.

[58] For the motto see Eire, *Reformations*, 447–49.

[59] An in-depth treatment of the Council of Trent is John O'Malley, *Trent: What Happened at the Council* (Cambridge, MA: The Belknap Press of Harvard University Press, 2013). Excellent brief discussions of the Council of Trent can be found in Eire, *Reformations*, 378–413; Lindberg, *European Reformations*, 338–45; Chadwick, *Reformation*, 273–81.

[60] Eire, *Reformations*, 379.

[61] Eire, *Reformations*, 44.

CHAPTER 7

"Given, Surrendered, and Sacrificed Wholly to God"
Evangelical Anabaptists Part 1

A violent and tragic chapter in the history of the sixteenth-century Reformations was the episode known as the German Peasants' War, or more recently as the Revolution of the Common Man.[1] It began in 1524, primarily as a series of protests against abuses the landowners and church hierarchy perpetuated against the peasants or commoners. In Luther's Reformation, many of the commoners saw hope for a reform of society in addition to church reform. Many believed that, in Christ, social distinctions should be abolished and there should be no more exploitation of the commoners. Concerns of the commoners included such things as freedom to hunt, fish, and gather firewood on landlords' estates; the right to approve their own clergy and who would preach the gospel without adding human doctrines; abolishment of serfdom; and relief from the burden of mandatory tithes and rents. The legitimacy of these requests was to be considered in light of the Bible alone.[2] By 1525, the protests had turned violent, but ultimately the revolt was mercilessly and brutally put down. Nevertheless, the desire for radical social change was not squelched.

It was in the context then of both the Protestants' reform of the church and the commoners' attempts to reform society that the rise of various movements that came to be known derisively as Anabaptism took place.[3] *Anabaptism* is a term meaning *rebaptism*, and it was applied in the sixteenth century to those who rejected infant baptism and generally practiced adult baptism. Thus, since practically everyone in sixteenth-century Europe had been baptized as an infant, adult baptism was understood as a rebaptism. Those known as Anabaptists, however, did not view infant baptism as baptism at all and rejected the idea that they were rebaptizing. As we shall see, however, the concerns of the Anabaptists were far broader than simply the proper subjects for baptism.

Until the twentieth century, most people grouped all those who had rejected infant baptism into the same basket labeled *Anabaptists*.[4] By the twentieth century, however, scholars began to recognize that there were significant differences between groups that had been labeled as Anabaptists and that grouping all of them together was inaccurate and unfair. Scholars now recognize distinct strands of radical sixteenth-century reformation.[5] One way of differentiating between the various strands is to think in terms of where they located religious authority. The Inspirationalists, or Spiritualists,[6] found ultimate authority in the Holy Spirit and new revelation. Their approach led to tragic excesses, the most famous of which was the Münster disaster. The Rationalists,[7] while generally accepting the teachings of the Bible, ultimately found authority in their own reason, rejecting those doctrines, such as the doctrine of the Trinity, for which they could find no rational explanation. The evangelical Anabaptists found their authority first and foremost in Scripture itself, primarily in the New Testament. They generally referred to themselves as brethren, evangelicals, believers, or simply as Christians. It is to the evangelical Anabaptists as New Testament restorationists that we will devote the remainder of this and the following chapter. Specifically, this chapter will consider the groups known as the Swiss Brethren, the Hutterites, and the Mennonites, and the following chapter will consider more closely some of the distinctive theological positions and practices of the evangelical Anabaptists.

The Swiss Brethren and South German Anabaptists

One of the first movements that came to be known as Anabaptists had its beginnings with the Swiss Brethren of Zurich, who emerged from the reforms of Ulrich Zwingli.[8] Zwingli had begun preaching at the Great Minster Church in Zurich in January 1519, calling for moral reform and beginning his program of a verse-by-verse exposition of Scripture (*lectio continua*). By the time he completed preaching through the New Testament six years later, reform in Zurich was well underway. In addition to Zwingli's normal ministerial duties, he had also gathered around himself a group of young men for special training. He met regularly with this group, and together they studied the Bible in Latin, Greek, Hebrew, and German. It was from this group, marked by their "zeal for Bible study,"[9] that significant and disturbing developments would come.

Following the January 1523 disputation in Zurich, a second disputation was held in October of the same year in order to specifically address issues related to changes in the celebration of the Mass. Earlier in the year, however, an imperial edict had been issued from Nuremberg that allowed for preaching the "holy gospel" while prohibiting changes from being made in the church services. The edict created a dilemma for reformers: How could they preach the holy gospel without implementing the actions the gospel called forth?[10] In light of the edict, although the council ruled largely in favor of Zwingli and the Reformation, it did prescribe a temporary halt in some of the reforms, pending further teaching. Zwingli submitted. At this point, disagreements surfaced between Zwingli and some of his more radical followers, such as Conrad Grebel (1498–1526), Simon Stumpf, and Felix Manz (1498[?]–1527), over the question of the authority of the Zurich city council in determining the pace of reform. The radicals, who were eager to push on with reforms, felt that Zwingli had agreed to abolish the Mass and celebrate a more apostolic Lord's Supper, regardless of the decision of the council. Perhaps Zwingli and they had anticipated that the council would rule definitively, either approving or disapproving the abolishment of the Mass, and had not foreseen that the council, mindful of the imperial edict, might decree, "Yes, but not yet." The radicals interpreted Zwingli's willingness to submit to the will of the council as a betrayal. Grebel wrote that Zwingli and the council had "disregarded the divine will" and that, because of this, the "Word was overthrown."[11]

This created what became a permanent rift between Zwingli and his radical disciples. Zwingli was convinced that, given time, he could persuade the populace and the council to accept his reforms. His approach was to be patient, introducing change gradually and under the auspices of the city magistrates. He once wrote, "Therefore, good Christians, do not try to push ahead too quickly: for to press on regardless of the weak is the mark not of a strong but a restless spirit which cannot wait until the poor sheep can catch up behind."[12] For the radicals, however, the issue was whether or not one was willing to be obedient to God's decrees. To wait on the emperor or the council was to give them authority that properly belonged to God alone.

The rift between Zwingli and his disciples expanded throughout the following year as the radicals began meeting in homes and apparently holding Communion services according to their understanding of the New Testament pattern.[13] Their attention turned to the question of the very nature of the church as a separated gathered congregation of the faithful versus the church as including everyone in society. Additionally, they began questioning the authority of the civil government in matters of faith. The concept of the church being composed only of the faithful was a revolutionary concept because it was a rejection of the idea of Christendom—that is, the idea that the church was composed of all within society.[14] An important symbol of Christendom was infant baptism, by which all those born into society were also incorporated into the church. This naturally raised the question of the role of baptism.

Sometime in 1524, several among the radicals began to question the validity of infant baptism, arguing that New Testament baptism was appropriate only for repentant believers (thus the term *believers' baptism*), and William Reublin (1484–c. 1559), the preacher at Zollikon, just outside of Zurich, was openly preaching against infant baptism. The radicals maintained that even Zwingli privately recognized that infant baptism was unnecessary and, in fact, was no baptism, but that he refused to come out publicly against it because he feared an uprising. Zwingli, for his part, feared that the radicals were a threat to the peaceful progress of reformation and opposed them.[15] Agitation reached the point that the city council called for a disputation on the question of infant baptism, which took place on the tenth and seventeenth of January 1525. The council ruled against the radicals and gave them three choices: Conform to the ruling of the council and cease opposing infant baptism, leave Zurich, or face imprisonment. The radicals responded that they must obey God rather than men.[16]

This led to a momentous decision four days later. In spite of their defeat before the council, "the Radicals (radical purists) still hoped for the success of their idea of a complete restitution of New Testament Christianity."[17] Several of the radicals gathered on the evening of January 21 at the home of Felix Manz to take the next step. As the *Hutterite Chronicle* describes: "Fear came over them and struck their hearts. They fell on their knees before the almighty God in heaven. . . . They prayed that God grant it to them to do his divine will and that he might have mercy on them. Neither flesh and blood nor human wisdom compelled them. They were well aware of what they would have to suffer for this."[18] A former priest named George Cajacob Blaurock (1491–1529) begged Conrad Grebel to baptize him with true Christian baptism. After Grebel did so, Blaurock baptized the others, and the movement of the Swiss Brethren was born.[19] According to William Estep, "Here, for the first time in the course of the Reformation, a group of Christians dared to form a church after what was conceived to be the New Testament pattern."[20]

Over the next week, several more people were rebaptized, and a congregation of Swiss Brethren was established at Zollikon. In addition to rebaptism, these first Anabaptists appear to have practiced a form of community of goods patterned on Acts 2 and 4 in which property was put at the disposal of the group in order to ensure that no one was in need or idle.[21] Another feature of the community was that before the practice had been adopted in the Zwinglian churches in Zurich, the Swiss Brethren were already celebrating Communion in both kinds and using regular bread instead of unleavened wafers. By the end of the week, the authorities struck by arresting twenty-seven Anabaptists, including Manz and Blaurock, and driving the rest out of Zurich and Zollikon. Nevertheless, baptizing continued in the towns and villages near Zurich. The Swiss Brethren were convinced that, in spite of persecution and the decrees of the authorities, each of the baptized was bound to do what he or she could to fulfill the Great Commission. This meant that they did not feel themselves to be limited to particular geographic or political boundaries, and they certainly did not feel that they needed the support of the civil authorities to proclaim their views, as was often the case for the magisterial reformers. After being released, Blaurock and Manz joined Grebel, Reublin, and others in traveling extensively, preaching and teaching wherever they could. They also suffered repeated imprisonments whenever the authorities could catch up with them.[22]

The normal baptismal practice of most Anabaptists was affusion or sprinkling rather than immersion. Near the village of Schaffhausen, however, Grebel immersed Wolfgang Ulimann (c. 1500–1528/30) in the Rhine River, because Ulimann insisted that he did not wish to be baptized "out of a platter."[23] A couple of months later, in April 1525, Grebel joined Ulimann in St. Gall, and, capitalizing on the previous work of others, baptized as many as five hundred people in the river outside of town. Given that a creek ran through St. Gall, it is interesting that the crowd traveled out of the city for the mass baptisms in the river. Were they looking for water sufficient for immersion?[24]

As a result of Anabaptist success in St. Gall, Zwingli entered the fray against them. Zwingli accused the Swiss Brethren of sedition, believing that "the practice of adult baptism leads to the isolation of a group of people . . . and therefore they [are not] ready to assume responsibility for the well-being of the community."[25] In other words, for Zwingli, the issue at stake was not so much baptism per se, but it was the threat to social stability that the rejection of infant baptism represented.

After the Anabaptists had been driven out of Zurich and Zollikon, Reublin made his way to the town of Waldshut, where the reform-minded Balthasar Hubmaier (1481–1528) was working. Hubmaier, who had received the Doctor of Divinity in 1512 from the University of Ingolstadt, came to be considered by many contemporaries as the most important leader of the Anabaptists. He became parish priest at Waldshut near Basel in 1521, where he was exposed to Protestant thought through the writings of Luther, correspondence with the Swiss reformers, and his own study of the New Testament. By 1522, his immersion in Scripture had convinced him that many of the practices and teachings of the Roman Catholic Church were not biblical, and by 1523, Hubmaier had broken with Roman Catholicism.

That same year, Hubmaier visited Zurich and participated in the October disputation as an ally of Zwingli's. He also, however, met Grebel and other radicals and was convinced about their views regarding the abolishment of the Mass. He returned to Waldshut, where he not only preached his new ideas but also married Elspeth Hugline. During a brief exile away from Waldshut, Hubmaier wrote the important work *Concerning Heretics and Those Who Burn Them*, in which he argued that faith cannot be coerced.[26] One characteristic of Hubmaier's writing was the regular inclusion of his motto, "Truth is immortal," and for him, that immortal truth was found in the Scriptures. By January 1525, Hubmaier, who, along with the town of Waldshut, had become involved in the German Peasants' Revolt, had also come to reject infant baptism, though he was still willing to baptize babies if their parents insisted. He was convinced that hearing the word, repentance, faith, and confession must precede baptism.[27] Previously, he had even corresponded with Zwingli concerning the lack of biblical support for infant baptism and claimed that Zwingli had agreed with him.[28] By this point, Hubmaier, believing that the New Testament was the sole authority for the church, wanted to reproduce the pattern of New Testament faith and practice in the church in Waldshut.[29] When Reublin arrived in Waldshut, he immediately baptized several eager disciples. He then baptized Hubmaier and several dozen others on Easter Sunday of 1525. Over the next several days, Hubmaier baptized more than three hundred people. For the first time, an entire congregation had joined the movement of the Swiss Brethren en masse.[30]

The first martyrdom of the Anabaptists occurred on May 29, 1525, when a banished coworker of Ulimann's named Eberli Bolt was burned at the stake by Roman Catholic authorities. Thousands of martyrdoms would follow over the years, making the story of the Anabaptists one of the most tragic and yet heroic chapters in the history of restoration movements.[31]

In fall 1525, Grebel, Manz, and Blaurock were all taken into custody in Zurich. Although this was Grebel's first imprisonment, it was already the second for Blaurock and the third for Manz.[32] They were sentenced to remain in prison either until they renounced their errors or until they rotted. In the meantime, the city of Waldshut fell to Austrian Roman Catholic forces in December 1525, but an ill Hubmaier managed to escape to Zurich, where he was placed under arrest. Hubmaier was allowed to debate Zwingli and, during the debate, quoted passages from Zwingli's own writings, in which Zwingli himself advocated waiting until children could be instructed before being baptized. Nevertheless, Hubmaier was returned to prison and tortured on the rack until he recanted. Zwingli then arranged for Hubmaier to publicly preach the error of his previous Anabaptist views, but instead, Hubmaier publicly recanted his recantation! He was put back in prison and tortured again until he once more recanted, following which he was expelled from Zurich. Prior to Hubmaier's departure from Zurich, two other important events took place. First, in March 1526, the city council decreed the sentence of death by drowning for anyone guilty of rebaptizing.[33] The drowning of Anabaptists was to become known mockingly as "The Third Baptism." Second, that same month, Grebel, Manz, Blaurock, and several others escaped their prison through an unlocked window.[34] Their preaching continued in homes, fields, woods, or wherever they had opportunities.

The months in the dungeon, however, had weakened Grebel's health, and sometime in summer 1526, probably in August, he contracted the plague and died. By December, both Manz and Blaurock had been recaptured. After their trials, Manz was condemned to death, and Blaurock was sentenced to public whipping and expulsion from the city. Manz's sentence was more severe because it was confirmed that he had performed rebaptism since the edict declaring it a capital offense had been issued, whereas there was no available evidence of this against Blaurock. The sentences were carried out on January 5, 1527. Manz was drowned in the river with the prayer, "Lord, into your hands I commit my spirit" on his lips.[35] Felix Manz was thus the first Anabaptist to be martyred at the hands of Protestants.

By 1527, Anabaptism had spread not only throughout Switzerland, but also throughout southern Germany. Many of the leading Anabaptists of southern Germany had Spiritualist leanings, so in February, a gathering of more biblically oriented Swiss Brethren, under the leadership of the German Michael Sattler (1490–1527), met at Schleitheim in the Swiss canton of Schaffhausen to consolidate their views and curb some of what they perceived to be the excesses of the Spiritualists. Sattler had been a Roman Catholic priest who converted to Anabaptist views by 1525. In the vacuum created by the deaths of Grebel and Manz and the exile of Blaurock and Hubmaier, Sattler briefly played a leading role in the expanding movement.

One of the reasons that Sattler was important is that he is considered the primary author of the *Schleitheim Confession* that was affirmed at the Schleitheim meeting on February 24. This document begins with a warning against false brothers who "have missed the truth," believing that faith and love permitted them to do anything they wished. It includes seven articles that summarize distinctive points of the faith and practice of the Swiss Brethren at the time. The first article affirms that baptism was for those who repent and believe, and it excludes infant baptism as an "abomination of the pope." The second article declares that Brethren who slipped into sin were to be warned twice in private, and then they were to be admonished publicly. The ban was to be implemented prior to the celebration of the Lord's Supper in both kinds. The third article deals with the Lord's Supper or "the breaking of bread," which was to be done in remembrance of the body and blood of Christ and was permitted only to those who had been united in the body of Christ by baptism. According to the fourth article, the Brethren were to separate themselves from the evils of the world, including all practices of the Roman Church and all practice of violence. Organizationally, the fifth article provides for each congregation to have a pastor whose responsibility was to preside over the worship services, preach and teach, warn, admonish, and ban. The pastor was to be supported by the congregation, and if he should be lost due to persecution, he was to be immediately replaced by the congregation. The sixth article affirms absolute pacifism. The sword was for those outside the perfection of Christ; the ban was used within the perfection of Christ. Christians were not to use the sword, even against the wicked or to defend the good. Christians were not to be involved in civil lawsuits, and they were forbidden from serving as magistrates. "The government magistracy is according to the flesh, but the Christians' is according to the spirit. . . . The worldlings are armed with steel and iron, but the Christians are armed with the armor of God, with truth, righteousness, peace, faith, salvation, and the word of God." The seventh article states that even though oaths were permitted in the Old Testament, no oaths or swearing were permitted in the New Testament. The *Schleitheim Confession* did not deal with theological doctrinal formulations and was not to be understood as an officially binding confession of faith for all Anabaptists. Instead, it was an affirmation of and exhortation to the distinctive order and discipline that were characteristic of and united the Swiss Brethren.[36]

A second reason that Sattler was important was his dramatic martyrdom. Upon his return from Schleitheim to his home in Horb, just west of Rottenburg, Sattler and his wife, along with several other Anabaptists, were arrested. After his trial, Sattler was horribly tortured but remained steadfast throughout the ordeal. Part of his tongue was cut off and, several times, hot tongs were used to tear chunks of flesh from his body. Then he was tied to a ladder and pushed into the fire. In spite of the horrific nature of his torture and execution, Sattler was still able to give a signal with his fingers to assure the brethren who were witnessing the spectacle that such a death was bearable.[37] A few days later, Sattler's wife was drowned in the Neckar River. Although several of the Anabaptists who were apprehended in the vicinity of Horb and Rottenburg recanted, others remained steadfast, and due to written accounts of his martyrdom receiving wide circulation, the example of Sattler became an inspiration and source of strength to others.

After his final banishment from Zurich, George Blaurock fled to Austria, preaching and establishing congregations all along the way. He finally settled near Innsbruck, where he enjoyed a most successful ministry. By this time, Blaurock had become known as "the new Paul," and Estep refers to him as the "Hercules of the Anabaptists" because of the effectiveness of his evangelistic ministry.[38] Unfortunately, his success led to his capture, as so many converts could not fail to come to the attention of the authorities. He was apprehended a final time in Innsbruck and, after torture, was burned at the stake on September 6, 1529.

Moravian Anabaptism and the Hutterites

Anabaptist refugees began to infiltrate Moravia as early as 1526. Among these was Balthasar Hubmaier, recently expelled from Zurich. Hubmaier found refuge in Nikolsburg (Mikulov) on the estates of the lords of

Liechtenstein. In fact, Hubmaier converted Leonard von Liechtenstein, along with the Lutheran pastor, Oswald Glait. Hubmaier's short ministry in Moravia was productive. He did much of his writing during this time, and as many as six thousand people were baptized from 1526–27.[39]

In addition to his evangelistic and apologetic activities, Hubmaier spent a great deal of time trying unsuccessfully to unite the various Anabaptist groups that were seeking refuge in Moravia. Two major lines of thought characterized the Anabaptists of Nikolsburg. One group, led by Hubmaier and supported by Lord Leonard von Liechtenstein, affirmed that, in some cases, Christians could serve as magistrates and defensive warfare might be permissible.[40] This was a pressing question due to the threat of Turkish invasion. This group also affirmed the Christian responsibility of sharing with those in need but rejected the idea of an obligatory community of goods. Because of their acceptance of the occasional legitimacy of the use of the sword, this group came to be referred to as the *Schwertler* (German for *people of the sword*). The other line of thought, exemplified by Hans Hut (d. 1527) and Jacob Wiedemann (d. 1535/6), rejected any Christian participation in government and advocated a more robust community of goods among the Brethren, though they were not yet pooling all their resources. This group came to be referred to as the *Stäbler* (*people of the staff*) for their total rejection of violence, even in cases of self-defense.[41] A disputation between Hubmaier and Hut was held at Nikolsburg in May 1527, but it failed to resolve the differences between the *Schwertler* and *Stäbler*.[42] A few months later, as a result of mounting pressure by King Ferdinand I to rid his territories of heretics, Hubmaier and Elspeth were arrested and taken to Vienna. After several months of interrogation and torture, Hubmaier was burned at the stake on March 10, 1528. His wife, Elspeth, was drowned in the Danube three days later.

In the meantime, the *Stäbler*, who were perceived by the Liechtensteins as a liability because of their divisiveness and their refusal to bear arms in defense of their estates, were asked to depart from Nikolsburg. Although Lord Leonard then changed his mind and requested that they return, the *Stäbler* refused to return because they could not in good conscience remain on the estates of someone who was willing to use arms in their defense. As they departed, about two hundred of them placed all their worldly goods on a large garment to be pooled for the common good, according to the example of the primitive church recorded in Acts 2, 4, and 5.[43] Thus, in Moravia, the previously theoretical notion of the community of goods among the faithful began in actual practice.

The *Stäbler* found refuge to the north of Nikolsburg at Austerlitz on the estates of four brothers who were the lords of Kaunitz and were already providing refuge to a group from the Unity of the Brethren. At Austerlitz in 1529, they formed a new communitarian colony of believers known as a *Brüderhof*.[44] The *Brüderhof* found the ideal of the community of goods to be difficult to actualize. Nevertheless, the community grew as refugees from all over Europe joined them. William Reublin joined the community at Austerlitz in 1530, but he and others were put off by Wiedemann's authoritarian style of leadership. They charged Wiedemann with distributing goods inequitably, forcing the young women to marry whomever the elders chose, and false teaching—especially the teaching that baptism was necessary for salvation. Soon thereafter, Reublin, along with more than half the community, established a new *Brüderhof* at Auspitz.[45]

It was about this time that Jacob Hutter (d. 1536) entered the story of Moravian Anabaptism. Hutter was from the Austrian province of Tyrol, had been trained in Prague as a hatter (hence his name), and was converted to Anabaptism about the year 1529. Hutter had returned to the Tyrol and soon found himself in the role of one of the leading Anabaptist pastors. About that same time, his sister Agnes, who was also an Anabaptist, was captured and executed. Hutter led a successful ministry in the Tyrol, but increasing persecution led him to seek refuge for his community in Moravia, to which many of them immigrated. With a price on his head, Hutter joined the *Brüderhof* at Auspitz in 1533 and immediately, though not without opposition, assumed leadership of the congregation there. Hutter firmly believed that he was called by God to be a leader, and his organizational and pastoral skills saved the *Brüderhof* from dissolving by giving it the stability and viability that it had previously lacked in establishing the communal ideal.

By 1535, persecution had increased in Moravia, scattering the Hutterites. From time to time over the next twenty years, many were forced to take refuge in forests, caves, and even underground tunnels.[46] Hutter himself returned to the Tyrol with his pregnant wife, but they were captured almost as soon as they got there. He was subjected to horrible tortures, including whipping and the rack. Perhaps the most horrific of his tortures was when he was put in freezing water and then beaten with rods until his body was lacerated. Then brandy was poured into his wounds and ignited.[47] In spite of all the torture, Hutter refused to recant or reveal the hiding places of his brethren. Eventually, he was burned at the stake on February 25, 1536. His wife managed to escape but was recaptured two years later and also martyred. When the Brethren who had remained at the *Brüderhof* in Auspitz learned of their beloved leader's courageous death, they took his name and, from that point on, were known as Hutterites or Hutterian Brethren.[48]

After the death of Hutter, leadership fell to his colleague John Amon (d. 1542). Organizationally, the Hutterites typically selected a single bishop called the *Vorsteher*.[49] Each *Brüderhof* was led by ministers of the Word, also called elders, who were in charge of teaching and the spiritual health of the community, and by ministers of service who were in charge of the economic life of the community. Each member had particular duties assigned to him or her for the benefit of the whole community. Hutterites constructed buildings with shops and common rooms on the ground floors and sleeping rooms upstairs.[50]

Under the leadership of Amon, the Hutterites became perhaps the most mission-minded of all the Anabaptist groups, taking the gospel all over Europe and especially throughout the German-speaking lands. They encouraged immigrants to join them in Moravia, and thousands did. They established at least one hundred *Brüderhofs* with as many as thirty or forty thousand members.[51] One of their greatest missionaries and leaders was Peter Riedemann (1506–56). He traveled tirelessly throughout German-speaking territories, enjoying success as an evangelist, as a pastor for struggling congregations, and also as a peacemaker among various Anabaptist factions. Over the course of his career, Riedemann suffered at least three different imprisonments for a total of nine years of incarceration. From prison, he wrote many pastoral letters to encourage the Brethren. During his third imprisonment, he wrote an important confession or *Account* (*Rechenschaft*) that has continued as the major Hutterite statement of doctrine. It was also during this third imprisonment that

Riedemann received a call to return to Moravia, if possible, and take up the mantle as *Vorsteher*. He made his escape, returned to Moravia, and spent the rest of his life fulfilling this ministry.

The great missionary zeal of the Hutterites, however, was accompanied by great sacrifice. Although Riedemann spent nine years in prison, he was comparatively fortunate. Up to 80 percent of Hutterite missionaries ultimately gave their lives as martyrs.[52] Their attitude could be summed up in the words of missionary martyr Claus Felbinger (d. 1560): "We have given, surrendered, and sacrificed ourselves wholly to God. Where He sends us and will use us, there we will go, in obedience to His divine will, regardless of what we must suffer and endure."[53]

From about 1565 to the outbreak of the Thirty Years' War in 1618, the Hutterites in Moravia enjoyed a period of relative peace. Their particular form of communal living contributed to their being considered valued residents on many Moravian noblemen's estates during this time. Each member received an education and learned a craft. Because the Hutterites eschewed the profit motive, they sold their goods at low prices. They were known as hard workers and skillful craftsmen, producing all sorts of commodities that were in demand throughout Europe. They were in demand as clock and furniture makers; weavers; doctors; carpenters; farmers; managers of castles, breweries, and mills; and practitioners of other specialties. This led to Hutterite communities becoming wealthy, though the wealth was owned communally rather than individually.[54] This also made them an appealing target when war and persecution resumed. Not everyone who joined the Hutterites remained with them, either. Over the years, many became disillusioned or disgruntled by the demands of *Brüderhof* life and left the community.[55]

Just as the Thirty Years' War had devastating consequences for the Unity of the Brethren, so it did for the Hutterites. They were driven out of Moravia once and for all and spent much of the next two centuries trying to find a land where they could practice their faith in peace. In spite of great persecution, near annihilation, and many forced migrations to such places as Slovakia, Transylvania, Romania, Ukraine, Russia, and finally, in the nineteenth century, to South Dakota and some Canadian provinces, the

Hutterites have survived and continue to perpetuate the ideals of pacifism, communal living, and caring for the needs of the Brethren.

Dutch Anabaptism and the Mennonites

Just as Anabaptism was spreading throughout Switzerland, southern Germany, Austria, and Moravia, it was also spreading northward throughout Germany and into the Netherlands.[56] A significant difference between many but not all Anabaptists in northern Germany and the Swiss Brethren was that many Anabaptist preachers in northern Germany tended to have chiliastic Spiritualist leanings. One such preacher was Melchior Hoffman (1495–1543/4). Hoffman had converted to Lutheranism and then to Zwinglianism before finally adopting Anabaptism sometime around 1530. He rejected infant baptism and believed in the imminent return of Christ. Hoffman's ministry was successful in converting large numbers of people to the Anabaptist faith, and he is generally credited with introducing Anabaptism in northern Germany and the Netherlands.

Meanwhile, the first Anabaptist martyr in the Netherlands was Sicke Freercks Snijder, who was beheaded on March 20, 1531, for being rebaptized.[57] Another Dutchman, Menno Simons (1496–1561), who had been ordained as a Roman Catholic priest in 1524, heard about this beheading and was intrigued by the crime of receiving second baptism.[58] Already, from about 1528, Simons, who had never previously studied the Bible, "got the idea to examine the New Testament diligently" and to follow it more closely.[59] So, when he heard about second baptism, he naturally decided to examine the New Testament on this subject as well, and to his surprise, he discovered that the Bible had no mention of infant baptism. His study of the arguments of ancient church leaders and the German and Swiss reformers in favor of infant baptism convinced him that they had all been deceived. It was several more years, though, before Menno Simons accepted believers' baptism for himself.

Two violent episodes involving Spiritualists provided the impetus for Simon's eventual conversion to Anabaptism. The first was the debacle of Münster. The climactic event of the Spiritualist efforts in Germany came when several of them, under the leadership of Bernard Rothmann (1495–c. 1535), gained control of the city council of Münster in late 1533 and early 1534. Additional, more radical Spiritualists, including John of Leyden (1509–36) and John Matthys (d. 1534), arrived in Münster and took over leadership of the city. They demanded that all who refused adult baptism leave the city, and they instituted the practices of the community of goods and polygamy. Their aim was to initiate a theocratic regime for the purpose of violently establishing God's kingdom on earth. Catholic forces, however, besieged the city, the Spiritualists were defeated, killed in battle or executed, and a permanent stain was left on all those who rejected infant baptism.

The second episode took place just about two months before the fall of Münster. In April 1535, several hundred Dutch Spiritualists were making their way to join the besieged city and took possession of the Old Cloister at a place called Bolsward. After a short siege, the cloister was attacked, and the defenders were practically wiped out. Among the slain was Simons's own brother. Simons, who had written against the excesses of Münster, now felt it his obligation to act on his beliefs and to minister to the beleaguered remnant of those who had been so deceived by the grandiose dreams of Münster: "I began in the name of the Lord to preach . . . the word of true repentance, to point the people to the narrow path . . . and to present the true worship; also the true baptism and the Lord's Supper, according to the doctrine of Christ."[60] Still, he continued to preach from his pulpit for another nine months before he made his decisive break. So it was, that around 1435 or 1436, after serving some twelve years as a Roman Catholic priest, Menno Simons received believers' baptism. He anticipated what would be the cost, stating that he had "renounced all my worldly reputation, name and fame . . . , and my easy life, and I willingly submitted to distress and poverty under the heavy cross of Christ." He continued, "I sought out the pious and though they were few in number I found some who were zealous and maintained the truth."[61]

Interestingly, not only was Simons rebaptized, but when he was called to serve as an Anabaptist minister and elder, he felt that he also needed to be reordained. This service was performed in 1537 by Obbe Philips (1500–1568). Philips was a Spiritualist Anabaptist leader who had been influenced by Hoffman and for a while led an Anabaptist congregation in Amsterdam.[62] Simons engaged upon his ministry of evangelism, encouraging the scattered and disheartened Brethren, preaching, and writing.

Ultimately, Simons was so important to the evangelical Anabaptist cause that not only did his Dutch followers come to be called Mennonites (or Menists), but the Swiss and South German Brethren took his name as well.[63]

Simons's life as an Anabaptist minister was the life of a wandering fugitive. He had no permanent residence and was constantly in hiding and on the lookout for the authorities. One can sense the pathos in his words as he described the life he led: "We [he and his wife Gertrude] generally have to hide ourselves in out-of-the-way corners. . . . We have to be on our guard when a dog barks for fear the arresting officer has arrived."[64] By 1541, he had become so important as an Anabaptist leader that an offer was extended for a full pardon for any Anabaptist who turned him in. When that failed to produce results, in 1542, Emperor Charles V offered a reward of five hundred gold guilders for his capture.[65] The story is told of Elizabeth Dirks, perhaps the first Mennonite deaconess, who was mistakenly assumed to be Simons's wife. She was arrested and tortured in hopes that she would reveal the whereabouts of Simons. Though she was subjected to both the Spanish boot and thumbscrews so blood squirted from her nails and she passed out, she refused to give any information and ultimately was martyred.[66] By 1543, Simons had to flee from the Netherlands to northwestern Germany, where he would work the final eighteen years of his life.

As important as Menno Simons was for the survival and spread of Dutch Anabaptism, he did not work alone. Perhaps his most important coworker was Dirk Philips (1504–68), the brother of Obbe. Dirk, who, like Simons, was ordained as an elder by Obbe, had received theological education and was an outstanding theological writer. Together, Simons and Philips helped the Mennonites navigate perilous times of persecution and various doctrinal challenges that the movement faced.[67]

A significant controversy in the history of Mennonite Anabaptism concerned the practice of the ban (excommunication) and shunning (total social avoidance). All Mennonites were in agreement that discipleship demanded the highest standards of ethical and moral behavior within the community of faith. This required the exercise of discipline when a member did not live up to these standards. The normal practice would be to admonish the fallen brother or sister multiple times and then, barring repentance, ban him or her from the congregation's Lord's Supper, according to Matthew 18:15–18. When the banned member truly repented and made confession to the congregation, he or she would be reinstated. Some, however, began the practice, based on their interpretation of 1 Corinthians 5:11, of shunning or totally avoiding any social contact with the offending member.[68] Some even expanded this to require husbands or wives to shun their spouses. At first, Simons tended to advocate a lenient view in the case of spouses, whereas Philips and others were stricter. As the controversy intensified, however, and Simons began to sense a lack of serious discipline within the movement, he moved toward a more rigorous position as well. The controversy over the ban and shunning led in 1555 to the separation of a more lenient group that came to be known as the Waterlanders, though they referred to themselves simply as Baptizers.[69] The schism that resulted in the Waterlanders' going their separate way was just one of several schisms that would plague the Mennonites throughout their history.[70] In spite of their divisiveness, however, Mennonites spread throughout and eventually beyond Europe, and today the various Mennonite denominations make up the largest number of those who trace their roots back to the sixteenth-century evangelical Anabaptists.

For Simons, the church was always important, and a restoration of the New Testament church was dependent on a Christocentric interpretation of the Bible. Simons was fond of quoting the text, "For other foundation can no man lay than that is laid, which is Jesus Christ" (1 Cor. 3:11).[71] From Simons's perspective, teachers whose doctrines were consistent "with the word and ordinance of God" were sound. Otherwise, their teaching should be considered a "doctrine of men, and accursed by to the Scriptures."[72] A renewed church was a church in which the inner reality of true faith would be expressed by the visible imitation of Christ and in which discipleship was manifested in holy living and a disciplined membership. Dirk Willems (d. 1569) was an outstanding example of this type of committed discipleship. After being imprisoned, Willems managed to escape and fled for his life. He safely crossed a frozen river, but the deputy, who was following close on his heels, broke through the ice and fell into the river. In obedience to Jesus's command to love your enemies and do good to those who hate you (Luke 6:27), Willems turned back and pulled his pursuer from the water. The deputy wanted to allow Willems to go free, but upon receiving orders to take him into custody, the deputy returned him to the village, where Willems was burned to death.⁷³

Fortunately, by 1577, freedom of religion was decreed for the Anabaptists in the Netherlands, and persecution in those lands had come to an end.

Questions for Thought or Discussion

1. To what extent could the evangelical Anabaptist movements be considered restoration movements?

2. Against what were the evangelical Anabaptists such as the Swiss Brethren, Hutterites, and Mennonites reacting?

3. What in particular were the evangelical Anabaptists emphasizing in their renewal efforts?

4. What were various strengths or weaknesses of these groups?

5. How were the movements of this chapter similar to or different from the previous movements discussed in this book?

6. What did you find particularly interesting or attractive about the evangelical Anabaptists?

7. What lessons or applications can you draw from these groups?

NOTES

[1] The change in terminology reflects modern scholarship's recognition that the "war" was not limited to Germany or to peasants. See Carlos M. N. Eire, *Reformations: The Early Modern World, 1450–1650* (New Haven, CT: Yale University Press, 2016), 200.

[2] A summary of *The Twelve Articles* detailing the commoners' demands can be found in Eire, *Reformations*, 202–4. Tithing had been general practice in some areas of Europe since the fifth century and had been made compulsory in the eighth century under Pippin III. The Fourth Lateran Council of 1215 also made them obligatory, Peter Brown, *The Rise of Western Christendom: Triumph and Diversity, A.D. 200–1000* (Malden, MA: Wiley-Blackwell, 2013), 452–53; Norman Tanner and Sethina Watson, "Least of the Laity: The Minimum Requirements for a Medieval Christian," *Journal of Medieval History* 32, no. 4 (2006): 414.

[3] James Stayer has explored the connections between the Peasants' War and Anabaptism and demonstrates that there were greater links between the German

Peasants War and Anabaptism than has generally been recognized, James M. Stayer, *The German Peasants' War and Anabaptist Community of Goods* (Montreal: McGill-Queen's University Press, 1991). In addition to individuals who were involved in both movements, he finds this link primarily in the egalitarianism of the Anabaptist practice of community of goods, concluding "that Anabaptist community of goods was the logical continuation of the social Gospel of the Reformation . . . a very radical, albeit non-violent, expression of the Peasants' War," Stayer, *Peasants' War*, 7.

[4] Luther had referred to them, and others, as *Schwärmer*, that is, "swarmers." For Luther's relationship to the *Schwärmer*, see Amy Nelson Burnett, "Luther and the *Schwärmer*," in *The Oxford Handbook of Martin Luther's Theology*, ed. Robert Kolb, Irene Dingel, and L'ubomir Batka (Oxford: Oxford University Press, 2014): 511–24.

[5] George Huntston Williams, *The Radical Reformation*, 3rd ed. (Kirksville, MO: Sixteenth Century Journal, 1992), xxix–xxx; and James B. North, *A History of the Church from Pentecost to Present*, 6th printing (Joplin, MO: College Press, 2005), 348–50, distinguish the strands as Spiritualists, Evangelical Rationalists, and simply Anabaptists. Eire, *Reformations*, 254–55, preserves Williams' terms, but modifies them, dividing the Anabaptists into Pacifists, Apocalyptic Activists, and Moderates. William R. Estep, *The Anabaptist Story*, 3rd ed. (Grand Rapids: Eerdmans, 1996), 21–22, suggests the terms *Inspirationalists*, *Rationalists*, and *Anabaptists*, and on several occasions (170, 171, 176, 182, 190) refers to the Anabaptists as biblical Anabaptists. Leonard Allen, *Poured Out: The Spirit of God Empowering the Mission of God* (Abilene, TX: Abilene Christian University Press, 2018), 40–41, refers to Spiritualist Anabaptists and Evangelical Anabaptists, omitting the Rationalists. We will use the term *evangelical Anabaptists* or simply *Anabaptists* to distinguish the subject of this chapter from the Spiritualists/Inspirationalists and the Rationalists.

[6] Represented by such figures as the so-called Zwickau prophets, as well as Thomas Müntzer, Caspar Schwenkfeld, Bernard Rothmann, John of Leyden, and John Matthys.

[7] Represented by such figures as Michael Servetus, Fausto Sozzini, and the Polish Brethren. They were forerunners of modern Unitarianism.

[8] Scholars have recognized various roots of Anabaptism in addition to the Swiss Brethren, such as the efforts of Thomas Müntzer in central Germany, Hans Hut in south Germany, and Melchior Hoffman in and around Strasbourg and the Netherlands, Carter Lindberg, *The European Reformations*, 2nd ed. (Malden, MA: Wiley-Blackwell, 2010), 189–90.

[9] Gunnar Westin, *The Free Church Through the Ages*, trans. Virgil A. Olson (Nashville: Broadman, 1958), 57.

[10] Although in circulation earlier, the edict was published on March 6, 1523. See the excellent discussion of this edict and its effect on the rise of the Swiss Brethren in Daniel Rhodes, "Against the World: The Doctrine of Separation within the Political Context of the Origins of Swiss Anabaptism," *Baptist Heritage and History* 54, no. 1 (Spring 2019): 38–53.

[11] Leland Harder, ed., *Sources of Swiss Anabaptism* (Scottdale, PA: Herald Press, 1985), 276.

[12] Huldrych Zwingli, "Of Baptism," in *Zwingli and Bullinger*, vol. 24 of *The Library of Christian Classics*, ed. G. W. Bromiley (Louisville, KY: Westminster John Knox, 2006), 158.

[13] Williams, *Radical Reformation*, 190–91.

[14] Rhodes argues that the "instinct to separate was driven by the larger political powers, which intentionally set out to drive a wedge between the preaching of the gospel and the socio political implications of living it out," concluding that "the possibility of relying on the Reformation to bring forth a full institution of the divine law vanished with the issuance of the Nuremberg Edict. As a result, to live out the gospel fully, the Anabaptists determined that a form of ecclesial and political separation from the world was the only possibility left," Rhodes, "Against the World," 43, 50.

[15] "In Zwingli's eyes the rise of the Zurich Anabaptists was therefore a clear and present danger.... Indeed, Zwingli saw these people as social revolutionaries whose teaching would overthrow society and religion alike," Lindberg, *European Reformations*, 190.

[16] From Heinrich Bullinger's account of this disputation, translated in Hans Hillerbrand, ed., *The Reformation: A Narrative History Related by Contemporary Observers and Participants* (Grand Rapids: Baker, 1989), 228–29. This was the same response the Waldensians had given when they were told to stop preaching. See above, Chapter Two.

[17] Williams, *Radical Reformation*, 189.

[18] *The Chronicle of the Hutterian Brethren*, vol. 1, trans. and ed. by the Hutterian Brethren (Rifton, NY: Plough Publishing House, 1987), 45, hereafter cited as *Hutterian Chronicle*.

[19] Initially, the group referred to themselves simply as brothers in Christ. The term *Swiss Brethren* was used from the 1540s and was initially applied to them by the Hutterites and the Marpeck brotherhood to distinguish them from their own groups. "The term 'Swiss Brethren' referred to all Anabaptists who were direct successors of Conrad Grebel . . . and Michael Sattler," whether in Switzerland or elsewhere, Stayer, *Peasants' War*, 95.

[20] Estep, *Anabaptist Story*, 14.

[21] Stayer, *Peasants' War*, 95–96; Williams, *Radical Reformation*, 218. The Swiss Brethren made it clear that they did not advocate involuntary seizure of goods, but voluntary use of their goods for the common good.

[22] Williams, *Radical Reformation*, 218–21.

[23] Estep, *Anabaptist Story*, 38

[24] See Estep, *Anabaptist Story*, 233–34n58.

[25] Ulrich Gäbler, *Huldrych Zwingli, His Life and Work*, trans. Ruth C. L. Gritsch (Philadelphia: Fortress Press, 1986), 128.

[26] Translation found in *Balthasar Hubmaier: Theologian of Anabaptism*, trans. and ed. H. Wayne Pipkin and John H. Yoder (Scottdale, PA: Herald Press, 1989), 59–66.

[27] Hubmaier, *Theologian*, 99–101.

[28] Williams, *Radical Reformation*, 149n18.

[29] Estep, *Anabaptist Story*, 88.

[30] Williams, *Radical Reformation*, 231; Donald F. Durnbaugh, *The Believers' Church: The History and Character of Radical Protestantism* (Scottdale, PA: Herald Press, 1985), 71. On Hubmaier's involvement in the Peasants' Revolt/War, see Stayer, *Peasants' War*, 61–71.

[31] Many of their stories are told in Thieleman J. van Braght, *The Bloody Theatre or Martyrs' Mirror of the Defenseless Christians*, trans. Joseph F. Sohm (Scottdale, PA: Herald Press, 1951).

[32] Williams, *Radical Reformation*, 234.

[33] On August 14, 1527, all the Swiss cantons officially decreed the death by drowning for all Anabaptists, not just those guilty of the act of rebaptizing.

[34] Williams, *Radical Reformation*, 239.

[35] From Heinrich Bullinger's account, translated in Hillerbrand, *Reformation*, 234.

[36] Michael Sattler, *The Schleitheim Confession* in *Creeds of the Churches: A Reader in Christian Doctrine from the Bible to the Present*, ed. John H. Leith, 3rd ed. (Atlanta: John Knox, 1982), 282–92. Carter Lindberg calls attention to several parallels between the concerns of the peasants and the *Schleitheim Confession*, Lindberg, *European Reformations*, 205–7.

[37] Estep, *Anabaptist Story*, 72. An account of Sattler's trial is found in van Braght, *Martyrs' Mirror*, 781–85. The sentence against him was as follows: "'In the case of the Governor of his Imperial Majesty versus Michael Sattler, judgment is passed, that Michael Sattler shall be delivered to the executioner, who shall lead him to the place of execution, and cut out his tongue; then throw him upon a wagon, and there tear his body twice with red hot tongs; and after he has been brought without the gate, he shall be pinched five times in the same manner.' After this had been done in the manner prescribed, he was burned to ashes as a heretic," van Braght, *Martyrs' Mirror*, 785.

[38] Williams, *Radical Reformation*, 219; Estep, *Anabaptist Story*, 49.

[39] Estep, *Anabaptist Story*, 94.

[40] Hubmaier's involvement in the Peasants' War has already been mentioned.

[41] Interestingly, however, Hans Hut secretly taught that four years after the Peasants' War, God would authorize the Anabaptists to execute God's vengeance by eliminating governments and killing all those who had not accepted baptism and community of goods, Stayer, *Peasants' War*, 114.

[42] A contemporary account of this controversy can be found in the *Hutterian Chronicle*, 47–50, 80.

[43] *Hutterian Chronicle*, 80–81. The *Chronicle* also mentioned Isaiah 23:18.

[44] Although other Anabaptist groups practiced the community of goods to varying extent, they generally did so at the level of single-family households rather than in a communitarian setting such as the *Brüderhof*, which set the community over the family, Stayer, *Peasants' War*, 145–46.

[45] Estep, *Anabaptist Story*, 130.

[46] Bob Scribner, "Practical Utopias: Pre-Modern Communism and the Reformation," *Comparative Studies in Society and History* 36, no. 4 (October 1994): 760; Williams, *Radical Reformation*, 1,066.

[47] *Hutterian Chronicle*, 145.

[48] *Hutterian Chronicle*, 146.

[49] However, on at least one occasion they were led by two co-bishops, Williams, *Radical Reformation*, 1065.

[50] For descriptions of the *Brüderhof*, see Estep, *Anabaptist Story*, 141–44; Stayer, *Peasants' War*, 146–53; Scribner, "Practical Utopias," 762–65; and Durnbaugh, *Believers' Church*, 87.

[51] Scribner, "Practical Utopias," 761; see also n77.

[52] Estep, *Anabaptist Story*, 134; Williams, *Radical Reformation*, 646.

[53] Robert Friedmann, "Claus Felbinger's Confession of 1560," *The Mennonite Quarterly Review* 39 (April 1955): 147. Felbinger was beheaded on July 19, 1560.

[54] See Scribner, "Practical Utopias," 764–65.

[55] Scribner, "Practical Utopias," 771–72.

[56] An excellent overview of Mennonite history is Cornelius J. Dyck, *An Introduction to Mennonite History: A Popular History of the Anabaptists and the Mennonites*, 3rd ed. (Scottdale, PA: Herald Press, 1993).

[57] Williams, *Radical Reformation*, 540.

[58] Simons gives his own account of his conversion to Anabaptism in Menno Simons, *The Complete Writings*, trans. Leonard Verduin, ed. John C. Wenger (Scottdale, PA: Herald Press, 1956), 668–74.

[59] Simons, *Complete Writings*, 668.

[60] Simons, *Complete Writings*, 671.

[61] Simons, *Complete Writings*, 671.

[62] Estep, *Anabaptist Story*, 168. Interestingly, Obbe Philips eventually deserted the Anabaptist cause.

[63] The term *Mennonite* or *Menist* is first attested either in 1544 or 1545; cf. Estep, *Anabaptist Story*, 170–71; and Williams, *Radical Reformation*, 595.

[64] Simons, *Complete Writings*, 674.

[65] Estep, *Anabaptist Story*, 169; Williams, *Radical Reformation*, 595.

[66] Williams, *Radical Reformation*, 595–96; cf. the account in van Braght, *Martyrs' Mirror*, 902–4.

[67] On the work of Simons and Philips, see Dyck, *Introduction*, 101–27.

[68] Williams, *Radical Reformation*, 598.

[69] Not believing that any group should be named for a human being, they rejected the name of Mennonite. In the seventeenth century, the Waterlanders were to influence the views of John Smyth, the founder of the first English Baptist congregation.

[70] Dyck, *Introduction*, 123–25. A similar issue resulted in the seventeenth-century Amish schism, Dyck, *Introduction*, 153–54.

[71] He prefaced practically all of his writings with this text. See the title pages in Simons, *Complete Writings*.

[72] Simons, *Complete Writings*, 695.

[73] Lee C. Camp, *Mere Discipleship* (Grand Rapids: Brazos), 76. See the account in van Braght, *Martyrs' Mirror*, 1,380–81.

CHAPTER 8

"OVERTHROWING RELIGION AND CIVIL ORDER"
Evangelical Anabaptists Part 2

Given the variety of the evangelical Anabaptist groups, any attempt to generalize their basic theology and practices will necessarily result in some degree of distortion. Various scholars have attempted to determine the "essence" or "center" of sixteenth-century Anabaptism, and there is debate about the relationship between the theological convictions and the social, political, and economic factors that gave rise to and shaped the various Anabaptist groups. Was the essence of Anabaptism their rejection of infant baptism? Was it their commitment to some form of community of goods? Was it their rejection of the church/state relationship and all that entailed? Was it something else? Can we even speak of an "essence" or "center" of sixteenth-century Anabaptism?[1] William Estep acknowledged that believers' baptism was the "most effective single distinguishing mark of the sixteenth-century Anabaptist movement," but he identified their "distinctive view of the church ... patterned after the New Testament example ... as the most determinative insight of sixteenth-century Anabaptism."[2] While James Stayer found the common thread among all Anabaptist groups in their commitment to the practice of community of goods,³ and Daniel Rhodes argued that, for the Swiss Brethren at least, "while it is by no means the case that there was one solidified theology among these radicals... The center of this movement... was... a radically social gospel that directly challenged the traditional hierarchical society strongly confirmed in the imperial edict" of Nuremberg,⁴ Cornelius Dyck identified core values or the essence of the evangelical Anabaptists in biblical authority, Christ as Savior and norm for Christian living, the importance of the congregation as the community of faith, and discipleship.⁵ Furthermore, Carlos M. N. Eire identified "an essential set of [five] features" that distinguished all the categories of Anabaptists: (1) belief in the fall and disappearance of the church, (2) belief in a chasm between Christians and "the world," (3) belief in a voluntary church composed only of believers, (4) rejection of infant baptism, and (5) belief in human free will and a role for human effort in the salvation process.⁶ Without attempting to resolve these debates, we will attempt a basic description of several significant sixteenth-century evangelical Anabaptist positions, bearing in mind that these descriptions would not necessarily apply to every group.

Sixteenth-Century Evangelical Anabaptist Theology and Practice

Because people do not debate issues about which they agree, it should not be surprising that the evangelical Anabaptists wrote comparatively little about some of the great theological truths of the historical Christian faith. Their writings were forged in the fires of persecution and were primarily designed to defend those positions for which they were being persecuted. With few exceptions, the evangelical Anabaptists affirmed the orthodox positions of the Christian faith regarding the Trinitarian view of the oneness of God in the persons of the Father, Son, and Holy Spirit. They believed in the incarnation of Christ,⁷ in his atoning death as the only means of human redemption, in his bodily resurrection, and in his second coming in judgment. For the most part, they accepted the Apostles' Creed as an accurate statement of Christian truth and may have recited it as a part of their devotional and worship practices, though they valued it not because it was in itself an authoritative statement of truth, but because they believed it to be an accurate statement of biblical truth. Additionally, they generally accepted the Protestant doctrine of justification by faith, though they emphasized that saving faith would always be manifested in lives of holy discipleship more than was typical of the Protestants. The following describes areas in which the evangelical Anabaptists differed significantly with others.

The Evangelical Anabaptist View of Scripture

Although the Protestant reformers championed the idea of *sola scriptura*, or Scripture alone, as the authority for the faith and practice of the church, it has been argued that the evangelical Anabaptists were more consistent in their application of this principle.[8] Whether or not that was actually the case, the Anabaptists certainly believed it to be so; thus, they believed that their distinctive beliefs and practices were based on Scripture. Accordingly, it is appropriate that this discussion begin with the evangelical Anabaptist approach to Scripture.

Like the restorationists we have already examined, the evangelical Anabaptists made a much sharper distinction between the Old Testament and the New Testament than the Protestants and Roman Catholics did. The typical view of the evangelical Anabaptists regarding the relationship between the Old and New Testaments was clearly articulated by Pilgram Marpeck (c. 1495–1556).[9] Marpeck was born in Rattenberg, Austria, and became involved in the town government in the 1520s, serving on the town council and as an engineer for the local silver mines. At some point, he became attracted to the Anabaptist cause and was dismissed from his position in January 1528 for refusing to aid in their apprehension. He fled to Strasburg, where he purchased citizenship and soon found himself exercising leadership among the local Anabaptists. In spite of his Anabaptist views, Marpeck had skills that were valued in the city, and he was given a post as a city engineer responsible for transporting lumber into the city. By 1531, Marpeck was involved in a religious debate with Martin Bucer that resulted in Marpeck's banishment from the city. After a dozen years of wandering, he eventually arrived in Augsburg, where he was once again given a position as a city engineer, and in spite of occasional reprimands for his Anabaptist faith, he was able to live out the rest of his life in relative peace.

His most important contribution to Anabaptist thought was his view of the distinction between the Old and New Testaments.[10] For Marpeck, although both Old and New Testaments were the Word of God, there were important differences between the two. Marpeck rejected the position of Zwingli and others of the magisterial reformers that the covenant made with Abraham was the same covenant that Christians were living under. It was in the supposed unity of the covenant of both Testaments, for example, that the reformers found the analogous connection between circumcision and infant baptism or between the nation of Israel and the Reformed church/state societies.[11] Marpeck recognized that the purpose of the Old and New Testaments was different. For Marpeck, "the old covenant is merely a covenant of promise."[12] Marpeck argued that the covenant of the Old Testament was for "yesterday" and the covenant of the New Testament represented "today."[13] God's revelation to human beings through the Bible was progressive. The Old Testament represented the "first grace," but "in the New Testament . . . there is a different reality."[14] The old covenant community of Israel was not the same as the new covenant community in Jesus Christ, the church. The Old Testament "church" was built on the foundation of the promise of God, but the New Testament church was built on the foundation of the Lord himself.[15] To confuse the distinction between the Testaments was to devalue the uniqueness of Christ and his new covenant.[16] According to William Estep, for Marpeck, the Old Testament was like the foundation, and the New Testament was like the house.[17] The foundation was important, even necessary, but it was preliminary and preparatory. One did not live in the foundation, but in the house. What was partial in the Old Testament had been completed in Jesus in the New Testament. According to Marpeck, "The figures and shadows of the Old Testament have held up the light. The essence and truth is now present. After all, we are now no longer under the Old Testament; we are under the New."[18] Therefore, the New Testament, which revealed Jesus Christ, was the normative authority for the Brethren. Treating the Old Testament as equally authoritative with the New blurred the distinction between the two Testaments and led to such serious and unfortunate excesses as religious war, the burning of "heretics," and attempts to regulate theocracies based on Israel's Old Testament law. According to Marpeck, the Roman Catholics, the magisterial reformers, and many of the Spiritualists were guilty of this fundamental mistake.[19]

In addition to the primacy the evangelical Anabaptists gave to the New Testament, they also tended to hold to the regulative principle in terms of what would be allowed in the church. Typical was the thought of Conrad Grebel: "Whatever we are not taught by clear passages or examples must be regarded as forbidden, just as if it were written: 'This do not.'"[20] This principle resulted in simplification of ceremonies and rituals, much like within the Reformed churches of Zwingli, and perhaps even more so.

This approach could certainly become problematic as not everyone always agreed on the meaning of "clear passages." Once freed from both the authoritative interpretations of the Roman Catholic Church and the controlling influence of the magistrates, Anabaptists were free to interpret the Bible according to their own whims and idiosyncrasies. Unfortunately, this often led to schism and division, as each group that fractured away tended to equate its own perceptions with absolute truth, and they often tended to be intolerant of other opinions. For example, the Hutterites came to believe that the communitarian *Brüderhof* system was the only valid expression of New Testament Christianity and rejected anyone who did not agree. Various Anabaptist groups went into schism over such issues as eschatology, the role of the magistracy in the church, nonresistance, community of goods, divorce from non-Anabaptist spouses, dress, foods, and the list could go on.[21] This, perhaps, was one of the costs of freedom of conscience.

Because of the Anabaptist emphasis on the authority of Scripture, they generally were cautious about official creeds and confessions of faith. As has been mentioned, although many accepted the Apostles' Creed, the creed in and of itself held no authoritative position. It was useful because it was considered to be faithful to scriptural truth. Even such a confession as the *Schleitheim Confession* was not considered necessarily binding or permanent. It was simply held as an accurate summary of what the Brethren believed was taught by Scripture. The evangelical Anabaptists never made confessions or creeds tests of Christian fellowship.[22]

The Evangelical Anabaptist View of the Church and Its Relationship to the State

Although the practice of believers' baptism was the most obvious visible difference between the evangelical Anabaptists and others, it may have been their view of the church that was the real point of theological difference. Their rejection of infant baptism and their practice of believers' baptism was simply a logical implication of their view of the church. Of course, they believed that their understanding of the church was derived from Scripture. Concisely stated, for the evangelical Anabaptists, the concept of the church of committed believers who voluntarily gathered themselves together replaced the concept of the church as a mixed multitude composed of all who were born and baptized into society.

Like most European Christians at the time, the evangelical Anabaptists took the position of Cyprian, the third-century bishop of Carthage, that outside of the church there was no salvation. They were convinced from their study of Scripture, however, that neither the churches of the magisterial reformers nor the Roman Catholic Church represented the true church.[23] Furthermore, they were convinced that the church had experienced a "fall," generally understood to have taken place with the union of church and state during the reign of Constantine. Because the fall had been so complete, it was not possible to repair the institution, as the magisterial reformers were trying to do.[24]

What was needed was a restoration of the church of the apostolic times, which the Brethren viewed as "a genuine expression of God's will,"[25] and thus as an appropriate prototype and pattern for the restored church of their time. Such a church could only be gathered when those who responded to the preaching of the gospel were baptized and joined themselves to the visible manifestation of the church in a given locality. Hubmaier argued that the marks of the true church consisted in regeneration, baptism, discipline, and holiness.[26] The Anabaptists rejected the concept of an invisible church made up of the predestined who were comingled with the masses. Membership in the church could never be coerced and was the result of a voluntary or free will decision by those who had experienced the regeneration of the Holy Spirit.

Because the means for gathering the church out of the world was the preaching of the word, the Anabaptists took Jesus's Great Commission seriously. This was in part because persecution often forced them to "go into all the world." More importantly, however, the Brethren understood that the church was not confined within the national or regional geopolitical boundaries within which the developing Protestant churches of the magisterial reformers were limited.[27]

In relation to the state, the evangelical Anabaptists recognized the legitimacy of the authority of the state. When accused of not obeying the magistracy, Simons replied, "We publicly and unequivocally confess that the office of a magistrate is ordained of God, even as we have always confessed. . . . And . . . we have obeyed them when not contrary to the Word of God."[28] With the exception of Hubmaier and a few others, however, in general they did not believe that it was proper for Christians to serve as magistrates, nor did they believe the state should be involved in religious coercion. To put it in modern language, we could say that the evangelical Anabaptists advocated for the freedom of religion and a return to the pre-Constantinian separation of church and state. It was not fitting for Christians to serve as magistrates on several grounds. Magistrates were expected to wield the sword against evildoers, which was incompatible with the Christian calling. Typical was the thought of Peter Riedemann: "Thus no Christian is a ruler and no ruler is a Christian, for the child of blessing cannot be the servant of wrath."[29] Additionally, for Christians to serve as magistrates would be to divide their loyalties between the affairs of worldly government and their heavenly citizenship.[30]

This perspective was significantly different from the magisterial reformers and the Roman Catholics who could not envision a concept of separation of church and state and who assumed that one role of the magistracy was to protect the church and even to coerce people into conformity with the teachings of the church. They also assumed that the church had a role in determining laws for society and maintaining social stability.

The Anabaptist perspective on separation of church and state explains the severity of the persecution faced by the Anabaptists. Certainly, there was a historical legal basis for the persecution of those refusing infant baptism or practicing rebaptism. The fourth-century code of Theodosius and the sixth-century Code of Justinian forbade rebaptism. Additionally, an edict of the Roman bishop Innocent I in 407 attempted to make infant baptism compulsory, and a synod in Carthage in 418 ruled that infants should be baptized. Finally, under Charlemagne in the eighth century, a refusal to baptize infants was made subject to the death penalty.[31] Beyond this, the 1529 Diet of Speyer had renewed the prohibitions of rebaptism. Thus, if anyone needed it, there was plenty of legal justification for the execution of Anabaptists. Ultimately, however, it was the understanding of the church as a people gathered out of and separate from society that led to such severe persecution of the Anabaptists. For example, Luther's associate Justus Menius said, "They seek to assemble a pure Church and wherever that is undertaken the public order is sure to be overthrown."[32] Indeed, there was a tendency among Anabaptists toward exclusivity and nonengagement with their culture.[33]

At a time when Europe was rent by religious division and war between Protestants and Catholics, and when it was also under threat from Turkish invasions, the Anabaptists' refusal to take civil oaths, their denial of the authority of the civil government in religious affairs, their refusal to participate in civil government, and their refusal to bear arms all brought their civic loyalty into question.[34] John Calvin accused them of "overthrowing not only religion but also all civil order," and Zwingli charged, "You wish to destroy the magistracy and the power of which it consists. Take away the oath and you have dissolved all order. . . . You see good reader, all order is overthrown when the oath is taken away. . . . Good God, what confusion and up-turning of everything!"[35] The Anabaptists were persecuted because they were seen as a dangerous threat to communal identity and social stability.

The Evangelical Anabaptist View of Discipleship and Discipline

Organizationally, Anabaptists tended to favor congregational polity in which each congregation chose its own leaders, typically called elders or shepherds, though some particularly effective leaders came to have influence over multiple congregations.[36] The congregation would gather regularly, often multiple times each week, for preaching, teaching, the Lord's Supper, prayer, and usually singing, though some, such as Conrad Grebel, opposed singing in the assembly.[37]

The Brethren believed the church should follow the New Testament pattern in organization and worship, but even more important was to follow the pattern of Jesus's own life and teachings in daily living. The Sermon on the Mount played a significant role in their understanding of the life of a disciple. For the most part, evangelical Anabaptists rejected the predestinarian theologies of the Protestant reformers and recognized a level of human freedom in obediently choosing to follow Jesus.[38] Although salvation was freely given by God's grace, the Christian was expected to take discipleship seriously. Thus, evangelical Anabaptists had high expectations for the behavior and morals of their brothers and sisters who had freely chosen the path of discipleship. They were known, even by their enemies, for the uprightness of their lives. Anabaptists had such a reputation for the holiness of their lives that anyone known for holy living might be in danger of being suspected of being guilty of the heresy of Anabaptism. There are even examples of people brought to trial due to the blamelessness of their lives![39]

Four distinctive areas in particular illustrate the seriousness of the evangelical Anabaptists' commitment to discipleship: pacifism, oaths, mutual care, and the ban.

Other than Balthasar Hubmaier and the *Schwertler*, almost all evangelical Anabaptists were pacifists. They believed that Christ's teachings, particularly in the Sermon on the Mount about loving one's enemies and doing good to those who hate you, were incompatible with the notion of shedding blood, whether in warfare or as civil punishment. The fourth article of the *Schleitheim Confession* stated it this way: "Therefore there will also unquestionably fall from us the unchristian, devilish weapons of force—such as sword, armor and the like, and all their use [either] for friends or against one's enemies—by virtue of the word of Christ, Resist not [him that is] evil."[40]

Anabaptists, again with the exception of Hubmaier and his following, were known for their refusal to take oaths or swear, which also were based on the teachings of Jesus in the Sermon on the Mount. According to the seventh article of the *Schleitheim Confession*:

> Christ, who teaches the perfection of the law, prohibits all swearing to His [followers], whether true or false . . . and that for the

reason which He shortly thereafter gives, For you are not able to make one hair white or black. So you see it is for this reason that all swearing is forbidden. . . . Christ also taught us along the same line when He said, Let your communication be Yea, yea; Nay, nay; for whatsoever is more than these cometh of evil.[41]

True disciples were simply to speak the truth, which would make swearing superfluous.

As mentioned, Stayer has demonstrated that all evangelical Anabaptist groups were committed to the concept of community of goods on the basis of Acts 2 and 4, though the practical manifestations of this commitment might differ from group to group.[42] From the beginnings of the Swiss Brethren, Felix Manz "advocated mutual support and aid as an ideal for life among reformed Christians."[43] Frequently, Anabaptist groups gathered collections into a common purse for the needy, and some Brethren sold property and gave the proceeds for the common coffer. It is important to emphasize, however, that these donations were considered voluntary and were given according to the needs of the situation.[44] In general, the Anabaptists believed that "people who shared Christ, should share their possessions"[45] and that ownership of possessions was a barrier to loving one's neighbor as oneself, because it fostered selfishness. While only the Hutterites implemented a full-fledged communitarian community of goods among the evangelical Anabaptists, all of the Brethren taught that their material possessions were held as stewardships from God and that they had the responsibility for "bearing the burdens" of any brother or sister in need.[46] In addition to the New Testament basis for the practice of community of goods, Stayer has argued that there was also a political element: "Anabaptist community of goods was the logical continuation of the social Gospel of the Reformation . . . a very radical, albeit non-violent, expression of the Peasants' War."[47] In other words, community of goods was an attempt to establish a society in which there would be no more economic exploitation of the masses.[48]

Another distinctive practice of the Brethren was the use of the ban, or excommunication, to enforce discipline within the community. According to the second article of the *Schleitheim Confession*, the practice of the ban was directly related to the expectation of holiness as a mark of "all those who have given themselves to the Lord." When a person submitted himself or herself to believers' baptism, that person also understood that he or she was submitting to the discipline of the community. Based on the teachings of Matthew 18:15–18, an unrepentant brother or sister who fell into sin would be banned from the assembly of the Brethren.[49] This discipline was applied in practically all evangelical Anabaptist groups, but the Dutch Mennonites took discipline even further with the practice of shunning or total avoidance based on their interpretation of 1 Corinthians 5:11. As has been mentioned, some expected that even in cases of marriage, partners could be required to shun their own spouses. In all cases of banning or shunning, the purpose was to bring the sinner to repentance so that he or she might be once more welcomed into the fellowship of the community. The negative side of this commitment to community discipline was the frequency with which it produced schism and division, as illustrated by the separation of the Waterlanders from the main body of Mennonites, mentioned in the previous chapter.

The Evangelical Anabaptist View of Baptism and the Lord's Supper

Although baptism and the Lord's Supper were traditionally referred to as sacraments, the evangelical Anabaptists did not typically use this word when referring to these practices, nor did they understand them in a sacramental sense.[50]

The rejection of infant baptism and the practice of believers' baptism was the most obvious difference between the practice of the evangelical Anabaptists and their opponents, whether Protestant reformers or Roman Catholics.[51] The biblical arguments against infant baptism had to do with the nature of Christian baptism, the nature of the church, and the fact that Christ did not command infant baptism nor was any apostolic example of it found in the New Testament. In terms of the nature of baptism and the nature of the church, the Anabaptists repeatedly pointed out that the church and New Testament baptism were for those who were able to voluntarily believe, repent, and make their own commitment to follow Jesus, all things that an infant was unable to do.[52] Accordingly, they rejected the idea that baptism was analogous to Old Testament circumcision. As Marpeck pointed out, "Thus, there is a great difference between circumcision and the true baptism of Christ.... Like most other things in the Old Testament, circumcision is a figure and an image.... But one cannot extrapolate from this promise to Abraham that children are to be baptized."[53]

Positively, the evangelical Anabaptists taught that baptism was for those who had already experienced conversion or regeneration. Hubmaier wrote, "By the power of the internal 'Yes' in the heart . . . the person proclaims publicly in the reception of water baptism, that he believes and is already sure in his heart of the remission of sins through Jesus Christ."[54] One submitted to baptism in imitation of Jesus himself and in obedience to his commands in the Great Commission of Matthew 28 and Mark 16.[55] Menno Simons argued for the practice of believers' baptism on three grounds: because of the command of the Lord, because of the teachings of the apostles, and because of the practice of the apostles.[56] Although the Anabaptists did not generally regard baptism as having any salvific value, they did understand it to represent or be the sign of many blessings connected to salvation. They understood it variously as the sign or seal of the new covenant, as a sign of forgiveness of sins, as a witness of, or testimony to, faith and/or regeneration, as the dying of the old man and putting on of the new, as a burial with Christ, as a pledge of discipleship, or as the door into the visible church. The practice of believers' baptism was essential to the life of the church and to Christian discipleship, and it identified those who belonged to the visible church.[57] In the words of Hubmaier, "Where there is no water baptism, there is no church."[58]

As to the mode of baptism, only in rare exceptions did the evangelical Anabaptists practice full immersion. It is interesting, however, that Pilgram Marpeck did recognize that "in its natural sense, the meaning of the word 'baptize' is to dunk into water or to thrust into water," though he went on to suggest that "baptism is the same as immersion or sprinkling with water." It is unclear as to whether he advocated immersion himself.[59] Instead, the common practice was to continue the medieval practice of affusion, described in the words of Hubmaier: "Baptism in water according to the divine command is to pour outward water over the person who confesses his sins."[60]

Regarding the Lord's Supper, which was received in both kinds, most evangelical Anabaptists rejected doctrines of the physical presence of Jesus in the bread and the wine (such as transubstantiation or consubstantiation), though they did not necessarily reject the idea that Jesus might be present during the Supper in some (usually) undefined spiritual sense. For example, Menno Simons referred to it as "the communion of the body and blood of Christ" and continued, "For wherever this Holy Supper is celebrated with such faith, love, attentiveness, peace, unity of heart and mind, there Jesus Christ is present with His grace, Spirit, and promise."[61] Most accepted the Supper as a symbolic memorial that reminded the Brethren to be willing to sacrifice themselves for one another just as Christ had sacrificed himself for them.[62] The Lord's Supper was reserved for the baptized, and because of the importance they placed on the church as holy community, it was important that only those who were committed disciples partake. In other words, they practiced closed Communion. Often, the announcement of the ban might precede the Supper, ensuring that those who were unrepentant would not be allowed to participate.[63]

Legacy

In spite of relentless persecution and constant internal disagreements, groups of men and women who preached the gospel wherever they went, maintained high standards of morality and discipline, cared for one another with the love of Christ, and loved truth more than life itself was a force so powerful that neither the most severe persecution imaginable nor the trauma of schism could prevent its spread. Not only is the legacy of the sixteenth-century evangelical Anabaptists carried on in surviving churches such as the Hutterites and various forms of Mennonites and Amish, but they also restored several significant principles to the Christian world. Among these are the concept of the separation of church and state and the so-called free church—a gathered community to which people of free will voluntarily commit rather than being born, coerced, or predestined into, and which is not bound geographically by a magisterial apparatus. Additionally, they restored the concept of autonomous congregations tied together not by doctrinal or confessional decrees, ecclesiastical hierarchy, or geographic political boundaries, but by common faith founded on a Christocentric understanding of Scripture, particularly the New Testament, lived out in sacrificial discipleship, and cemented by communal discipline. Finally, their heroic missionary zeal in the face of staggering odds and horrific persecution has been an inspiration to generations of believers.

Questions for Thought or Discussion

1. Why did the evangelical Anabaptists write so little about the great themes of Christian theology?

2. What were the evangelical Anabaptists emphasizing in their renewal efforts?

3. Which of the theological issues or practices of the evangelical Anabaptists is most challenging to you and why?

4. What were various strengths or weaknesses in the theological perspectives of these groups?

5. What lessons or applications can you draw from the evangelical Anabaptists?

NOTES

[1] See the discussions in Carlos M. N. Eire, *Reformations: The Early Modern World, 1450–1650* (New Haven, CT: Yale University Press, 2016), 250–55; Daniel P. Rhodes, "Against the World: The Doctrine of Separation within the Political Context of the Origins of Swiss Anabaptism," *Baptist Heritage and History* 54, no. 1 (Spring 2019): 38–39; Cornelius Dyck, *An Introduction to Mennonite History: A Popular History of the Anabaptists and the Mennonites*, 3rd ed. (Scottdale, PA: Herald Press, 1993), 33–36, 134–49.

[2] William R. Estep, *The Anabaptist Story*, 3rd ed. (Grand Rapids: Eerdmans, 1996), 235, 237, 239.

[3] James M. Stayer, *The German Peasants' War and Anabaptist Community of Goods* (Montreal: McGill-Queen's University Press, 1991).

[4] Rhodes, "Against the World," 48.

[5] Dyck, *Introduction*, 149.

[6] Eire, *Reformations*, 250.

[7] Menno Simons did, however, advocate a controversial view of the incarnation, while still affirming both the full deity and full humanity of Christ. For Menno Simons's view, see Menno Simons, *The Complete Writings*, trans. Leonard Verduin, ed. John C. Wenger

(Scottdale, PA: Herald Press, 1956), 785–834; for a summary of his view, see Estep, *Anabaptist Story*, 188–90.

[8] For example, "Within the Reformation no group took more seriously the principle of *sola Scriptura* in matters of doctrine and discipline than did the true Anabaptists," or "The Anabaptist view of the Bible . . . became a dynamic center of a biblical and creative theology free from the entangling hindrances of tradition and scholasticism alike. At this point the Anabaptists were the most Protestant and yet the furthest removed from Protestantism. They took the principle of *sola Scriptura* seriously and sought to make the biblical witness a contemporary phenomenon," Estep, *Anabaptist Story*, 190, 196. Again, "In many ways, the Anabaptists merely took Zwingli's strict biblicism, his idea of *sola scriptura*, to its logical conclusion," Craig D. Atwood, *The Theology of the Czech Brethren from Hus to Comenius* (University Park, PA: Pennsylvania State University Press, 2009), 255. For helpful discussions on how the sixteenth-century reformers applied the concept of *sola scriptura*, see Phyllis Rodgerson Pleasants, "*Sola Scriptura* in Zurich?" and D. H. Williams, "Scripture, Tradition, and the Church: Reformation and Post-Reformation," in D. H. Williams, ed., *The Free Church and the Early Church: Bridging the Historical and Theological Divide* (Grand Rapids: Eerdmans, 2002), 77–99 and 101–26.

[9] For a biographical summary of Marpeck, see Pilgram Marpeck, *The Writings of Pilgram Marpeck*, trans. and ed. William Klassen and Walter Klaassen (Scottdale, PA: Herald Press, 1978), 15–41; and David C. Steinmetz, *Reformers in the Wings* (Philadelphia: Fortress Press, 1971), 222–25.

[10] Estep, *Anabaptist Story*, 193–94.

[11] See Steinmetz, *Reformers*, 222, 224; and Dyck, *Introduction*, 89–92.

[12] Marpeck, *Writings*, 225; cf. 116, 222–23.

[13] Marpeck, *Writings*, 557–66, 559; cf. 561–62.

[14] Marpeck, *Writings*, 118–19, 123.

[15] Marpeck, *Writings*, 226–27, 232.

[16] Marpeck, *Writings*, 119, 556–57; cf. Steinmetz, *Reformers*, 226.

[17] Estep, *Anabaptist Story*, 126.

[18] Marpeck, *Writings*, 240–41.

[19] See Estep, *Anabaptist Story*, 126, 194; cf. Marpeck, *Writings*, 150, 556, 557.

[20] Conrad Grebel, "Letter to Thomas Munster" (1524), in Keith D. Stanglin, ed., *The Reformation to the Modern Church: A Reader in Christian Theology* (Minneapolis: Fortress Press, 2014), 137–38.

[21] Stayer, *Peasants' War*, 81–82, 141–42, 155, 158.

[22] Estep, *Anabaptist Story*, 180–82.

[23] Cf. Carter Lindberg, *The European Reformations*, 2nd ed. (Malden, MA: Wiley-Blackwell, 2010), 211.

[24] See the discussion in Estep, *Anabaptist Story*, 241–43.

[25] Walter Klaassen, "The Anabaptist Understanding of the Separation of the Church," *Church History* 46 (1977): 433.

[26] See discussion in Estep, *Anabaptist Story*, 245–52.

[27] George Huntston Williams, *The Radical Reformation*, 3rd ed. (Kirksville, MO: Sixteenth Century Journal, 1992), 221.

[28] Simons, *Complete Writings*, 549.

[29] Peter Riedemann, "Account of our Religion, Doctrine, and Faith," in Michael G. Long, ed., *Christian Peace and Nonviolence: A Documentary History* (Maryknoll, NY: Orbis Books, 2011), 85.

30 See Estep, *Anabaptist Story*, 254; cf. Riedemann, "Account," 84–85.
31 See Leonard Verduin, *The Reformers and Their Stepchildren* (Grand Rapids: Baker, 1964), 190; and Estep, *Anabaptist Story*, 242.
32 Verduin, *Reformers*, 104.
33 Given the persecution they faced, this was understandable. Rhodes puts it this way: "The radicals' instinct to separate was driven by the larger political powers, which intentionally set out to drive a wedge between the preaching of the gospel and the sociopolitical implications of living it out," Rhodes, "Against the World," 43.
34 See Lindberg, *European Reformations*, 192.
35 John Calvin, *John Calvin: Selections from His Writings*, ed., John Dillenberger (Garden City, NY: Anchor Books, 1971), 27; Ulrich Zwingli, *Selected Works of Huldreich Zwingli*, ed., Samuel Macauley Jackson (Philadelphia: University of Pennsylvania Press, 1901), 208–9.
36 "No type of connectionalism existed among the autonomous congregations of Anabaptists, with the exception of the Hutterites, until Menno reorganized the Mennonites," Estep, *Anabaptist Story*, 254.
37 Grebel, "Letter," 137–38. Grebel argued that "since we find nothing taught in the New Testament about singing, no example of it," it was therefore forbidden.
38 See, for example, two treatises by Balthasar Hubmaier on "Freedom of the Will" in *Balthasar Hubmaier; Theologian of Anabaptism*, trans. and ed. H. Wayne Pipkin and John H. Yoder (Scottdale, PA: Herald Press, 1989), 427–91.
39 Harold S. Bender, "The Anabaptist Vision," *Church History* 13 (1944): 17.
40 Michael Sattler, *The Schleitheim Confession* in *Creeds of the Churches: A Reader in Christian Doctrine from the Bible to the Present*, ed. John H. Leith, 3rd ed. (Atlanta: John Knox, 1982), 287. The quotation from the Sermon on the Mount is found in Matthew 5:39.
41 Sattler, *Schleitheim Confession*, 289–91.
42 Stayer, *Peasants' War*. See also Bob Scribner, "Practical Utopias: Pre-Modern Communism and the Reformation," *Comparative Studies in Society and History* 36, no. 4 (October 1994): 743–74.
43 Scribner, "Practical Utopias," 753.
44 Scribner, "Practical Utopias," 754–56.
45 Stayer, *Peasants' War*, 122.
46 See for example, Simons, *Complete Writings*, 558.
47 Stayer, *Peasants' War*, 7.
48 Stayer, *Peasants' War*, 106.
49 Sattler, *Schleitheim Confession*, 284–85.
50 For example, Menno Simons referred to baptism and the "Supper" as "ceremonies," Simons, *Complete Writings*, 236. Pilgram Marpeck believed "the term sacrament can be used correctly" only when it was properly understood, *Writings*, 169. He also frequently used the term *ceremonies*, 44, 47.
51 The following discussion is largely dependent on Estep, *Anabaptist Story*, 201–35.
52 For example, Hubmaier, *Theologian*, 99–101; and Marpeck, *Writings*, 130, 208, 212–13.
53 Marpeck, *Writings*, 223.
54 Hubmaier, *Theologian*, 118.
55 Hubmaier, *Theologian*, 121–22, 129–30.
56 Simons, *Complete Writings*, 237. For his whole discussion on "Christian Baptism," see 229–87, in which he also points out reasons why he opposes infant baptism.

[57] See discussion in Estep, *Anabaptist Story*, 201–35.
[58] Hubmaier, *Theologian*, 127.
[59] Marpeck, *Writings*, 185, 172. The rationalist Polish Brethren were probably the largest group that consistently practiced immersion. See Wes Harrison, "The Renewal of the Practice of Adult Baptism by Immersion during the Reformation Era, 1525–1700," *Restoration Quarterly* 43, no. 2 (2001): 95–112. On Marpeck's view, 100.
[60] Hubmaier, *Theologian*, 99.
[61] Simons, *Complete Writings*, 146, 148.
[62] Marpeck, *Writings*, 272, 288; Hubmaier, *Theologian*, 147–48.
[63] Sattler, *Schleitheim Confession*, 285.

CHAPTER 9

"A Personal Religion of the Heart"
Pietism, Schwarzenau Brethren, and the Moravian Brethren

The Protestant Reformations of the sixteenth century had contributed to what are known as the wars of religion that plagued Europe throughout the latter half of that century. The culmination of these wars of religion was the Thirty Years' War that began in 1618 and raged until 1648. Although the war began ostensibly as a religious war with sides being determined along confessional lines, pitting Protestants against Roman Catholics, by its conclusion, it had become a purely political conflict such that Catholic France was allied with the Protestant powers against the Catholic Hapsburgs. Religiously, the Thirty Years' War confirmed the principle *cuius regio eius religio* (*whose the region, his the religion*), meaning that the secular rulers of each region of the Holy Roman Empire could determine the religion of their territories.[1] But this did not result in a comfortable peace. Christopher Gehrz and Mark Pattie III described it as "a highly polarized time. The peace was tenuous. Territorial, societal, and ecclesial boundaries were becoming increasingly rigid throughout central Europe."[2] In the aftermath of the Thirty Years' War, many in seventeenth-century Germany, which had been particularly devastated by the war, recognized the need for a return to Christian moral decency, and many desired cooperation rather than animosity between the various confessional branches of Christianity. Of course, others were completely disillusioned, blaming religion for the war. In this social climate, it seemed to many people that Protestantism had grown stale with its endless disputes about theological minutiae and that the pastors and theologians had lost touch with the spiritual concerns of everyday people. In Germany, both church and civil authorities tried to enforce conformity, and those who were seen as nonconformists were denounced and persecuted.[3] For many, the prevailing church systems had become too dogmatic and too institutionalized, too concerned with "dead orthodoxy." Some were even turning to the writings of the Anabaptist Spiritualists and to various mystics. As early as 1610, the Lutheran Johann Arndt (1555–1621) had published a work called *Four Books of True Christianity* in which he argued that "the scholarly study of the Scriptures without love and a holy Christian life is simply worthless."[4] What people were looking for was a personal religion of the heart; they needed something to feed their souls. Some innovative religious leaders responded to this longing by advocating meeting in private homes for prayer, Scripture reading, and spiritual growth.

Philip Jacob Spener and German Pietism

It was within this context that among both Dutch Calvinists and German Lutherans the renewal movement called Pietism arose. This movement was so influential that historian Douglas Shantz called it perhaps "the most significant Protestant renewal movement since the sixteenth century,"[5] and he drew attention to important features of Pietism that distinguished it from traditional Protestantism: the experience of renewal and new birth, gatherings of Christians outside the regular church assemblies for mutual encouragement featuring "the central place of Bible reading in association with the practice of the universal priesthood of believers," missions to the world, and an imminent expectation of Christ's kingdom on earth.[6] Gehrz and Pattie have identified the ethos of Pietism as shared instincts, impulses, or inclinations "that start in the heart before they reach the head." They suggested that these instincts include emphases on the message of personal faith, unity among Christians, a truly transformative encounter with Jesus accompanied by few doctrinal essentials, and an expectation that God will break into the world in unexpected ways.[7] All of these emphases are consistent with a restorationist orientation; concisely stated, "groups of Pietists sought to recapture the flavor and core ecclesiology of first-century Christianity."[8]

The beginnings of German Pietism proper are found in Frankfurt in the activities of the Lutheran minister Philip Jacob Spener (1635–1705), who is generally regarded as the originator of German Pietism, and Johann Jakob Schütz (1640–90), a converted atheist. Spener had been educated in Strasburg, Basel, and Geneva, where he had been influenced by Reformed doctrine and practice, making him open to ideas beyond orthodox Lutheranism. He began his ministry in Frankfurt in 1666, where he sought to bring about the renewal of spirituality in the local Lutheran churches. Schütz was a lawyer who had lost his faith and embraced atheism before becoming acquainted with Spener. Schütz then experienced conversion in 1668 as a result of his discovery of the Bible, the reading of which "moved his soul and . . . spoke to his conscience."[9] In August 1670, Schütz and another man approached Spener about beginning a small group, or conventicle, in Spener's home for the purpose of edifying discussion. This group grew from six men in 1670, who gathered on Sunday and Wednesday evenings to discuss devotional books, to nearly one hundred "brothers" and "sisters" by 1677, who gathered to read, study, and discuss the Bible. Spener argued in his *Pia Desideria*, "Accordingly, *all* scripture, without exception, should be known by the congregation if we are all to receive the necessary benefit."[10] According to Shantz, Spener, following Schütz, believed that the reading of Scripture was the way in which people were able to experience the working of the Holy Spirit in coming to faith.[11]

The group founded by Spener and Schütz was Frankfurt's first *collegium pietatis* (school of piety) from which the term *Pietism* is derived. It was composed not only of Lutherans, but also of Reformed Calvinists; this was not problematic because the group intentionally avoided doctrinal controversy and focused on spiritual renewal and holy living. Believing that, for the truly converted, "doctrinal differences were relatively unimportant,"

Spener instead taught "the necessity of the new birth, a personal, warm Christian experience, and the cultivation of Christian virtues."[12]

For Spener, these small groups were a key for church renewal because they allowed for a greater role in ministry for the laity. They represented a practical outworking of Luther's doctrine of the priesthood of all believers.[13] Nevertheless, Spener's intention had been that the *collegia* would remain under his or other clergy supervision and would remain within the larger Lutheran church, functioning somewhat as small churches within the state church.[14] More and more conventicles sprang up, however, some even without Spener's knowledge, and the connection to the established church became impossible to maintain for all the groups. For example, dissatisfied with being forced to sit in a separate room from the men and having to remain silent during the discussions, two women, Maria Juliana Baur von Eyseneck (1641–84) and Johanna Eleonora von Merlau (1644–1724), started a new conventicle in the home of von Eyseneck on her Saalhof estate. Eventually, the Saalhof conventicle completely separated itself from the Lutheran church. It is important to point out the important role played by women, especially in the beginnings of the Pietist movement. According to Shantz, "Women, in large measure, made up the rank and file of Pietist conventicles and networks. Though they held no official office and had no formal theological education, women played prominent roles in the formative phase of the Pietist movement."[15] For example, von Merlau, who had mastered Greek and Hebrew, published fifteen books, including an autobiography and several books on biblical interpretation.[16]

Conventicles formed not only in Frankfurt but throughout Germany as people responded to a Christianity of the heart fueled by a return to Scripture. For many within the conventicles, their religion of the heart was accompanied by millenarian hopes for a better future and the reign of Christ on earth. Naturally enough, controversy arose from opponents within orthodox Lutheranism, accusing Spener of forsaking Lutheran doctrine and complaining that many of those who were attending his groups were ceasing to attend church.

Spener believed that the church of his day should resemble that of the early Christians. To that end, in 1675, he published his most important writing, *Pia Desideria* (*Pius Longings*).[17] In this work, he attacked society and the orthodox Lutheranism of his day and gave his vision for the renewal of the church. He also expressed his desire for unity among Christians: "If there is any prospect of a union of most of the confessions among Christians, the primary way of achieving it, and the one that God would bless most, would perhaps be this, that we do not stake everything on argumentation, for the present disposition of men's minds, which are filled by as much fleshly as spiritual zeal, makes disputation fruitless."[18] He proposed six remedies for the ills of the church: (1) More extensive use should be made of the Word of God, particularly through diligent reading of Scripture, both publicly and privately, with an emphasis on the New Testament. (2) The spiritual priesthood of not only ministers, but of all Christians, should be put into practice. (3) It was necessary that knowledge of the Christian faith should be accompanied by the practice of Christian love. (4) Christians should be careful in how they conducted themselves with those with whom they disagreed, with unbelievers, and with heretics. Christians should conduct themselves with love and firm but gentle persuasion, praying for them and providing them with a good example, recognizing that "disputation [was] not the only means of maintaining the truth . . ." but also "recognizable and unalloyed love of our neighbors, including those who are heretics . . ." was necessary.[19] (5) Only suitable persons ought to be called to the ministry, and their preparation should consist in training in holiness and practical ministry, in addition to training in theology. (6) Sermons should be prepared in order to achieve the purpose of producing faith and its fruits.[20]

According to Gehrz and Pattie, Spener and his fellow workers looked "to the past and the early church's example of such kingdom work bearing great fruit," but they also "looked to the future to discern the kingdom purposes they were called to work toward." It was this looking both backward and forward that led them to action in the world.[21] The ministry of August Hermann Francke (1663–1727),[22] Spener's successor as a major leader of the Pietist movement, exemplified this perspective. Francke was a professor at the university in Leipzig, where he and some of his colleagues began a group they called a *collegium philobiblicum* (school of friends of the Bible) for the purpose of studying Scripture in its original languages. Spener, who by this time had moved to Dresden, heard about Francke's group and encouraged its activities, meeting Francke for the first time in 1687. A few months after their first meeting, Francke underwent a serious spiritual struggle that led him through what he considered his own conversion experience. He described a time when he got down on his knees to pray, not believing in God, and rose with full certainty of his new birth. This type of conversion experience with an emphasis on "new birth" would become a common mark of Pietism in the future.[23]

Francke's conversion led to a change in his teaching from formal scholarly lectures to devotional discussions and an emphasis on Christian living. This change led to revival not only among students, but also among the townspeople of Leipzig. Conventicles began to spread throughout the city, some of them led by laypersons with no clergy present. In some conventicles, there were reports of visions, prophecies (particularly by women), and millenarian expectations, and the authorities became concerned about the religious activities that seemed aimed at beginning a new sect. The upshot of it all was that, by 1690, conventicles had been banned in Leipzig, Francke had lost his position at the university, and most of the Pietist students had left Leipzig for other towns and universities, where they passed on the message and practices of Pietism.[24]

After a short ministry in Erfurt, from which Francke was also dismissed due to his association with conventicles, he ended up in 1692 teaching in Halle and preaching in Glaucha, just outside of Halle. Due to his work in these communities, Halle was to become known as the main center of German Pietism. Over the years, Francke was able to establish the Halle Foundations, consisting of, among other things, a school for poor children (1695), a famous orphanage where children were educated and taught work skills (1698), a theological college (1702), a seminary for teachers, a Latin school, a pharmacy, a bookstore, a print shop, homes for widows, and collection and distribution of alms for the poor. With help from Baron Carl Hildebrand von Canstein, as many as two million Bibles were published at Halle over the next one hundred years, at prices that even the poor could afford.[25]

In addition to all this, Halle became a base from which Protestant missionaries began to be sent. The impetus for this came from King Frederick IV of Denmark (1671–1730, reigned 1699–1730). Frederick, who was a supporter of Pietism, requested missionaries to evangelize his overseas territory of Tranquebar, on the Coromandel Coast of India. Two Lutheran Pietists, Bartholomew Ziegenbalg (1682/3–1719) and Heinrich Plütschau (1677–1747), responded, sailing for Tranquebar in 1705 and arriving in 1706. The work began with remarkable success, and within just more than a year of work, the pair had already baptized as many as forty Indians. This does not mean, however, that the work was without its difficulties. The missionaries faced significant opposition to their work from the Danish officials, and Ziegenbalg was even imprisoned. After six years, Plütschau was forced by poor health to return home, but Ziegenbalg served fourteen years until his death, completing a translation of the Tamil New Testament before his passing. In spite of the persecution faced by the Indians who converted to Christianity, at the time of Ziegenbalg's death, there was an Indian church of between 250 and 350 baptized members.[26] The significance of the mission of Ziegenbalg and Plütschau is that they were the first two Protestants to be sent out as missionaries to non-Christian lands, and this set the stage for the restoration of missionary zeal among Protestants. This was the beginning of the Danish-Halle mission that, during the eighteenth century, sent out dozens of Pietist missionaries, including some sixty to India. The most important of the Danish-Halle missionaries was Christian Frederick Schwartz (1726–98), who served in India for forty-eight years and, at the time of his death, left a church of about two thousand members.[27]

With its emphasis on personal spiritual renewal facilitated by conventicles with their focus on prayer, Bible study, and mutual edification that led to international mission work, interdenominational cooperation, and social activism, Pietism made a positive contribution to the renewal of the church of the seventeenth and eighteenth centuries, especially in Germany. On the other hand, Pietism also led to excesses, as many began to elevate their own spiritual insight above the teachings of Scripture and developed attitudes of spiritual superiority and elitism.[28] Many within Pietism saw no value in the church itself and separated themselves from organized church structures, valuing their private conventicles over the church. At the opposite extreme, Francke, for example, could appear judgmental and unreasonable in his application of church discipline, fostering expectations of perfectionism among his church members and withholding the Lord's Supper from those who did not meet his standards. Conventicles were often dependent on charismatic leaders, who themselves might be subject to moral failings, and the emphasis on the religion of the heart often led to an unhealthy anti-intellectualism and a devaluation of reason.[29]

The Schwarzenau Brethren

Another of the great weaknesses of the Pietist movement was its own divisiveness; this is certainly ironic, given Spener's aversion to doctrinal disagreement. This divisiveness resulted in the rise of numerous similar but distinct groups falling under the categorization of Pietism. The Pietism of Spener and Francke may be described as "church Pietism," while other expressions of Pietism are generally described as "radical Pietism."[30] A particular feature of "radical Pietism" was an orientation "on the life of Jesus and the congregational practice of the first Christians as their model and guiding principle."[31] Because of the variety within Pietism, it is not surprising that various Pietistic groups had differing understandings of such practices as Christian baptism. Many groups retained the normal Lutheran practice of infant baptism, and still others, under Quaker influence and perhaps under the influence of Spiritualist Anabaptists, did away with baptism altogether. Others, under the influence of evangelical Anabaptists, rejected infant baptism and accepted the practice of believers' baptism. One of these radical Pietist groups was the Schwarzenau Brethren, a restorationist group also known as the New Baptists and later in North America as the Church of the Brethren.[32]

Near the beginning of the eighteenth century, Countess Hedwig Sophie and Count Heinrich Albrecht had granted asylum to radical Pietists in the county of Wittgenstein to the northwest of Frankfurt, leading several hundred Pietists to settle in the town of Schwarzenau. One of these refugees was a miller and Pietist leader named Alexander Mack (1679–1735).[33] Although these radicals had broken with the establishment Reformed and Lutheran churches, and although they referred to themselves as "brother" and "sister," they themselves suffered from conflict and division. A group of these Pietists who had gathered around Mack believed that discipline and unity could be achieved if they would follow the model of the early

Christians and give "strict obedience to the letter of Scripture."[34] In summer 1708, Mack and seven other radical Pietists, four men and three women, decided that they needed to receive believers' baptism by immersion. Mack defended this conclusion by pointing to the scriptural evidence of the baptism of Jesus, the meaning of the Greek word *baptizo*, and the practice of the early church.[35] One morning in August, Alexander Mack, his wife Anna, Andreas and Johanna Boni, Johann and Johanna Kipping, Johan Georg Grebe, and Lukas Vetter made their way to the Eder River. Mack was to be baptized first. The drawing of lots determined who among Grebe, Vetter, Boni, and Kipping would perform the first baptism, but they intentionally kept secret the name of the man who was chosen. Following his immersion, Mack immersed the others.[36] Although Mack rejected a sacramental understanding of baptism and believed, along with other Protestants, that salvation was bound to faith alone and was the work of the Holy Spirit, he also believed that only in baptism does genuine rebirth take place. Though baptism was an external sign of the Spirit's work, it was also connected to actual forgiveness of sins. Thus, although salvation was not attained through baptism, it was obtained in baptism.[37] Based on Matthew 28:18–20, the Brethren practiced triune immersion (performed forward instead of backward), once in the name of the Father, then in the name of the Son, and then in the name of the Holy Spirit, by which they believed they had restored the practice of the Christians of the first and second centuries.[38] When questioned about whether they believed that for more than a thousand years there had been no true baptism, and consequently no true church, the Brethren responded that they believed that God had always preserved his true church, which had observed the true baptism and other ordinances, though its numbers were often few and hidden.[39]

Though others referred to them as New Baptists, the group rejected any type of self-designation and simply referred to themselves as "brethren."[40] By forming themselves as a church, the Schwarzenau Brethren set themselves up for even more severe opposition. On the one hand, the practice of rebaptism was still illegal and subject to severe penalties, and on the other hand, many Pietists rejected any ecclesiastical organization and attacked the Brethren for being sectarian. Mack believed the marks of a true church were the practice of baptism, the ban, and the Lord's Supper.[41]

The Brethren insisted on baptism upon confession of faith, pacifism, strict discipline, including the exercise of the ban, and a rejection of oaths. It appears that, initially, the Brethren practiced sexual abstinence and the community of goods but quickly abandoned these positions. They were committed to congregational polity, and it was necessary for leaders, or "householders," in the church to have the Holy Spirit as evinced by exemplary conduct. Unlike many of the radical Pietists, the Brethren rejected a chiliastic expectation of the imminent establishment of the kingdom of God on earth, though they did accept the idea of the *apocatastasis panton* or the "restoration of all things," by which all people would eventually be purified and saved. Like many other restorationist groups, the worship services of the New Baptists were simple. They consisted of singing a few songs, reading and explaining the Bible, praying, and partaking in the love feast, celebrated in the evening. Mack rejected the eucharistic practice of giving only small portions of bread and wine, insisting on a full meal. This love feast, intended to form a close community, was the Brethren's Communion service, consisting of foot washing, an agape meal, and the Lord's Supper. An important manifestation of the love and unity of the Brethren was the practice of the holy kiss or kiss of peace.[42]

In spite of opposition, many people came to Brethren meetings at Schwarzenau and were then sent from Schwarzenau with the new Brethren message. The Brethren were mission-minded,[43] and like the Anabaptist missionaries before them, many of their missionaries also faced great opposition and persecution. Nevertheless, they founded new congregations, and the movement spread. At times, entire communities of the Brethren were banished from their homes. In one case, six members of the congregation at Solingen were arrested and tried. Roman Catholic, Lutheran, and Reformed theologians were consulted as to what should be done with the brothers. The Roman Catholics recommended execution, the Lutherans recommended that they be made galley slaves, and the Reformed recommended life in prison with hard labor. The suggestion of the Reformed was accepted. Fortunately, under diplomatic pressure, the authorities released the men after they had served not quite four years of their sentence.[44]

Because of increasing persecution, many Brethren decided to seek out safer territories. Between 1719 and 1735, hundreds of them immigrated to North America, where they eventually became known as the Church of the Brethren, or Dunkers. Most settled in Pennsylvania, but the movement spread to other states as well, almost exclusively among German settlers. Those who remained in Europe eventually either died out or merged with other groups.

The Moravian Brethren and the Eighteenth-Century Renewal of Missions

The influence of Pietism was not limited to groups that Pietism itself spawned. As previously mentioned, the Unity of the Brethren had originated in the lands of the Czech kings in the fifteenth century as a result of the reforms of the followers of John Hus. After surviving as an illegal sect for almost one hundred years, the Unity linked up with the Protestants of the sixteenth-century Reformation. However, in the seventeenth century, most of the Unity was driven out of the Czech lands and Moravia as a result of the Catholic victory in those territories during the Thirty Years' War. Various groups of the Brethren began searching for a place of refuge.

Nicolaus Ludwig von Zinzendorf (1700–1760) was a German nobleman whose godfather was none other than Philip Jacob Spener, the father of German Pietism. At the age of ten, Zinzendorf went to study for about six years at Halle, where he was immersed in Pietistic thought before continuing his studies at Wittenberg. While at Halle, he met Bartholomew Ziegenbalg and Heinrich Plütschau and heard of their mission work. Zinzendorf and four of his friends committed that, upon adulthood, they would labor as patrons for missions for the conversion of the heathen.[45]

It was in 1722 that Zinzendorf had a meeting that was to change his life and ultimately lead to the renewal of missionary fervor among Protestants. Zinzendorf met a carpenter from Moravia, Christian David (1690–1751), who had been raised as a Roman Catholic but had converted to the faith of the Unity of the Brethren as a young man.[46] David told Zinzendorf of the plight of the underground Brethren in Moravia who had nowhere to safely live and practice their faith. Zinzendorf was touched by their plight and agreed to give asylum on his estate in Saxony to the refugees from the

Czech lands and Moravia. The refugees arrived at their new home on June 17, 1722, and named it Herrnhut, "The Lord's Watch," to signify both that they were under the Lord's watch and care and that they were on watch for the Lord.[47] Although the first group of refugees consisted of only ten people, the little community grew, and by 1725, there were ninety people living and working at Herrnhut. The community encouraged its members to form small groups for the study and application of the Bible.[48] Although a number of these refugees had indeed come from the remnants of the Unity of the Brethren, a larger number of them had come from other places and other religious backgrounds, and this, along with the disparity of social character among the refugees, became a source of tension between the various groups.[49] Nevertheless, because of the Moravian origins of the first refugees, this group was to become known as the Moravian Brethren, though officially, they considered themselves the Renewed Unity of the Brethren.[50]

In 1727, Zinzendorf received a copy of the *Ratio Disciplinae*, compiled by the former bishop of the Unity of the Brethren, John Amos Comenius, which impressed him greatly. He saw in the writings of Comenius similarities to his own thinking, and he became more sympathetic to the Moravians' desire to reconstitute the Unity of the Brethren. In order to better organize the Herrnhut community, which consisted not only of the Brethren but of refugees from other religious movements as well, Zinzendorf produced two important documents: "Principle Things Required and Forbidden" and "Statutes of Brotherly Union." Desiring that the community should live "according to the pattern of the first Christians" as described in the New Testament, he proceeded to establish an eldership among the Brethren.[51] Shortly after this, during a Communion service on August 13, the group at Herrnhut, now numbering between two hundred and three hundred people, experienced a great spiritual revival attributed to the coming of the Holy Spirit. Two weeks later, on August 27, they began an around-the-clock prayer vigil made up of twenty-four men and twenty-four women, each taking shifts determined by lot. This prayer vigil ended up lasting some one hundred years.[52]

In addition to the prayer vigil, the community worshiped together on a daily basis, both morning and evening. Also, the community organized as many as ninety bands made up of three to five people who would meet together two or three times each week for prayer and sharing with one another.[53] The following February, twenty-six unmarried men offered themselves to begin preparing for mission work, so Zinzendorf began leading classes for them in the fields of geography, writing, medicine, and theology.[54] Almost three years into the prayer vigil, another important step in the life of Herrnhut was taken. Anna Nitschmann (1715–60) and seventeen other single women committed themselves to submitting their entire lives to the service of Christ on May 14, 1730.[55] The community was moving toward a significant commitment, though it was not yet clear what that was to be.

Most Protestants in the early eighteenth century were not interested in missions outside of Europe.[56] A variety of reasons contributed to this neglect, including the feeling among some that the Great Commission had been given only to the apostles and had been fulfilled in their time. Additionally, for many, the Calvinistic doctrine of predestination made missions superfluous. After all, if God had predetermined who would be saved, what was the point in trying to evangelize?[57] Zinzendorf, however, had not forgotten the pact that he and his friends had made years before to do all that they could for the conversion of the heathen. This was completely in line with the thinking of Comenius himself, who, according to J. Taylor Hamilton and Kenneth G. Hamilton, had argued almost a century earlier that "the evangelization of the heathen [was] an imperative obligation for a living church."[58] On a visit to Copenhagen in 1731, Zinzendorf and David Nitschmann (1695/96–1772) met two converts from a Pietist Lutheran mission to Greenland and also heard reports from a former slave named Anthony Ulrich about the terrible condition of the African slaves in the West Indies. Ulrich suggested that the only way a missionary could reach the slaves, however, would be for the missionary himself to become a slave.[59]

The decisive action came in 1732. It was at that point that, in the words of Hamilton and Hamilton:

> The little community of Herrnhut—some six hundred people all told—heard and answered a divine call. The Lord to whom all authority in heaven and earth is given used these humble

refugees to demonstrate again that the weakness of God is stronger than men. Through their dedicated interest the Church of Christ was stirred, and a new era of foreign missions began.[60]

From this moment, the Herrnhut community was completely dedicated to the propagation and spread of the Christian faith. The 1730s became "the Great Missionary Decade" of the Moravians.[61] During this decade, the Moravians sent missionaries to the West Indies, Surinam, the Gold Coast, Algeria, Russia, Ceylon, Greenland, South Africa, throughout Europe, and to Native Americans and slaves of North America. Some of their missionaries even expressed a willingness to follow Anthony Ulrich's suggestion and become slaves in order to reach the New World so they could proclaim the gospel.[62] As we shall see, however, the reality of the Moravians' approach to slavery was not as noble as this might suggest. Nevertheless, the missionaries labored at great personal cost. As many as 160 Moravian missionaries died in the field during their first fifty years of work.[63]

The first two missionaries of the Moravian Brethren were Leonhard Dober (1706–66) and David Nitschmann. After being commissioned with prayer and the laying on of hands, they departed from Herrnhut for Copenhagen on foot and with practically no money. In Copenhagen, Nitschmann was hired as a ship's carpenter, and they sailed for the Danish West Indies on October 8, arriving at St. Thomas on December 13, 1732. Slaves named Abraham and Anna, the brother and sister of Anthony Ulrich, facilitated the Moravians' introductions to the slaves, and the work was begun. As he had done on the ship, Nitschmann supported the work through his carpentry. According to their plan, however, Nitschmann stayed only long enough to help Dober become settled in the work, and in April 1733, Nitschmann returned to Europe, though his missionary career was far from over.

Dober persevered in spite of opposition from the white colonists, who, because of a violent slave insurrection on a neighboring island, were especially wary of any white man who identified too closely with the slaves. Dober also took a job on a cotton plantation, where one of his duties was to serve as overseer of the slaves. Unsurprisingly, this "dual status as teacher and overseer" was confusing to the slaves.[64] A year and a half after the arrival of the first two missionaries, in June 1734, eighteen more Moravians (fourteen men and four women) arrived on St. Thomas to take over that work and begin a new work on St. Croix. Dober returned to Herrnhut to become the new chief elder of the community. He had made one convert.

The replacements continued to face tremendous opposition and suffering, and by January 1735, eight of the eighteen replacements had died.[65] Nevertheless, more missionaries continued to arrive, and die, and the work went on. Within the first six years, the church on St. Thomas had grown to three hundred members, and by 1750, the Moravians had established a church on St. Thomas with 425 members. They had reached many of the other islands of the West Indies as well.[66]

Friedrich Martin arrived on St. Thomas in 1736 and became a leader among the Moravians in bringing literacy to the slaves, teaching them both reading and writing. However, one of the methods that the Moravians used in their mission was the acquisition of a plantation, including its slaves. In other words, the Moravians themselves became slaveholders, and there were many other instances of Moravian missionaries owning slaves. There is debate as to the extent to which the Moravians' methods compromised with the institution of slavery versus the extent to which their activities, such as providing slaves with education and opportunities for church leadership, and even encouraging interracial marriage, led to emancipation in the West Indies. On the one hand, the Moravians owned slaves and taught slaves that they were to be obedient to their masters. Their teaching that slaves should obey their masters was one way the Moravians won the good will of the slaveholders. On the other hand, the motivation for getting involved in owning slaves was to have a better opportunity to teach them the gospel and to prevent the breakup of slaves' marriages. According to Helen Richards, stressing that all humans were creatures of God and teaching the slaves to read and write "was eventually to have the unintended consequence of aiding the cause of emancipation."[67] Nevertheless, the Moravians were complicit in the bondage of human beings.

The second mission the Moravians undertook was to Greenland. A Norwegian Pietist Lutheran missionary, Hans Egede (1686–1758), with his wife and four sons, had arrived in Greenland in 1721, but the work had been difficult, and the Egedes had little to show for their labors. The Moravians were under the impression that Egede had become so discouraged that he was giving up the mission, so they made plans to send missionaries to Greenland to continue the work. Their contingent, led by Christian David, arrived in Greenland in 1733, only to discover that Egede had no intentions of leaving and was not particularly happy about the arrival of his uninvited coworkers. In fact, about the time the Moravians arrived, Egede started seeing some progress. Nevertheless, Egede welcomed the Moravians and gave them what assistance he could. On the other hand, at times the Moravians and Egede had trouble getting along, with Egede justly accusing the Moravians of reaping the benefits of his labors. Another contingent, including sisters Rosina and Anna Stach and their stepmother, arrived to work in Greenland in 1735. At that time, Christian David returned to Herrnhut. The Moravians' first converts in Greenland came after five years of difficult work, but in 1738, significant numbers of Greenlanders began to be converted. The work grew, and by 1745, more than two hundred were attending worship services.[68]

Another example of early Moravian Brethren mission work is that of George Schmidt (1709–85) to South Africa. Schmidt had been born in Kunvald (now Kunin) in Moravia[69] and had come to Christ among underground Brethren. At the age of seventeen, he arrived at Herrnhut and was there for the great revival of 1727. Schmidt was a zealous proclaimer of the gospel and was commissioned along with two coworkers to preach back in Moravia. Upon their arrival, he and his companions were captured and spent several days in jail. After their release, Schmidt was then commissioned with Melchior Nitschmann to preach in Austria. As the two traveled through the Czech lands, they organized religious gatherings along the way until they were arrested. Nitschmann died in prison in 1729, but Schmidt spent three years in a dungeon, where he was constantly badgered by the Jesuits to recant his faith. After three years in the dungeon, he was subjected to three more years of hard labor. Finally, he was broken to the point that he agreed to recant his Brethren faith and converted to Catholicism in exchange for his release. When Schmidt returned to Herrnhut, the Moravians were scandalized to learn that he had recanted.

Perhaps feeling a need to prove his faith to his brethren, in 1736 Schmidt accepted the call to preach to the Hottentots of South Africa, arriving there in 1737. After living for a while on a military post, he moved to the Baboon Valley to live and work among the Hottentots, where he established a school for fifty students. Both life and ministry were difficult in South Africa. Food was scarce, and opposition from the colonists and the authorities was stout. The colonists did not want the Hottentots, whom they were trying to enslave, to have their social status raised by a missionary, and Dutch Calvinist Reformed religious leaders questioned Schmidt's ministerial credentials. Several of his potential converts fell back into sin, and he was accused of being a hypocrite, committing fornication, and being a spy. While it is true that Schmidt could be arrogant and difficult to get along with, there is no evidence of his immorality or being a spy.

Eventually, Zinzendorf ordained him by letter so he could perform baptisms and serve Communion. Several Hottentots were baptized, but this raised more opposition from the Dutch Calvinists, who considered Schmidt's ordination to be invalid. In 1743, the Dutch authorities banished Schmidt from South Africa. He was never allowed to return. Schmidt left behind a congregation of forty-seven Hottentot believers, plus he had converted thirty-nine colonists to Christ.[70] Fifty years later, three Moravians were able to return to the Baboon Valley and resumed the work. Under the leadership of Hans Peter Hallbeck (1784–1840), the work met with great success in the nineteenth century. By the mid-twentieth century, the Moravians claimed nearly fifty thousand members in the area.[71]

Efforts of the Moravians to reach North America should also be noted. Zinzendorf was able, in 1734, to negotiate a land grant in the new colony of Georgia as a potential refuge for religious exiles and as a base from which to evangelize among the Native Americans. The following year, the first nine Moravians, led by August Gottlieb Spangenberg (1704–92), arrived in Georgia. They were joined in 1736 by twenty more Moravians, led by the former missionary to St. Thomas, Bishop David Nitschmann.[72] Spangenberg, Nitschmann, and others worked not only in Georgia but began mission work throughout the colonies, especially in Pennsylvania and New York.

An important encounter took place in 1735 and 1736 with Nitschmann's group of missionaries to North America. Sailing on the ship with them were none other than John (1703–91) and Charles Wesley (1707–88). The ship encountered a storm during which the passengers despaired of life. While the English were screaming in fear of their lives, and John Wesley himself realized that he was uncertain of his own salvation in the event of his death, the Moravians were calmly singing. The display of calmness during the storm impressed Wesley.[73] After safely arriving in Georgia, the Wesleys had opportunities to visit with Spangenberg, and they learned about Herrnhut and the Moravians' understanding of the personal assurance of salvation. In February 1738, after the Wesleys had returned to England, they met a young Moravian missionary named Peter Böhler (d. 1775), who was himself on his way to do mission work in North America. The Wesleys had several conversations with Böhler, who spoke to them "about the fruits of living faith, the holiness and happiness which he affirmed to attend it," a happiness the brothers had not known.[74] It was after several conversations with Böhler that the Wesley brothers had their famous conversion experiences. Additionally, John Wesley and Peter Böhler had worked together on drawing up statutes for a religious "society" in London.[75] After his conversion, John Wesley traveled to Europe, where he met with Zinzendorf in Marienborn in Wetteravia and with Christian David at Herrnhut. Through these interactions, the Moravian Brethren had a profound influence on the development of the thought of the Wesleys.

Meanwhile, the Moravians at Herrnhut aroused the suspicion of neighbors and the nobles, which was compounded by Zinzendorf's own ordination as Lutheran pastor in 1734. The authorities, who had become jealous and worried by the growing influence of the Herrnhut community, exiled Zinzendorf from Herrnhut in 1736 (until 1747), but this ultimately proved to be a blessing to the new movement, as it forced Zinzendorf to spend the next several years traveling throughout the world, supporting and encouraging the Moravian missionaries. In 1737, Zinzendorf, who was both a German nobleman and a Lutheran clergyman, was ordained as a bishop of the Moravian Brethren. One peculiarity of the organization of the Moravian church was that, although the Brethren ordained their own bishops, they decided by lot on September 16, 1741, that Jesus Christ himself would be the church's only chief elder.[76]

Zinzendorf arrived in North America in 1741 and worked for Christian union among all the German Protestants of Pennsylvania. For a while, he served as pastor of both a Lutheran and Reformed congregation in Philadelphia and then later with an English Moravian congregation. In June 1742, Moravians in North America developed a twofold system of membership, with one group being dedicated to missionary work and education and the second group supporting the first group. Spangenberg returned to North America in October 1744 after having been consecrated as a bishop in Europe. Spangenberg was a skilled administrator and "supervised Moravian itinerant evangelism among the German settlers, directed their missions among the Indians, managed the economic life and enterprises of the settlements . . . and presided over all the undertakings controlled by the Pennsylvania Synods."[77]

The Moravians developed a communal system known as the Economy, by which they all pooled their labor for the work of the church. According to Hamilton and Hamilton, "the Economy nurtured a race of men and women who did not count their lives dear but held themselves in readiness for any task, no matter how arduous, that would further the kingdom of their Lord."[78]

The Moravians were not perfect. Zinzendorf himself greatly neglected his first wife, Erdmuth, and according to Ruth Tucker, "the last fifteen years of their marriage was a marriage in name only."[79] Nevertheless, Erdmuth supported the work of the Moravians and played a vital role in the success of their mission, particularly in legal matters, property management, and the writing of hymns.

Due to a Pietistic lack of emphasis on doctrinal teaching and a strong emphasis on meditating on the death of Christ, many Moravians, including Zinzendorf, drifted into what many perceived as an arrogant mysticism that for a time took their focus away from missions and marred their reputation with others.[80] Also, because they understood that faith was a gracious gift of God, they encouraged the unconverted not to pursue saving faith through such practices as Bible reading, prayer, taking Communion, or trying to live a Christian life. Instead, they taught that one must first simply "be still" and wait passively for God to give faith before one should engage in religious activities.[81]

Another weakness had to do with the Moravians' approach to finances.[82] Zinzendorf himself financed many of their projects, but often by securing enormous loans. Because Zinzendorf did not believe that voluntary offerings would ever be enough to finance all the projects that needed to be done, the missionaries were usually expected to be self-supporting, and in turn, they generally failed to teach new converts of the importance of freewill giving. Unfortunately, self-support was not always viable for the missionaries, and they often suffered a lack of basic necessities. To supply these shortfalls, the Brethren became engaged in massive business and educational enterprises that themselves proved unsustainable. All of these issues often caused the movement to face tremendous financial burdens and crises that ultimately led to pulling out of areas the Moravians had previously entered. Additionally, they discovered that "even in financially successful years the attempt to combine commerce with evangelism adversely affected their ministry to their people."[83]

Additionally, because of their view of the necessity of ordination for the performance of the sacraments, the Moravians often neglected or delayed baptism of converts and were sometimes slow in developing national leaders.

Finally, we have already mentioned the Moravians' collaboration with slave owners and their own participation in owning slaves, ostensibly as a way to reach them with the gospel. Hamilton and Hamilton pointed out, "That in the end this practice would militate against the success of their spiritual labor is hardly to be wondered at. It laid under suspicion the disinterestedness of men who sought at the same time to be taskmasters and religious teachers."[84] Like many others, the Moravian Brethren accepted the institution of slavery as compatible with Christianity. Although the early Moravian practice had been to teach literacy to the slaves, within a decade of their arrival in the West Indies, the Moravians had discontinued teaching literacy for two primary reasons. First, the plantation owners feared that slave literacy would facilitate the freedom of slaves, and the Moravians wanted to earn the good will of the owners. Second, the Moravians were concerned that through the reading of the Bible, literate slaves were reaching theological conclusions that were unacceptable to the Moravians. Nowhere was this more obvious than when literate slaves began to argue for polygamy from numerous texts that they read in the

Old Testament. The missionaries soon grew tired of arguing with slaves about the conclusions they drew from Scripture.

Choices, then, made by Moravian missionaries in the 1700s regarding the relationship between missionaries, slave owners, and slaves set in motion templates that would be copied throughout the Atlantic world. Missionaries endeared themselves to planters by explaining that evangelizing blacks would help cultivate better slaves, and they championed the idea of spiritual salvation that would not change one's material status in the world. In other words, slaves would remain slaves.[85]

In spite of these weaknesses, the Moravian Brethren played a vital role in the renewal of efforts among Protestants to fulfill the Great Commission. They insisted that Scripture was "the only standard and rule both of [their] doctrine and practice" and that its teachings must be lived out.[86] Based on this, they were convinced that the evangelization of the world was the primary purpose of the church and, unlike any Protestant group before them and few after, they were fully invested in the task of taking the gospel to the world. They bought or constructed several ships to transport their missionaries and supplies throughout the world. They established productive communities wherever they went and became leaders in educational work, establishing many schools. Unlike other later Protestant groups, the Brethren did not view missions as simply the work of a missionary society composed of a small minority of interested members. Instead, for them, the whole church was to be actively engaged in spreading the gospel. Moreover, not only was evangelization of the world the purpose of the church in some general, institutional sense, it was the responsibility of each individual member of the community.[87] In their first century of existence, their ratio of missionaries to members was estimated to be better than one missionary for every sixty members.[88]

Some figures illustrate the seriousness with which the Moravian Brethren went about this task. Though always a relatively small group at Herrnhut,[89] the Moravian Brethren furnished more than half the Protestant missionaries from Europe in the eighteenth century, and from the 1730s to the 1750s, the Moravians sent out more missionaries than all the other Protestant groups combined had done in the previous two hundred years. By 1760, the year of Zinzendorf's death, the Moravians had sent out no fewer than 226 missionaries and had baptized three thousand people, and in the century between 1733 and 1833, the Moravians sent 102 missionaries to Greenland alone.[90]

Over the years, the Moravian Brethren faced many challenges—theological, missiological, logistical, political, methodological, organizational, and financial. Some of their missionaries faced martyrdom, poor health, lack of supplies, and natural disasters, but in spite of all the challenges, they never lost sight of their ultimate mission, which was to be constantly and fully engaged in the mission of God to the lost souls of the world. God did great things with such a small movement that was willing and dedicated to his mission. With the understanding that "missions was not an adjunct to church life, it was church life,"[91] the Moravian Brethren were the forerunners of and became a model and inspiration for the Protestant missionary work of the nineteenth-century "Great Century" of Protestant missions.

Legacy

The legacy of Pietism is seen in several areas. First and foremost, Pietism brought about a renewal of the concept of Christianity as a religion of the heart and a personal relationship with Christ, sensitive to the leading of the Spirit rather than simply as a religion of doctrine. The emphasis on "new birth" has continued to be important in many strands of Christianity. The legacy of the *collegia pietatis*, where Christians gather for encouragement, Bible study, worship, and edification, thrives today in many Christian fellowships of home Bible study groups, cell groups, and house churches. Related to this is the emphasis in many Christian groups on lay involvement in teaching and evangelizing. The legacy of the Schwarzenau Brethren lives on in several historic "peace churches" such as the Church of the Brethren, the Old German Baptist Brethren, the Brethren Church, the Fellowship of Grace Brethren churches, the Dunkard Brethren, and the Conservative Grace Brethren. Through Count Zinzendorf, Pietism played an important role in the beginnings of the Renewed Unity of the Brethren, and this group had a significant influence on John and Charles Wesley and thus on the movement that became Methodism. Finally, and perhaps most importantly, fueled by the Pietistic impulse to prayer and openness to the guidance of the Holy Spirit, the work of the Moravian Brethren led to a renewal of missions among Protestants.

Questions for Thought or Discussion

1. How did the Moravian Brethren differ from the German Pietists?

2. To what extent could the movements discussed in this chapter be considered restoration movements?

3. Against what were these various groups reacting?

4. What in particular were these groups emphasizing in their renewal efforts?

5. What were various strengths or weaknesses of the various Pietistic movements?

6. How were these movements similar to or different from the previous movements discussed in this book?

7. What did you find particularly interesting or attractive about the Pietistic movements?

8. What lessons or applications can you draw from the Pietistic movements?

NOTES

[1] In effect, this simply confirmed the understanding of the 1555 Peace of Augsburg, but it expanded it to include the Reformed (Calvinists) as well as Roman Catholics and Lutherans.

[2] Christopher Gehrz and Mark Pattie III, *The Pietist Option* (Downers Grove, IL: InterVarsity Press Academic, 2017), 72.

[3] Douglas H. Shantz, *An Introduction to German Pietism: Protestant Renewal at the Dawn of Modern Europe* (Baltimore: Johns Hopkins University Press, 2013), 152.

[4] Shantz, *Introduction to German Pietism*, 27. The German original is Johann Arndt, *Von wahrem Christenthumb, heilsamer Busse, wahrem Glauben heyligem Leben und Wandel der rechten wahren Christen. Das erste Buch. Durch Johannem Arndt Dienern der Kirchen Christi zu S. Marten in Braunschweig* (Frankfurt am Main: Nicolao Hoffmann, 1605), 283. In 1605, Arndt published a shorter version known simply as *Of True Christianity*.

[5] Shantz, *Introduction to German Pietism*, 1.

[6] Shantz, *Introduction to German Pietism*, 4, 279.

[7] Gehrz and Pattie, *Pietist Option*, 5–9.

[8] John Howard Smith, *The Perfect Rule of the Christian Religion: A History of Sandemanianism in the Eighteenth Century* (Albany: State University of New York Press, 2008), 19.

[9] Shantz, *Introduction to German Pietism*, 75. "The key feature of Schütz's new orientation was his discovery of the Bible."

[10] Philip Jacob Spener, *Pia Desideria*, trans. Theodore G. Tappert (Minneapolis: Fortress Press, 1964), 88.

[11] Shantz, *Introduction to German Pietism*, 76. Furthermore, Shantz asserts that during the seventeenth century, "the ideal of Christians reading and knowing the Bible for themselves was taken seriously only with Spener's Pietism," 89. Although Shantz's assertion is surely an exaggeration, it does call attention to the priority of personal Bible study within Pietism. According to Gehrz and Pattie, "Pietists held that the Scriptures are primarily a God-inspired gift for transformation," *Pietist Option*, 43. Gunnar Westin states, "It is to Pietism's everlasting credit that . . . it placed the Bible and Bible studies in the center for private and church spiritual life," *The Free Church Through the Ages*, trans. Virgil A. Olson (Nashville: Broadman, 1958), 277.

[12] Kenneth Scott Latourette, *A History of Christianity*, vol. 2: *Reformation to the Present*, rev. ed. (Peabody, MA: Prince, 1999), 895.

[13] John D. Woodbridge and Frank A. James III, *Church History*, vol. 2: *From Pre-Reformation to the Present Day* (Grand Rapids: Zondervan, 2013), 263.

[14] *Ecclesiola in Ecclesia*.

[15] Shantz, *Introduction to German Pietism*, 181.

[16] Von Merlau married Johann Willhelm Petersen in 1680 and took his name. She published under the name Johanna Eleonora Peterson, breaking the practice of women publishing anonymously. Shantz calls her "the most significant female Pietist author of her day," *Introduction to German Pietism*, 81–82.

[17] The full title is *Pious Longings, or Heartfelt Desires for Improvement Pleasing to God of the True Evangelical Churches, Including Some Christian Recommendations to That End*. For examples of Spener's holding up of the early church as worthy of imitation, see Spener, *Pia Disederia*, 80–82.

[18] Spener, *Pia Desideria*, 99.

[19] Spener, *Pia Desideria*, 101, 102.

[20] For discussion of these points, see Spener, *Pia Desideria*, 87–122; Shantz, *Introduction to German Pietism*, 87–91; Keith D. Stanglin, ed., *The Reformation to the Modern Church: A Reader in Christian Theology* (Minneapolis: Fortress Press, 2014), 299–302; James B. North, *A History of the Church from Pentecost to Present*, 6th printing (Joplin, MO: College Press, 2005), 406–7; William Cardwell Prout, "Spener and the Theology of Pietism," *Journal of Bible and Religion* 15 (1947): 48–49.

[21] Gehrz and Pattie, *Pietist Option*, 31.

[22] On Francke's ministry, see Shantz, *Introduction to German Pietism*, 98–143.

[23] Shantz, *Introduction to German Pietism*, 106–7. See also Woodbridge, *Church History*, 263.

[24] Shantz, *Introduction to German Pietism*, 102–11.

[25] Shantz, *Introduction to German Pietism*, 208.

²⁶Jon Hinkson, "Missions among Puritans and Pietists," in *The Great Commission: Evangelicals and the History of World Missions*, ed. Martin I. Klauber and Scott M. Manetsch (Nashville: B & H Publishing, 2008), 38, gives the figure of 250, whereas Shantz, *Introduction to German Pietism*, 252, gives the number 350.

²⁷Ruth A. Tucker, *From Jerusalem to Irian Jaya: A Biographical History of Christian Missions*, 2nd ed. (Grand Rapids: Zondervan, 1983), 98–99. For an overview of Schwartz's ministry, see Robert Eric Frykenberg, "The Legacy of Christian Friedrich Schwartz," *International Bulletin of Missionary Research* 23, no. 3 (1999): 130–35. Frykenberg suggests that perhaps as many as six thousand Tamils were converted as a direct result of Schwartz's work, 134.

²⁸Shantz, *Introduction to German Pietism*, 115–16.

²⁹Shantz, *Introduction to German Pietism*, 285–88. Shantz provides several examples of these weaknesses, including the Saalhof Pietists in Frankfurt and the "deranged and immoral behaviors" of prophets like Anna Margaretha Jahn.

³⁰After distinguishing "church Pietism" from "radical Pietism," Shantz identifies "a fourfold typology of expressions of radical Pietism": (1) the spiritualist-alchemist model; (2) the millennialist model; (3) the conventicle model; (4) the sect model, *Introduction to German Pietism*, 154–58.

³¹Marcus Meier, *The Origin of the Schwarzenau Brethren*, trans. Dennis L. Slabaugh (Philadelphia: Brethren Encyclopedia, 2008), 42.

³²Meier, *Origin*, demonstrates the influences of both radical Pietism and Anabaptism, among others, including the Philadelphians of Jane Leade, on the Schwarzenau Brethren. On the differing views of baptism among Pietists, see, for example, 72, 119.

³³Meier, *Origin*, 73–79. For a biographical sketch of Mack, see 7–16.

³⁴Meier, *Origin*, 81–83. Meier points out that the emphases on the practice of the early Christians and obedience to the letter of Scripture as "norms that gave the Brethren congregation its unmistakable character," 86; cf. 128.

³⁵Alexander Mack, *Kurtze und einfältige Vorstellung der äußern aber doch heiligen Rechten und Ordnungen deß Hauses Gottes wie es der wahre Hauß-Vatter Jesus Christus befohlen und in seinem Testament schrifftlich hinterlassen: Vorgestellt in einem Gespräch unter Vater und Sohn durch Frag und Antwort*, 2nd ed. (Germantown, PA: Sauer, 1774), 24–33; cf. Meier, *Origin*, 121–23.

³⁶Meier, *Origin*, 88.

³⁷Alexander Mack, *Eberhard Ludwig Grubers Grundforschende Fragen, welche denen neuen Täufern im Witgensteinischen, insonderheit zu beantworten vorgelegt waren* (Germantown, PA: Sauer, 1774), 16–17, 27, 33; Mack, *Kurtze und einfältige Vorstellung*, 8, 26, 31. See discussion in Meier, *Origin*, 124–25.

³⁸On triune immersion, see Meier, *Origin*, 88, 90, 122–24.

³⁹Meier, *Origin*, 126–27; cf. Donald F. Durnbaugh, *The Believers' Church: The History and Character of Radical Protestantism* (Scottdale, PA: Herald Press, 1985), 124.

⁴⁰Meier, *Origin*, 92–93.

⁴¹Mack, *Eberhard Ludwig Grubers*, 8; cf. Meier, *Origin*, 127.

⁴²For a summary of Schwarzenau Brethren beliefs and practices, see Meier, *Origin*, 53, 84–86, 111–41; and Durnbaugh, *Believers' Church*, 121.

⁴³"Wherever Brethren appeared, they became active missionaries," Meier, *Origin*, 131.

⁴⁴Durnbaugh, *Believers' Church*, 126–27.

⁴⁵ J. Taylor Hamilton and Kenneth G. Hamilton, *History of the Moravian Church: The Renewed Unitas Fratrum, 1722–1957* (Bethlehem, PA: Interprovincial Board of Christian Education, Moravian Church in America, 1967), 19.

⁴⁶ There is some question as to whether David had simply converted to Protestantism or whether he had actually converted to the Unity. See Hamilton and Hamilton, *History of the Moravian Church*, 14–16; W. R. Ward, "The Renewed Unity of the Brethren: Ancient Church, New Sect or Interconfessional Movement?," *Bulletin of the John Rylands Library* 70, no. 3 (1988): 82–84; J. E. Hutton, *A History of the Moravian Church* (Coppell, TX: Pantianos Classics, 2020 [originally published in 1909]), 68–69.

⁴⁷ Hamilton and Hamilton, *History of the Moravian Church*, 24. For most of the basic facts related to the Moravian Brethren, I depend on Hamilton and Hamilton; Tucker, *Jerusalem to Irian Jaya*, 97–113; and Shantz, *Introduction to German Pietism*, 253–69. See also Hutton, *History of the Moravian Church*.

⁴⁸ Ian M. Randall, "A Moravian Spirituality: Moravian Brethren and Eighteenth-Century English Evangelicalism," *Transformation* 23, no. 4 (2006): 207.

⁴⁹ Ward, "Renewed Unity," 84–85; cf. Hutton, *History of the Moravian Church*, 71–72.

⁵⁰ Craig Atwood cautions against seeing too direct a connection between the original Unity of the Brethren and the Moravian Brethren. Without denying the connection of the original Herrnhut settlers to the Unity of the Brethren, he suggests, "There are reasons to doubt that the Moravian refugees had preserved their old church . . . or that it was revived by Zinzendorf," Craig D. Atwood, *The Theology of the Czech Brethren from Hus to Comenius* (University Park, PA: Pennsylvania State University Press, 2009), xiii.

⁵¹ Shantz, *Introduction to German Pietism*, 257; cf. Randall, "Moravian Spirituality," 207.

⁵² Tucker, *Jerusalem to Irian Jaya*, 101.

⁵³ Robert L. Gallagher, "Zinzendorf and the Early Moravians: Pioneers in Leadership Selection and Training," *Missiology* 36, no. 2 (2008): 238.

⁵⁴ Hamilton and Hamilton, *History of the Moravian Church*, 43.

⁵⁵ Hamilton and Hamilton, *History of the Moravian Church*, 36.

⁵⁶ The real exception to this was mission work among Native Americans in the North American colonies of Great Britain.

⁵⁷ For a summary of reasons Protestants did not engage in missions, see Tucker, *Jerusalem to Irian Jaya*, 97. An illustration of the Calvinist perspective is the famous statement of John Ryland Sr. to William Carey, "Young man, sit down. When God pleases to convert the heathen, He will do it without your aid or mine," in Timothy George, *Faithful Witness: The Life and Mission of William Carey* (Birmingham, AL: New Hope, 1991), 53.

⁵⁸ Hamilton and Hamilton, *History of the Moravian Church*, 43–44.

⁵⁹ Hamilton and Hamilton, *History of the Moravian Church*, 44.

⁶⁰ Hamilton and Hamilton, *History of the Moravian Church*, 41.

⁶¹ Hamilton and Hamilton, *History of the Moravian Church*, 52.

⁶² Hamilton and Hamilton, *History of the Moravian Church*, 76.

⁶³ Hinkson, "Missions among Puritans," 40.

⁶⁴ Helen Richards, "Distant Garden: Moravian Missions and the Culture of Slavery in the Danish West Indies, 1732–1848," *Journal of Moravian History* 2 (2007): 60.

⁶⁵ Hamilton and Hamilton, *History of the Moravian Church*, 48.

⁶⁶ Hamilton and Hamilton, *History of the Moravian Church*, 51; Hinkson, "Missions among Puritans," 40.

⁶⁷ Richards, "Distant Garden," 61–65. Moravians continued to own slaves until 1843, Richards, "Distant Garden," 72. On the Moravians and their complicity with slavery, see also Jan Hüsgen, "Religion and Rebellion: Moravian Mission and (Post)-Emancipation Revolts in the British and Danish Caribbean," *Journal of Moravian History* 13, no. 1 (2013): 76–100; and Katharine Gerbner, *Christian Slavery: Conversion and Race in the Protestant Atlantic World* (Philadelphia: University of Pennsylvania Press, 2018), 164–88. On preventing the breakup of slave marriages, see Gerbner, *Christian Slavery*, 176.

⁶⁸ Hamilton and Hamilton, *History of the Moravian Church*, 55; cf. Stephen Neill, *A History of Christian Missions* (Harmondsworth, England: Penguin, 1964), 236–38.

⁶⁹ Not to be confused with the birthplace of the Unity of the Brethren. On Schmidt's work, see Hamilton and Hamilton, *History of the Moravian Church*, 56–57; and Tucker, *Jerusalem to Irian Jaya*, 110–13; cf. Hutton, *History of the Moravian Church*, 85–86.

⁷⁰ Hamilton and Hamilton, *History of the Moravian Church*, 57.

⁷¹ Tucker, *Jerusalem to Irian Jaya*, 112.

⁷² Nitschmann had become the first bishop of the Renewed Unity in 1735.

⁷³ John Wesley, *The Journal of the Rev. John Wesley, A. M. in Four Volumes*, vol. 1 (London: J. M. Dent & Sons, 1913), 1: 20 (entry for January 25, 1736).

⁷⁴ Wesley, *Journal of the Rev. John Wesley*, 1: 87–88; cf. 89 (entries for March 23 and April 21, 1738).

⁷⁵ Hamilton and Hamilton, *History of the Moravian Church*, 79.

⁷⁶ Hamilton and Hamilton, *History of the Moravian Church*, 73–74. The use of the lot for making major decisions and discerning the Lord's will, based on Acts 1:21–26, was common practice for the Moravian Brethren.

⁷⁷ Hamilton and Hamilton, *History of the Moravian Church*, 134.

⁷⁸ Hamilton and Hamilton, *History of the Moravian Church*, 138.

⁷⁹ Tucker, *Jerusalem to Irian Jaya*, 103.

⁸⁰ Tucker, *Jerusalem to Irian Jaya*, 103–4.

⁸¹ Timothy J. Crutcher, *John Wesley: His Life and Thought* (Kansas City, MO: Beacon Hill, 2015), 55.

⁸² Tucker, *Jerusalem to Irian Jaya*, 104.

⁸³ Hamilton and Hamilton, *History of the Moravian Church*, 533.

⁸⁴ Hamilton and Hamilton, *History of the Moravian Church*, 149.

⁸⁵ Gerbner, *Christian Slavery*, 164–88. Interestingly, in the nineteenth century, the Moravians were once more taking the lead in educating both free blacks and slaves in the West Indies, Richards, "Distant Garden," 68–69, 72.

⁸⁶ Randall, "Moravian Spirituality," 206–7.

⁸⁷ "Theirs was a missionary congregation in which each and every person was mobilized for ministry," Hinkson, "Missions among Puritans," 43.

⁸⁸ Tucker, *Jerusalem to Irian Jaya*, 99, gives the ratio of one to sixty; cf. Hinkson, "Missions among Puritans," 43, who gives the figure of one missionary for every twelve members!

⁸⁹ They probably never numbered more than about six hundred congregants at Herrnhut, Gallagher, "Zinzendorf," 237.

⁹⁰ These figures found in J. Herbert Kane, "A Prime Obligation; A Personal Responsibility," *Christian History* 1 (1982): 6; Tucker, *Jerusalem to Irian Jaya*, 101; Shantz, *Introduction to German Pietism*, 253; and Hamilton and Hamilton, *History of the Moravian Church*, 263.

⁹¹ James W. Reapsome, "Solely to Send Laborers," *Christian History* 1 (1982): 5.

CHAPTER 10

"No Such Thing as a National Church"
Scottish Restorationists

Since the rise of sixteenth-century Puritanism in Great Britain, a multiplicity of nonconformist groups had come on the scene. Many of these, certainly as early as the seventeenth century, had decidedly restorationist tendencies, but we know little about most of these groups. For example, one group near Edinburgh, Scotland, published a confession in 1644 and 1653 in which it affirmed the headship of Christ, leadership by elders and deacons, baptism by immersion upon a profession of faith, and congregational autonomy that, however, still allowed for cooperation among like-minded congregations.[1] Other nonconformist churches in and near the county of Somerset published a confession in 1656 referring to themselves simply as Churches of Christ and admitting to membership only those who had experienced the new birth, but beyond that, we have little information about them.[2] We also know that in 1669 in Lancashire, England, eight congregations were organized that also called themselves Churches of Christ. These congregations practiced immersion of adult believers, celebrated the Lord's Supper every week, and were led by elders and deacons, ideas that were based on the pattern they discerned in the New Testament.[3] By the eighteenth century in Ireland, Scotland, England, and Wales, additional nonconformist restorationist movements began among Baptists and Presbyterians. Several of the Scottish restorationists were willing to be regarded as outside the established Church of Scotland, and it is to some of these movements that we now turn.

Glasites and Sandemanians

By the eighteenth century, the Presbyterian Church of Scotland had begun to splinter into a variety of distinct Presbyterian denominations such as the Seceders, Burghers, and Anti-Burghers. Increasingly, people were feeling free to study Scripture for themselves and even to establish new congregations based on their understanding of that Scripture. One such person was a minister in the Church of Scotland by the name of John Glas (1695–1773).[4] Glas was born at Auchtermuchty in Fife, Scotland, the son of a minister in the Scottish Kirk. He was well educated for ministry, graduating from St. Andrews University in 1713 with a good grasp of church history and a proficiency in the biblical languages. Ordained in the Church of Scotland in 1719, he began his ministry with a rural church at Tealing, and in 1721, he married Catherine Black, who became one of his most loyal coworkers. As a good Church of Scotland Presbyterian minister, Glas intended to exhort his congregants to renew their allegiance to the National Covenant.[5] However, as he studied the matter, he determined to be guided only by the word of Jesus and thus concluded that the New Testament knew nothing of a National Covenant. Furthermore, he concluded that because Christ's kingdom is a spiritual kingdom, civil authorities should have no function at all in Christ's church. In his 1727 treatise *The Testimony of the King of Martyrs*, Glas argued for the complete separation of church and state.[6] From this time, Glas began preaching against the National Covenant. Already in 1725, about one hundred members of the Tealing church had formed the Independent Church of Tealing and committed themselves to following the New Testament.[7] Glas, believing that the Roman Catholic Church had departed from New Testament Christianity, became a committed restorationist and argued in *Some Observations upon the Original Constitution of the Church* that "the Scriptures of the Old and New Testament contain the complete revelation of the whole counsel of God and are the perfect rule of the Christian religion which is still to be found pure and entire in these."[8]

For one to oppose the National Covenant was to bring one under suspicion of disloyalty and perhaps treason to Scotland. Obviously, Glas's position was met with disapproval from the Church of Scotland, and in 1728, he was deposed. He, however, continued to preach at Tealing and elsewhere, and within a few short years, Glasite churches had been established in Dundee, Edinburgh, Guthrie, and Perth. Eventually, more than twenty congregations were established in Scotland.[9] Glas attempted to form his congregations on the apostolic example he found in the book of Acts.[10]

In 1734, a young man who was studying at the University of Edinburgh, Robert Sandeman (1718–71), attached himself to the Glasite congregation there.[11] Sandeman fell in love with Glas's daughter, Catherine, and they were married. He supported himself from a family linen business while also working for the church. Having been ordained as an elder in the congregation at Perth in 1744 at the young age of twenty-six, before he and Catherine had any children, Sandeman became one of his father-in-law's greatest allies and coworkers in the movement. He was both a preacher and a writer and was influential in establishing many more congregations not only throughout Scotland, but in England and Wales as well.

Although both Glas and Sandeman were staunch Calvinists, Sandeman made an important theological contribution to the movement in his rejection of an understanding of "imputed righteousness," which held that humans were unable to come to faith without God first giving them the gift of grace that enabled them to believe. Faith, therefore, was a sign of election. Sandeman argued, on the other hand, that it was faith that led to salvation, and faith was possible through the hearing of the gospel without some sort of special predestined gift of grace.[12] One way that Sandeman illustrated how faith brought about salvation was to suggest that men in a pit who grasp a ladder to get out are saved by the ladder and not by themselves. The ladder represented God's salvation; their grasping it represented faith.[13] Eventually, in 1764, Sandeman immigrated as a missionary to the United States, where he established several Churches of Christ in New England. One of the ironies of the movement, however, was that by the nineteenth century, many within the movement were adamant in their opposition to foreign missions to non-British people, arguing that Christ had commissioned missions specifically and only to his apostles. After the apostles, no others had received such a commission. The church was simply to be the church, and God himself would take care of spreading the gospel; how God would do that without involving the church was not explained.[14]

Although the congregations attached to Glas and Sandeman referred to themselves as Churches of Christ, they preferred to designate themselves simply as "Christians" or "Disciples of Christ."[15] Outsiders referred to them as Glasite churches or, outside of Scotland, Sandemanian churches. They probably reached their peak numerically around 1800 with about one thousand members.[16] Glasite and Sandemanian churches had congregational polity, were led by a plurality of elders (synonymous with bishops), and were served by deacons, deaconesses, and ministering widows. Because it was their aim to restore New Testament Christianity, they naturally denied the authoritative value of creeds and official confessions of faith, though they might publish their interpretations of Scripture in order to combat error. In fact, Glas wrote seven volumes of *Notes on Scripture Texts*.[17]

Although Glas and Sandeman abolished the distinction between clergy and laity, they believed that no congregation could be properly organized without a plurality of elders. They were so committed to this pattern that they sometimes ordained very young men as elders—for example, the aforementioned ordination of Sandeman himself. This is significant in demonstrating the importance in Glasite and Sandemanian churches of what they perceived as the proper New Testament ordering of the church. In their view, the New Testament taught that each church must have elders, even when the congregation did not necessarily have men who met every specific New Testament qualification of elders as found in 1 Timothy 3 and Titus 1. For them, the pattern of having a plurality of elders carried greater weight than the pattern of what qualities were required to qualify one to be an elder, though they did take the biblical qualifications seriously. Nevertheless, when forced to choose between having elders who were perhaps less than literally qualified on every point and having no elders at all, they chose the former. Most importantly, elders had to demonstrate proven character and an ability to teach, though unlike in the Church of Scotland, a university education was not necessary.[18]

Like the Presbyterians from whom they were cast out, Glasite and Sandemanian churches rejected transubstantiation and consubstantiation, advocating that the Lord's Supper was a spiritual feast and a memorial.[19] Unlike the Presbyterians, however, they celebrated the Lord's Supper every Lord's Day, usually in the evening. In fact, the Lord's Supper was the central act of their Sunday assemblies. They believed, however, that it could only be served in a congregation with a plurality of elders. Once again, we see the primary importance of the eldership in the movement. Although the churches believed that Scripture taught that the Lord's Supper should be celebrated every Sunday, they also believed it taught that it could not be celebrated without elders (without whom a church was not properly constituted). If an assembly were faced with a choice between celebrating without elders or not celebrating at all, they chose the latter.[20] Because of their view that the Lord's Supper could only be served when the congregation was in harmony, they practiced strict discipline and insisted that problems be resolved each week before partaking of the Supper.[21]

Although Glas recognized there was no New Testament authority for the practice of infant baptism, he retained the practice as a concession to concerned parents.[22] Theologically, Glas viewed baptism as analogous to Old Testament circumcision—that is, as a sign and seal of the covenant. He believed that baptism was a washing of purification that was made effective by the blood of Christ, and he held that immersion and pouring were the proper modes of baptism as they both expressed the idea of washing.[23]

In Glasite and Sandemanian assemblies, singing was a cappella, and usually the only songs were Psalms set to common tunes. One typical practice would be to have a morning assembly, followed by a love feast held in an upper room. Following the love feast, the congregation would gather again for an afternoon service, which would then be followed by the Lord's Supper, at which at least two elders were required to preside. Interestingly, based on the decision of the Jerusalem conference in Acts 15, most Glasite and Sandemanian churches forbade the eating of blood, which was a ticklish matter given the Scottish preference for haggis and black pudding. Another common practice was the fellowship, or collection for their members who were in need, which was taken seriously. Church members practiced greeting with a holy kiss, and outside Scotland, sometimes congregations practiced foot washing, though not as "divine institutions, but rather as exemplary imitations of the primitive Christians."[24]

Unfortunately, the Glasite and Sandemanian churches were plagued at times with infighting over matters of discipline and doctrine. Glas and Sandeman were both considered by some of their opponents to be intolerant and hard to get along with. Additionally, they tended to be closed in terms of relationships with other religious groups, even toward groups that had similar aims. Although initially Glas expressed that uniformity among congregations of the Lord's church was not to be expected, his view later hardened to the point that he prohibited any kind of joint worship or intercommunion with those who did not follow the Glasite order.[25] According to John Howard Smith, Glas's view was that "true charity is essentially love of the truth, and in practice it 'must be precisely regulated by the New Testament.' Forbearance that ignores the truth is not Christian charity."[26] Perhaps this was a reason that the movement never truly gained the momentum to become great numerically, though some of its congregations survived until the late twentieth century.[27] However, this would not have troubled John Glas and Robert Sandeman, for they came to believe, based on Jesus's words in Matthew 7:13–14, that the true church would always be small.[28]

Scotch Baptists

A restorationist group that could be considered in some ways a spiritual heir of the Glasite and Sandemanian movement is the Scotch Baptists. In 1757 or 1762, Robert Carmichael (d. 1774) withdrew from his position as pastor in the Anti-Burgher Secession Presbyterian Church and became a minister for the Glasite church in Glasgow.[29] At that time, he published his *Declaration and Confession* in which he described his view of the church: "Christ's kingdom is altogether spiritual. There can be no such thing as a National Church. The Word of God alone is the test of orthodoxy, and there is no Church of Christ other than a society of Christ's disciples called to observe all the ordinances He hath commanded."[30]

In the meantime, Archibald McLean (1733–1812), a Presbyterian printer and bookseller living in Glasgow, read *The Testimony of the King of Martyrs* by John Glas and, convinced by its arguments, he also withdrew in 1762 from the Church of Scotland and joined the Glasite church in Glasgow in 1763. Carmichael and McLean became acquainted through the Glasite church, but shortly thereafter, both withdrew from the Glasites when a member was, from their perspective, unfairly disciplined.[31]

After separating from the Glasites, Carmichael moved to Edinburgh, where he established an Independent church. Before his move, however, he and McLean agreed to independently study the question of baptism and then later report their findings to each other. In 1764, McLean wrote to Carmichael that, based on his study of Scripture, he had concluded that proper baptism was believers' immersion in water. Carmichael was not yet convinced. The following year, however, Carmichael and five others of his little congregation meeting in the Magdalene Chapel in Edinburgh came to the same conclusion as McLean and began searching for someone to immerse them. In October 1765, a Baptist congregation in London invited Carmichael to come preach for them. While there, he requested immersion and was baptized by a Dr. Gill on October 9. It is intriguing to imagine what those Baptists in London must have thought of the idea of their guest preacher requesting baptism for himself! At any rate, Carmichael returned to Edinburgh and immersed the five members of Magdalene Chapel, thus beginning the Scotch Baptist movement. Shortly after this, McLean acted on his conclusions regarding baptism and was also immersed. He then moved to Edinburgh, where he became Carmichael's coworker while continuing his work in the printing business.[32]

As word of the Scotch Baptist teachings spread, people began to come to Edinburgh to request baptism, and eventually, congregations were initiated throughout Scotland, England, and Wales, and even in the United States. Carmichael moved to Dundee to help with a congregation there, and McLean moved to work with a new congregation in Glasgow. Additionally, at least one Glasite congregation accepted the teaching of believers' immersion and became a Scotch Baptist congregation.[33] Unlike the Glasite churches, the Scotch Baptists were evangelistic, and McLean himself was exemplary. He worked tirelessly to spread the gospel, both personally and in writing, and he also encouraged the Scotch Baptists to support the Baptist Missionary Society. The church in Edinburgh asked

McLean in 1785 to devote himself full-time to the ministry, so he gave up his secular work and became a salaried pastor.[34]

However, as the Scotch Baptist message spread, so did their controversies. McLean's personal ambiguity regarding the eternal generation of the Son from the Father, which he doubted, became a point of division among Scotch Baptist churches in the nineteenth century. Others advocated Sabellian modalism—that is, the idea that one God revealed himself successively as emanations of Father, Son, and Holy Spirit. Other controversies, such as whether the Lord's Supper could be celebrated in the absence of elders, plagued and divided the movement as well.[35]

Like other restorationists, Scotch Baptists considered the New Testament to be "very plain on matters of faith and practice."[36] Thus, in terms of authority, they rejected human systems as the standard of faith and practice, seeking the "Apostolic Plan" as the "only rule they profess[ed] to follow."[37] Doctrinally, Scotch Baptists had many similarities with the Glasites and Sandemanians who had so strongly influenced them. Of course, they differed on believers' baptism by immersion. Like the Glasites and Sandemanians, they organized with congregational polity with a plurality of elders (usually) and required unanimity on decisions. However, if they did not have a plurality of men who were qualified to be recognized as elders, Scotch Baptists went ahead and set a church in order with the ordination of one elder, though it was considered incomplete without a plurality. They practiced closed Communion each Lord's Day, presided over by at least one elder, instead of requiring at least two as did the Glasites and Sandemanians. Both the issue of closed Communion and whether it was necessary to have an elder present became matters of significant controversy. Additionally, they emphasized the reading of Scripture during assemblies and lay exhortation, and they practiced the fellowship or contribution. They advocated abstinence from blood, practiced love feasts and the kiss of charity, and practiced foot washing when it was "really serviceable as an act of hospitality."[38] They also practiced strict discipline among their members.

Socially, Scotch Baptists believed that it was a Christian duty to marry "only in the Lord," but that being married to an unbeliever did not dissolve the marriage. They discouraged extravagant dress as an indication of pride and vanity both for men and women, and they taught that it was shameful for men to have long hair, regardless of contemporary fashion. They also rejected many forms of entertainment, such as gambling and attending plays, as "unbecoming the gravity and sobriety of the Christian profession."[39]

The Haldanes

Another restoration movement that was in some ways an heir of the Glasite and Sandemanian movement was that of Robert (1764–1842) and James Alexander Haldane (1768–1851).[40] Their father, James, had been a ship captain in the East India Company, and their mother, Katherine, made sure the boys learned about God. The boys were orphaned at an early age, their father having died just before James was born and their mother passing when they were ten and six years old, respectively. In 1777, their grandmother, who had been raising the boys, also died, so their uncles enrolled them in the Royal High School in Edinburgh, where they boarded at the home of the rector.

Robert enlisted in the Royal Navy in 1780 and, while in port, attended the church services of an Independent church in Gosport. In 1783, he returned to the University of Edinburgh to study, and, in between terms, he also traveled throughout Europe. He married Katherine Oswald in 1785, and they moved to the family estate at Airthrey, near Stirling, where they lived in relative comfort for several years. The course of the French Revolution caused Robert to turn to religion and the study of the Bible.

In the meantime, James completed his studies at the Edinburgh high school and enrolled in the university. In 1785, he also went to sea, and by 1794, he was commanding an East India merchant ship. He had several voyages to the Far East and met the famous English Baptist missionary William Carey (1761–1834) in India. It was these experiences that instilled in James an evangelistic fervor for the lost. After about nine years at sea, James gave up the sailing life and got married, eventually settling back in Edinburgh.

Robert also became acquainted with the work of William Carey and was so touched that, in 1795, he proposed to sell the Airthrey estate to finance a mission to India. He recruited three coworkers: William Innes (1770–1855), who was a Baptist preacher in Stirling; David Bogue (1750–1825), who was a founding member of the London Missionary Society and the preacher in the Independent church in Gosport that Robert had attended while in the navy; and Greville Ewing (1767–1841), who was minister of Lady Glenorchy's Chapel in Edinburgh. Unfortunately, the opposition to the venture by the East India Company was so great that the group was not able to get permission to go, so the plan was aborted.

Instead, James became involved in a missionary effort at home when he joined with John Campbell (1766–1840) to begin establishing Sunday schools to provide opportunities for education and spiritual instruction to child laborers. Robert soon became involved in the Sunday school venture as well, and soon at least sixty schools were established.[41] Work with the Sunday schools provided James with his first opportunities as a preacher, and he discovered that he had a knack for this type of ministry. From July to November 1797, James participated in a preaching tour to more than forty towns in northern Scotland, speaking at times to audiences of as many as six thousand people and distributing more than twenty thousand tracts.[42] The Haldanes emphasized the ecumenical nature of their work, affirming, "The true church is not found in one sect or denomination, but scattered among all who have heard the gospel."[43] Following the tour, in January 1798, the Haldanes, along with twelve coworkers, began the Society for Propagating the Gospel at Home (SPGH). This was an interdenominational and nonsectarian organization that was "to be composed of persons of every denomination, holding unity of faith in the leading doctrines of Christianity."[44] The organizers stated, "It is not our design to form or to extend the influence of any sect. Our sole intention is to make known the Evangelical Gospel of our Lord Jesus Christ."[45]

The Haldanes then invited English Independent evangelist Rowland Hill (1744–1833) to conduct a preaching tour in Scotland, beginning in Edinburgh at the Edinburgh Circus Tabernacle. The first evening, two thousand five hundred people attended, and eventually, the crowds became so large that they had to move the preaching outside so more than ten thousand people might attend! Hill advocated that the New Testament pattern of church government was congregational, with each church having elders and deacons.[46] The Haldanes would later accept these principles as well.

Although Robert also preached from time to time, he became the financial backer of the brothers' efforts, selling the family estate and financing the SPGH and purchasing meeting places, constructed as Tabernacles, for preaching.[47] Greville Ewing joined the effort and began preaching throughout Scotland, as did other Presbyterian, Episcopal, Baptist, and Congregational preachers. The preachers were given advice that preachers today might do well to heed: "Let not your sermon and your prayer be too long. Much better your hearers should wish you had been longer than be wearied till you close. We are disposed to speak longest when we have least to say."[48]

Up to this point, the Haldanes focused their efforts on evangelism and were not particularly concerned with various doctrinal differences, believing that the preaching of the gospel could be done in a nonsectarian manner; nor were they intending to start any sort of new church.[49] When the movement began to face opposition from the established Church of Scotland, however, the Haldanes decided to formally organize the Tabernacle Circus Church in Edinburgh. Because of his theological training, Greville Ewing was called upon to draw up the principles for the organization of the new church, and James Haldane was ordained as the first preacher. Ewing, in particular, had become committed to the ideal of New Testament restoration, and he advocated congregational polity, weekly observance of the Lord's Supper, strict discipline, and the elimination of clergy/laity distinction. He also advocated the practice of mutual exhortation outside the Sunday assembly with one or two members invited to comment on the text chosen by the minister.[50] The new church began with more than three hundred members committing to the congregation in January 1799. Interestingly, thirty-eight of the initial members simultaneously continued their membership in the Church of Scotland.[51] According to one contemporary description of the new congregation, "There was a fervour of spirit; a love to each other for the truth's sake; a delight in all the ordinances of the Gospel, which makes it resemble more perhaps the Pentecostal period in Jerusalem, than any that has succeeded it. . . . The work of God in seeking the conversion of sinners was made the business of life."[52]

Although the Haldanes did not believe that theological education was a requirement for ministry, they did understand the value of good training with an emphasis on spirituality.⁵³ The same month that the Tabernacle Circus Church began in Edinburgh, Robert Haldane, at his own expense, also established a seminary for training young ministers, with Ewing as its head instructor. Tabernacle churches had been started in other towns, such as Glasgow and Dundee, so the Haldanes were able to offer seminary classes in those places as well. The method of training that developed was that students would study their first year under William Innes, followed by a summer preaching tour, and concluding with a year of instruction under Ewing. Curriculum included instruction in grammar and rhetoric, the biblical languages, and systematic theology, with other subjects available on demand. Over the next ten years, the seminaries trained some three hundred ministers. Several students from the Glasite and Sandemanian churches enrolled in the Haldane seminaries and brought with them the writings of Glas and Sandeman. In this way, the Haldane movement was influenced by the restorationist thought of the earlier movement.⁵⁴

As previously mentioned, in addition to their evangelistic zeal and desire to restore New Testament Christianity, the Haldanes were also interested in unity among believers in the great work of evangelism and were willing to work with other evangelicals in the spread of the gospel. The desire to cooperate in the proclamation of the gospel while also following the New Testament pattern of worship and church government, however, created inherent tensions.⁵⁵ How does a group that is committed to following its understanding of New Testament teaching maintain unity and fellowship with another group when their understanding of New Testament teaching differs?

A turning point in the movement came in 1808. Lachlan Macintosh (d. 1857), one of the Haldanes' students, had been immersed in a Scotch Baptist meeting house and had begun preaching believers' baptism. Up to this point, the Haldanes had continued the traditional Scottish Presbyterian practice of infant baptism and had not questioned the practice. When James received word of Macintosh's teaching, he called the young man in to be disciplined. A couple of incidents, however, caused a change in his thinking. A contemporary of the Haldanes reported that after having baptized an infant, James was asked by his young son whether the infant had believed, since, in the New Testament, everyone who was baptized had believed. This led James to begin a serious New Testament study of baptism. His reading of an article by the Scotch Baptist Archibald McLean against infant baptism also influenced James's thinking. Within a month, James concluded that Macintosh had been correct, and in spring 1808, James Haldane was immersed. Shortly thereafter, Robert Haldane was also immersed. Of his decision to be immersed, James revealed that he had feared such a decision might ultimately hinder his evangelistic work but that he finally realized "the more simply he followed the Lord, the more useful he should in reality be."[56] Whatever effect this decision may have had on his evangelistic work, it certainly damaged his aspirations for unity.

The Haldanes hoped their new understanding and practice of baptism would not harm their movement. They expressed that, although they would no longer baptize infants, they hoped that those who continued in that practice would remain in fellowship with those who did not and that all would demonstrate mutual forbearance. Unfortunately, both Greville Ewing and William Innes, along with others, rejected what appeared to be a new and suspect practice, and many of the Haldane churches split over this issue.[57] Tensions were further exacerbated when the Haldanes, understandably, withheld financial support from those congregations that refused them fellowship.[58]

One significant weakness of the movement was a result of the Haldanes' tremendous generosity. Because they gave so much of their own material wealth to finance much of the work, they naturally felt that they had an enormous stake in decisions that were made and practices that were implemented. They tended to exercise what others saw as too much individual control over the movement. On at least one occasion, Greville Ewing accused Robert Haldane of being "the POPE of independents."[59] Money almost always comes with strings attached.

As with most restorationist groups, the Haldanes developed their new beliefs gradually as they came to new understandings of Scripture. One of the criticisms that was levelled toward them was that they preached new teachings before they had become settled in their own minds.[60] Even their belief that the New Testament provided the model for the arranging of the church came gradually. When the movement began, the number one priority was evangelism, and the brothers did not much concern themselves with doctrine. However, once they established the Tabernacle Church at the Edinburgh Circus, it became necessary to think about doctrine and practice. After all, the church must be organized, perform certain acts during worship assemblies, and have a sense of what it will corporately confess and teach. The default setting for the Haldanes was the teaching and practice of the Church of Scotland because that was their background. However, as the Haldanes continually examined the teachings of the Church of Scotland in the light of the New Testament to discover what should be implemented in a new church, they began to reach new conclusions about many matters that they had never before considered, though, on other matters, their positions never changed. Many of these new conclusions led to difficulties and even divisions.[61]

Theologically, the Haldanes were good Protestants in terms of their affirmations of the classical doctrines of Christianity, along with their acceptance of the doctrine of justification by faith alone apart from any meritorious works. Additionally, the Haldanes never changed their acceptance of the Calvinistic teachings of the Westminster Confession, particularly in terms of unconditional election and limited atonement. It is essential, however, to realize that the Haldanes accepted Protestant and especially Calvinistic ideas because they believed the Bible taught them rather than because the Confession demanded them. They accepted the theology of the Confession, but not its authority.[62]

Although from the beginning, the Edinburgh Tabernacle Church accepted congregational polity, it was only after a matter of time that it appointed a plurality of elders. The church began with monthly observance of the Lord's Supper and only later implemented the weekly observance that Greville Ewing had originally advocated. Mutual exhortation was added to the Sunday assemblies only in 1808.[63] Their gradual acceptance of believers' immersion has already been described.

Additionally, the Haldanes recognized that there was no biblical distinction between an elder and a bishop, nor was there a distinction between teaching elders and ruling elders, as taught by the Presbyterian church. Deacons were appointed in each church to care for the poor. Like the Glasites and Sandemanians, they rejected the union of church and state, though they maintained a strong respect for the role of the state in society. They insisted on observing Communion each Sunday, although they did not reject the possibility of observing it on other days as well. The Haldanes saw the Lord's Supper as a memorial of the Lord's death and resurrection and as a representation of the Christians' union with one another through their union with Christ. Outsiders referred to their churches as "Haldanean" churches, but they simply referred to their members as "Christians" or "disciples" and to their churches as churches of Christ. They made no distinction between clergy and laity and even permitted lay baptism and administration of the Lord's Supper, though, as mentioned, they did emphasize training for ministers.[64]

Legacy

Although few, if any, churches remain from these Scottish restoration movements, their lasting legacy is not insignificant. As we have seen, the Glasite and Sandemanian movement spread throughout Great Britain and to North America, while it also played a role in the beginnings of the Scotch Baptists and the Haldane movement. It also influenced the birth of the Old Scots Independents and other restorationist groups.[65] About ten churches identified as Scotch Baptist survived into the late twentieth century in North Wales and Lancashire.[66] Others became part of the Baptist Union of Scotland or united with the English Baptists. The Haldane movement continued for several decades in its original evangelistic zeal, both in Scotland and abroad, even planting churches in Canada and the United States, in spite of defections over the question of baptism and other issues. Robert Haldane even taught his restoration principles in France and in Geneva, Switzerland. Ultimately, most of the Haldane congregations in Scotland that accepted the practice of believers' immersion became Scotch Baptist congregations. Most of those that did not either returned to the Church of Scotland or became Scottish Congregationalists.[67]

Perhaps the most enduring legacy of the Scottish restoration movements can be found in their connection to the Stone-Campbell Restoration Movement of the nineteenth century.[68] In the eighteenth century, Robert Sandeman became what Lynn McMillon referred to as the "cultivator of the first American restoration movement," which itself was a precursor of and had connections to the Stone-Campbell movement.[69] In the mid-nineteenth century, several Scotch Baptist congregations, as well as some of the former Haldane congregations, such as those at Kirkcaldy and Auchtermuchty, came to be called Churches of Christ and identified themselves with Alexander Campbell's Restoration Movement.[70]

Both Thomas Campbell and his son, Alexander, had been introduced to Haldane ideas in Ireland. Later, in 1808, after Alexander was shipwrecked off the coast of Scotland on his way to join his father in the United States, he spent several months in Glasgow before continuing his voyage. While in Glasgow, not only was Alexander Campbell exposed to the ideas of Glas and Sandeman, but he also met Greville Ewing, with whom he formed a strong friendship. It was Ewing who introduced Alexander to the restorationist teachings of the Haldanes.[71] About ten years later in Pittsburg, Walter Scott (1796–1861), who was to become the greatest early evangelist of the Stone-Campbell Restoration Movement, began teaching in a school run by the Haldane George Forrester. Forrester introduced Scott to restorationist ideals and immersed him into Christ.[72] Thus, all three Scottish restoration movements helped fuel a desire for the restoration of the New Testament church, a desire that was embraced by the nineteenth-century Stone-Campbell US Restoration Movement. But that is another story.

Questions for Thought or Discussion

1. How were the various Scottish groups discussed in this chapter similar to or different from one another?

2. To what extent could these Scottish movements be considered restoration movements?

3. Against what were the Scottish movements reacting?

4. What in particular were the Scottish groups emphasizing in their renewal efforts?

5. What were various strengths or weaknesses of the Scottish movements?

6. How were the Scottish movements similar to or different from the previous movements discussed in this book?

7. What did you find particularly interesting or attractive about the Scottish movements?

8. What lessons or applications can you draw from the Scottish movements?

NOTES

[1] John Renwick, *Reformation to Restoration: The Restoration Ideal in Europe from the 16th to the 19th Century and the Rise of New Testament Churches in Britain and America with a Special Focus on Scotland* (Kirkcaldy, Scotland: Hayfield Publications, 2004), 55.

[2] Renwick, *Reformation to Restoration*, 56.

[3] David Roper, *Voices Crying in the Wilderness* (Salisbury, South Australia: Restoration Publications, 1979), 36.

[4] For biographical information on Glas, I draw primarily from Lynn A. McMillon, *Restoration Roots: The Scottish Origins of the American Restoration Movement* (Henderson, TN: Hester Publications, 1983), 19–28; and John Howard Smith, *The Perfect Rule of the Christian Religion: A History of Sandemanianism in the Eighteenth Century* (Albany: State University of New York Press, 2008), 17–36. On Glas's theology, see Smith, *Perfect Rule*, 37–63.

[5] The National Covenant of 1581, revised and repromulgated in 1638, and The Solemn League and Covenant of 1643 were documents that established the presbyterian form of polity for the Church of Scotland. This was in response to efforts by the English kings James I and Charles I to enforce English episcopacy on Scotland. Good Scottish citizens were expected to *covenant*, that is, swear allegiance to these covenants, Lynn A. McMillon, *Restoration Roots, Third Annual Inman Bible Forum* (Parkersburg, WV: Ohio Valley College, 1985), 6–7. See also Smith, *Perfect Rule*, 10–17.

[6] See, for example, John Glas, *The Testimony of the King of Martyrs Concerning His Kingdom*, vol. 1: *The Works of Mr. John Glas* (Perth: R. Morison and Son, 1782), 33–38.

[7] McMillon, *Restoration Roots* [1985], 8.

[8] Quoted in Renwick, *Reformation to Restoration*, 80; and Smith, *Perfect Rule*, 37. Glas identified the beginnings of the corruption of the Roman Church with the time of Constantine, Smith, *Perfect Rule*, 46.

[9] McMillon, *Restoration Roots* [1985], 14.

[10] Smith, *Perfect Rule*, 36.

[11] For biographical information on Sandeman, see Smith, *Perfect Rule*, 65–120; and McMillon, *Restoration Roots* [1983], 39–59.

[12] McMillon, *Restoration Roots* [1985], 15–16.

[13] McMillon, *Restoration Roots* [1983], 63.

[14] Dyron Daughrity, "Glasite versus Haldanite Scottish Divergence on the Question of Missions," *Restoration Quarterly* 53, no. 2 (2011): 71–72.

[15] Smith, *Perfect Rule*, 44.

[16] Daughrity, "Glasite versus Haldanite," 70.
[17] Renwick, *Reformation to Restoration*, 83.
[18] On their views regarding elders and deacons, see McMillon, *Restoration Roots* [1983], 31–32; and Smith, *Perfect Rule*, 45–49.
[19] McMillon, *Restoration Roots* [1983], 34–35.
[20] McMillon, *Restoration Roots* [1983], 62–63.
[21] McMillon, *Restoration Roots* [1985], 20–21; Smith, *Perfect Rule*, 50–51.
[22] McMillon, *Restoration Roots* [1985], 21.
[23] McMillon, *Restoration Roots* [1983], 33–34; cf. Smith, *Perfect Rule*, 49–50.
[24] McMillon, *Restoration Roots* [1983], 66.
[25] Smith, *Perfect Rule*, 55–57, 84, 166.
[26] Smith, *Perfect Rule*, 56.
[27] The last known Glasite church in Scotland ceased operation as a church in July 1985 in Edinburgh, Daughrity, "Glasite versus Haldanite," 71. In North America, the last known Sandemanian church ceased operation in Halifax, Nova Scotia, in 1905 or 1906, Smith, *Perfect Rule*, 179.
[28] McMillon, *Restoration Roots* [1985], 8; and *Restoration Roots* [1983], 61.
[29] For the differing dates of Carmichael's withdrawal, see Renwick, *Reformation to Restoration*, 60, 82, 86.
[30] Quoted in Renwick, *Reformation to Restoration*, 60.
[31] McMillon, *Restoration Roots* [1985], 32.
[32] Renwick, *Reformation to Restoration*, 86–87.
[33] Renwick, *Reformation to Restoration*, 87; cf. D. B. Murray, "The Scotch Baptist Tradition in Great Britain," *The Baptist Quarterly Journal of the Baptist Historical Society* 33, no. 4 (1989): 188.
[34] Joseph Jackson Goadby, *Bye-Paths in Baptist History: A Collection of Interesting, Instructive and Curious Information Not Generally Known Concerning the Baptist Denomination* (London: Elliot Stock, 1871), 44.
[35] Murray, "Scotch Baptist Tradition," 189–90. Sabellius had been excommunicated for his teachings in the third century.
[36] Renwick, *Reformation to Restoration*, 88.
[37] McLain quoted by Goadby, *Bye-Paths*, 45.
[38] Goadby, *Bye-Paths*, 45.
[39] This summary of Scotch Baptist beliefs taken from Murray, "Scotch Baptist Tradition," 187–89; Renwick, *Reformation to Restoration*, 88–89; and Goadby, *Bye-Paths*, 44–46.
[40] For biographical information on the Haldanes, see Alexander Haldane, *Memoirs of the Lives of Robert Haldane of Airthrey, and of His Brother, James Alexander Haldane* (London: Hamilton, Adams, and Co., 1852). I draw primarily from McMillon, *Restoration Roots* [1983], 69–75; Renwick, *Reformation to Restoration*, 97–102. See also James L. Gorman, *Among the Early Evangelicals: The Transatlantic Origins of the Stone-Campbell Movement* (Abilene, TX: Abilene Christian University Press, 2017), 133–46. Gorman puts the Haldane movement in the context of a larger movement that he calls "transatlantic evangelical missions," 25.
[41] A. Haldane, *Memoirs*, 144.
[42] McMillon, *Restoration Roots* [1983], 72.

43 James Alexander Haldane, *Journal of a Tour through the Northern Counties of Scotland and the Orkney Isles, in Autumn 1797: Undertaken with a View to Promote the Knowledge of the Gospel of Jesus Christ* (Edinburgh: printed by J. Ritchie, 1798), 25.

44 Deryck W. Lovegrove, "Unity and Separation: Contrasting Elements in the Thought and Practice of Robert and James Alexander Haldane," in *The Stone-Campbell Movement: An International Religious Tradition*, ed. Michael W. Casey and Douglas A. Foster (Knoxville: University of Tennessee Press, 2002), 521.

45 A. Haldane, *Memoirs*, 191.

46 McMillon, *Restoration Roots* [1983], 73.

47 The Haldanes got the idea of erecting Tabernacles for preaching from George Whitefield, A. Haldane, *Memoirs*, 231.

48 Renwick, *Reformation to Restoration*, 101.

49 For example, of the establishment of the Edinburgh Tabernacle, James Haldane had asserted that it "was no separation from the Establishment. It was merely opening another place of worship for preaching the Gospel," A. Haldane, *Memoirs*, 352.

50 A. Haldane, *Memoirs*, 353–54; cf. Camille Dean, "Robert and James Alexander Haldane in Scotland: Evangelicals or Restorationists," *Restoration Quarterly* 42, no. 2 (2000): 104–5.

51 A description of the formation of the Circus Church and the ordination of James Haldane is found in A. Haldane, *Memoirs*, 232–44; cf. McMillon, *Restoration Roots* [1983], 73; and Dean, "Robert and James," 104.

52 A. Haldane, *Memoirs*, 243.

53 Lovegrove, "Unity and Separation," 532.

54 For the Haldanite seminaries, see A. Haldane, *Memoirs*, 330–31; cf. Dean, "Robert and James," 104; McMillon, *Restoration Roots* [1983], 74; and Renwick, *Reformation to Restoration*, 102, 104.

55 Dean, "Robert and James," 108; Lovegrove, "Unity and Separation," 536–37.

56 A. Haldane, *Memoirs*, 357; cf. Dean, "Robert and James," 105, for a slightly different rendering: "that his greatest usefulness would come by simply following the Lord"; for the Haldane conversion to believers' baptism, see McMillon, *Restoration Roots* [1985], 41, and Renwick, *Reformation to Restoration*, 102–3.

57 A. Haldane, *Memoirs*, 357–58.

58 A. Haldane, *Memoirs*, 360–61. See also Dean, "Robert and James," 105–6; and Renwick, *Reformation to Restoration*, 103.

59 Lovegrove, "Unity and Separation," 521; cf. Dean, "Robert and James," 108–11; McMillon, *Restoration Roots* [1983], 74.

60 Dean, "Robert and James," 110.

61 "Years elapsed before attention to the apostolic order of primitive Churches seriously distracted attention, and necessarily produced difference of opinion, accompanied by divisions," A. Haldane, *Memoirs*, 352.

62 Lovegrave, "Unity and Separation," 525, 527–28.

63 Lovegrave, "Unity and Separation," 533–36. They also allowed women to preach to women in private settings, Gorman, *Early Evangelicals*, 136.

64 For a summary of Haldane teaching, see McMillon, *Restoration Roots* [1983], 75–80. On lay administration of the sacraments, see Gorman, *Early Evangelicals*, 136.

65 Daughrity, "Glasite versus Haldanite," 71.

[66] Murray, "Scotch Baptist Tradition," 186, 196.

[67] Dean, "Robert and James," 106–7; Renwick, *Reformation to Restoration*, 103.

[68] So designated because of its early leaders, Barton W. Stone (1772–1844) and Thomas (1763–1854) and Alexander Campbell (1788–1866). The movement today is preserved in three major and distinct fellowships: the Christian Church (Disciples of Christ), Independent Christian Churches/Churches of Christ, and Churches of Christ. For the influence of some of the Scottish restorationists on Thomas and Alexander Campbell, see McMillon, *Restoration Roots* [1983], 81–93; Gorman, *Early Evangelicals*; and Smith, *Perfect Rule*, 157–58, 177–82.

[69] McMillon, *Restoration Roots* [1983], 51, 60–61.

[70] See, for example, Robert W. Hughes, *Churches of Christ in the County of Fife, Scotland* (Kirkaldy, Scotland: Hayfield Publications, 1998).

[71] McMillon, *Restoration Roots* [1983], 81–83.

[72] Scott also indicated that he read the writings of Glas and Sandeman from works available in Forrester's library, McMillon, *Restoration Roots* [1983], 84.

AFTERWORD

"Yet More Truth to Break Forth from His Holy Word"

In his work on the Waldensians, Amedeo Molnár suggested that "the only church that can reform . . . is one that never ceases to renew itself by taking on itself, over and over, the likeness of the death of Christ."[1] From almost the beginning of its existence, the Christian church has found itself in need of renewal. The New Testament documents themselves are full of passages exhorting Christians to live lives worthy of the calling they have received in Christ and to beware of various forms of false teaching to which many of them had succumbed.[2] The tendency to allow the world to have too much influence in the church and to drift from the ideals that God intended has always been present in the church, and each generation of Christians finds itself needing renewal.

As we have seen, restoration or restitution is the effort of Christians to reject perceived human corruptions in the church and to renew faithfulness to God's truth and his intended ideal for the church as revealed in the authoritative and normative teachings of the New Testament. Typically, restorationists have made a sharp distinction between the "primitive" church and later manifestations of the church. For many, it was the development of the Roman Catholic hierarchy, culminating in the papacy with all of its trappings, that represented the establishment of a church that was different from the church Jesus intended. A significant number of those who have called for renewal throughout history have been in agreement that the partnership between church and state that began in the fourth century with Constantine was not good for the church. For many, this was the point of the church's departure from the true faith; it was the time when Constantine poured poison into the church. This rejection of the church/state relationship distinguished restorationists from reformers who accepted the "Constantinian symbiosis."[3]

Usually, restoration-type movements originated when people gained greater access to Scripture than they previously had and when they took advantage of that greater access, leading to the discovery of truths and implementation of practices that had been forgotten or neglected. In their most simplistic expressions, some of these restoration movements saw themselves as trying to imitate a pattern they believed could be discerned in comprehensive detail from Scripture, particularly the New Testament. At their best, however, these movements were concerned with restoring the ideals of what God intended for his church in every place and time, regardless of how those ideals might be manifested in any specific time and place.

Our survey of the history of some of these movements calls for four final observations. First, the recognition that historical context has profoundly shaped each attempt at renewal should instill humility and caution among contemporary restorationists as they recognize that, had their movement sprung up in a different time and place, it might have taken a different shape. This should caution us about thinking that any one group of Christ followers possesses all truth. Tůma of Přeloučský, a fifteenth-century priest of the Unity of the Brethren, recognized this when he cautioned that "the existence of several churches proves that absolute certainty in religion is impossible."[4] In the pursuit of truth, we can all learn from each other.

Second, because restoration is an ongoing process rather than an accomplished fact, this means that each of us has more truth to learn from God's Word. John Howard Yoder expressed it this way:

When John Robinson bade farewell to the Plymouth dissenters with his since famous phrase, "The Lord has yet more truth to break forth from his holy Word," his claim was not that in the face of high-church persecution there was also a clandestine connection with Waldo and Wyclif. He believed that *the apostolicity* of the Pilgrim cause was certified *by its conformity with the apostolic documents*, reliably recognizable because even across the sea the same Spirit will lead again, *reading the same documents in fresh yet similar ways.* To trust this constancy despite the repetitiveness of men's infidelity is the most hopeful view of history, the one most free to read the facts as they stand in any century without either official apologetics or spiritualistic unconcern, the way most able to proclaim the continuing sovereignty of the Word Incarnate over all the words that seek to speak His echo.[5]

While God's truth does not change, our limited perception of it should change as our understanding grows. Our conclusions today may not be the same conclusions we reach tomorrow. Additionally, we should show forbearance toward those who have not yet come to the same conclusions we have. Perhaps tomorrow they will.

Third, we have noted similarities among the various movements covered in this volume beginning with an emphasis on the primary authority of the New Testament and extending to such areas as commitment to holy living and discipline, simplification of worship rituals and church organization, rejection of the role of the state in church affairs, evangelistic zeal, and brotherly concern for one another. In other words, the practice of reading the apostolic documents with the intention of conforming belief and practice to them will necessarily lead to a measure of similarity, though due to differences such as context and circumstance, it will not necessarily lead to uniformity.

Finally, these movements, in some ways similar to and yet in many ways different from one another due to their varying historical contexts, represent an important strand within the history of the church and bring important lessons to bear on the church today. Indeed, we are indebted to restorationists such as Valdes, Nicholas Biskupec, Petr Chelčický, Brother Gregory, Michael Sattler, Balthasar Hubmaier, Philip Jacob Spener, Alexander Mack, John Glas, Archibald McLean, the Haldanes, and others who, "even across the sea" and across the centuries, "read the same documents in fresh yet similar ways." They challenge us time and again to reexamine our traditional ways of viewing history, God, faith, Scripture, and the practice of the Christian way. We may not always agree with them, but we ought always to give them a hearing. By so doing, our own faith and practice may be immeasurably enriched as we, like them, seek to be renewed by the Word. We do so in faith, confident that God's truth shall prevail.[6]

Questions for Thought or Discussion

1. To what degree do you see the restoration ideal as valid or invalid?

2. What is the difference between restoring a pattern and restoring an ideal, and how are the two related?

3. Which of the movements discussed in this book appeals to you the most and why?

4. In what ways, if any, have your attitudes changed or been challenged through your reading about these movements?

5. How do you respond to the final four observations?

6. What are the most important lessons you have learned from reading about these movements?

NOTES

[1] Amedeo Molnár, *Valdenští* (Prague: Kalich, 1991), 358.
[2] For example, Matt. 7:15–23; Acts 20:28–31; Gal. 1:6–9; Eph. 4:1; Phil. 1:27–28; Col. 1:10, 2:4–23; 1 Tim. 3:1–9.
[3] William R. Estep, *The Anabaptist Story*, 3rd ed. (Grand Rapids: Eerdmans, 1996), 242.
[4] Craig D. Atwood, *The Theology of the Czech Brethren from Hus to Comenius* (University Park: Pennsylvania State University Press, 2009), 192.

⁵John Howard Yoder, *The Priestly Kingdom* (Notre Dame, IN: University of Notre Dame Press, 1984), 133–34 (emphasis mine).

⁶Adapted from Robert Allen Diles, "The Old Testament and Restoration: A Comparison of the Approach to and Use of the Old Testament in Restoration Movements of Fifteenth-Century Tabor and Nineteenth-Century North America, as Seen in the *Confessio Taboritarum* of Nicholas Biskupec of Pelhřimov and in Selected Works of Alexander Campbell" (ThD diss., Charles University, 2005), 248.

Selected Bibliography

Since the first citation of each source is complete in the endnotes for each chapter, it was not necessary to include all of them in the bibliography. I list here the most important works related to the material of this book.

Atwood, Craig D. *The Theology of the Czech Brethren from Hus to Comenius.* University Park: Pennsylvania State University Press, 2009.
Audisio, Gabriel. *The Waldensian Dissent, Persecution and Survival, c. 1170–c. 1570.* Translated by Claire Davison. Cambridge, UK: Cambridge University Press, 1999.
Bainton, Roland H. *Here I Stand: A Life of Luther.* New York: New American Library, 1950.
———. *The Medieval Church.* Malabar, FL: Robert E. Krieger, 1985.
Bartoš, František M. *The Hussite Revolution.* Edited by John M. Klassen. New York: Columbia University Press, 1986.
Bell, David N. *A Cloud of Witnesses: An Introduction to the Development of Christian Doctrine to AD 500.* Revised edition. Collegeville, MN: Cistercian Publications, 2007.
Bender, Harold S. "The Anabaptist Vision." *Church History* 13 (1944): 3–24.
Biller, Peter. *The Waldenses, 1170–1530: Between a Religious Order and a Church.* Aldershot, UK: Ashgate, 2001.
Biskupec, Nicholas. *Confessio Taboritarum.* Edited by Amedeo Molnár and Romolo Cegna. Rome: Istituto Storico Italiano Per Il Medio Evo, 1983.
———. *Mikuláš z Pelhřimova: Vyznání a obrana Táborů.* Edited by Amedeo Molnár and František M. Dobiáš. Prague: Československá akademie věd, 1972.
Boubín, Jaroslav. *Petr Chelčický:Myslitel a Reformátor.* Prague: Vyšehrad, 2005.

Brock, Peter. *The Political and Social Doctrines of the Unity of Czech Brethren in the Fifteenth and Early Sixteenth Centuries*. The Hague: Mouton & Co., 1957.

Brown, Peter. *The Rise of Western Christendom: Triumph and Diversity, A. D. 200–1000*. Revised edition. Malden, MA: Wiley-Blackwell, 2013.

Burnett, Amy Nelson. "The Social History of Communion and the Reformation of the Eucharist." *Past and Present* 211 (May 2011): 77–119.

Calvin, John. *Institutes of the Christian Religion*. Translated by Henry Beveridge. Peabody, MA: Hendrickson, 2008.

Cameron, Euan. *Waldenses: Rejections of Holy Church in Medieval Europe*. Malden, MA: Blackwell, 2000.

Chadwick, Owen. *The Reformation*. New York: Penguin, 1985.

Comenius, John Amos. *Unum Necessarium: The One Thing Necessary*. Translated by Vernon H. Nelson. Winston-Salem, NC: Moravian Archives, 2008. Accessed July 28, 2020. www.moravianarchives.org/images/pdfs/Unum%20Necessarium.pdf.

Cook, William R. "John Wyclif and Hussite Theology, 1415–1436." *Church History* 42 (1973): 335–49.

Crews, C. Daniel. *Faith, Love, Hope: A History of the Unitas Fratrum*. Winston-Salem, NC: Moravian Archives, 2008.

Crutcher, Timothy J. *John Wesley: His Life and Thought*. Kansas City, MO: Beacon Hill, 2015.

Daughrity, Dyron. "Glasite versus Haldanite Scottish Divergence on the Question of Missions." *Restoration Quarterly* 53, no. 2 (2011): 65–79.

Dean, Camille. "Robert and James Alexander Haldane in Scotland: Evangelicals or Restorationists." *Restoration Quarterly* 42, no. 2 (2000): 99–111.

Deanesly, Margaret. *A History of the Medieval Church, 590–1500*. London: Routledge, 1969.

DeGroot, Alfred. T. *The Restoration Principle*. St. Louis: Bethany, 1960.

Diles, R. Allen. "The *Confessio Taboritarum* of Nicholas Biskupec of Pehhrimov: His Eight Suppositions and His Approach to the Old Testament." *Communio Viatorum* 56, no. 2 (2014): 119–35.

Dowley, Tim, ed. *Introduction to the History of Christianity*. 2nd edition. Minneapolis: Fortress Press, 2013.

Durnbaugh, Donald F. *The Believers' Church: The History and Character of Radical Protestantism*. Scottdale, PA: Herald Press, 1985.

Dyck, Cornelius. *An Introduction to Mennonite History: A Popular History of the Anabaptists and the Mennonites*. 3rd edition. Scottdale, PA: Herald Press, 1993.

Eire, Carlos M. N. *Reformations: The Early Modern World, 1450–1650*. New Haven, CT: Yale University Press, 2016.

Estep, William R. *The Anabaptist Story*. 3rd edition. Grand Rapids: Eerdmans, 1996.

Ferguson, Everett. *Church History*. Volume 1: *From Christ to the Pre-Reformation*. 2nd ed. Grand Rapids: Zondervan, 2013.

———. *The Early Church and Today*. Volume 2: *Christian Life, Scripture, and Restoration*. Abilene, TX: Abilene Christian University Press, 2014.

Fudge, Thomas A. *The Magnificent Ride: The First Reformation in Hussite Bohemia*. Brookfield, VT: Ashgate, 1998.
Gäbler, Ulrich. *Huldrych Zwingli, His Life and Work*. Translated by Ruth C. L. Gritsch. Philadelphia: Fortress Press, 1986.
Glas, John. *The Works of Mr. John Glas*. Perth: R. Morison and Son, 1782.
Gordon, Bruce. *Calvin*. New Haven, CT: Yale University Press, 2009.
Gorman, James L. *Among the Early Evangelicals: The Transatlantic Origins of the Stone-Campbell Movement*. Abilene, TX: Abilene Christian University Press, 2017.
Haldane, Alexander. *Memoirs of the Lives of Robert Haldane of Airthrey, and of His Brother, James Alexander Haldane*. London: Hamilton, Adams, and Co., 1852.
Hamilton, J. Taylor, and Kenneth G. Hamilton. *History of the Moravian Church: The Renewed Unitas Fratrum, 1722–1957*. Bethlehem, PA: Interprovincial Board of Christian Education, Moravian Church in America, 1967.
Harder, Leland, ed. *Sources of Swiss Anabaptism*. Scottdale, PA: Herald Press, 1985.
Harrison, Wes. "The Renewal of the Practice of Adult Baptism by Immersion during the Reformation Era, 1525–1700." *Restoration Quarterly* 43, no. 2 (2001): 95–112.
Hillerbrand, Hans, ed. *The Reformation: A Narrative History Related by Contemporary Observers and Participants*. Grand Rapids: Baker, 1989.
Hinkson, Jon. "Missions among Puritans and Pietists." In *The Great Commission: Evangelicals and the History of World Missions*, edited by Martin I. Klauber and Scott M. Manetsch, 23–43. Nashville: B & H Publishing, 2008.
Hubmaier, Balthasar. *Balthasar Hubmaier; Theologian of Anabaptism*. Translated and edited by H. Wayne Pipkin and John H. Yoder. Scottdale, PA: Herald Press, 1989.
Hus, John. *De Ecclesia. The Church*. Translated by David Schley Schaff, 1915. https://en.wikisource.org/wiki/De_Ecclesia._The_Church.
The Hutterian Brethren, ed. and trans. *The Chronicle of the Hutterian Brethren*. Volume 1. Rifton, NY: Plough Publishing House, 1987.
Hutton, J. E. *A History of the Moravian Church*. Coppell, TX: Pantianos Classics, 2020.
Janz, Denis R., ed. *A Reformation Reader: Primary Texts with Introductions*. 2nd edition. Minneapolis: Fortress Press, 2008.
Jordan, William Chester. *Europe in the High Middle Ages*. London: Penguin Books, 2001.
Kaminsky, Howard. *A History of the Hussite Revolution*. Berkeley: University of California Press, 1967.
Kejř, Jiří. *The Hussite Revolution*. Prague: Orbis, 1988.
Klaassen, Walter. "The Anabaptist Understanding of the Separation of the Church." *Church History* 46 (1977): 421–36.
Latourette, Kenneth Scott. *A History of Christianity*. Volume 1: *Beginnings to AD 1500*. Revised edition. Peabody, MA: Prince, 1997.
——— . *A History of Christianity*. Volume 2: *Reformation to the Present*. Revised edition. Peabody, MA: Prince, 1999.

Lindberg, Carter. *The European Reformations*. 2nd edition. Malden, MA: Wiley-Blackwell, 2010.
Littell, Franklin. *The Anabaptist View of the Church*. Boston: Star King, 1958.
Lovegrove, Deryck W. "Unity and Separation: Contrasting Elements in the Thought and Practice of Robert and James Alexander Haldane." In *The Stone-Campbell Movement: An International Religious Tradition*, edited by Michael W. Casey and Douglas A. Foster, 520–43. Knoxville: University of Tennessee Press, 2002.
Maxfield, John A. "Luther, Zwingli, and Calvin on the Significance of Christ's Death." *Concordia Theological Quarterly* 75 (2011): 91–110.
McMillon, Lynn A. *Restoration Roots: The Scottish Origins of the American Restoration Movement*. Henderson, TN: Hester Publications, 1983.
Meier, Marcus. *The Origin of the Schwarzenau Brethren*. Translated by Dennis L. Slabaugh. Philadelphia: Brethren Encyclopedia, 2008.
Molnár, Amedeo. *Valdenští*. Prague, Czech Republic: Kalich, 1991.
Molnár, Enrico C. S. "A Study of Peter Chelčický's Life and a Translation from Czech of Part One of His Net of Faith." Master's thesis, Pacific School of Religion, 1947. Transcribed, formatted, and edited by www.nonresistance.org, Oberlin, Ohio, 2006. Accessed March 12, 2020. https://archive.org/details/TheNetOfFaith/mode/2up.
Morée, Peter C. A. *Preaching in Fourteenth Century Bohemia*. Slavkov, Czech Republic: Evangelické manufakturní alternativní nakladatelství, 1999.
North, James B. *A History of the Church from Pentecost to Present*. 6th printing. Joplin, MO: College Press, 2005.
O'Malley, John. *Trent: What Happened at the Council*. Cambridge, MA: The Belknap Press of Harvard University Press, 2013.
Pánek, Jaroslav. *Comenius, Teacher of Nations*. Prague: Orbis, 1991.
Pelikan, Jaroslav, and Helmut T. Lehmann, eds. *Luther's Works: American Edition*. 55 vols. St. Louis: Concordia; Philadelphia: Muhlenberg Press; Philadelphia: Fortress Press, 1955–87.
Pleasants, Phillis Rodgerson. "*Sola Scriptura* in Zürich." In *The Free Church and the Early Church*, edited by D. H. Williams, 77–99. Grand Rapids: Eerdmans, 2002.
Polidoro, Gianmaria. *St. Francis of Assisi*. Gorle, Italy: Velar, 2006.
Prout, William Cardwell. "Spener and the Theology of Pietism." *Journal of Bible and Religion* 15 (1947): 46–49.
Renwick, John. *Reformation to Restoration: The Restoration Ideal in Europe from the 16th to the 19th Century and the Rise of New Testament Churches in Britain and America with a Special Focus on Scotland*. Kirkcaldy, Scotland: Hayfield Publications, 2004.
Rhodes, Daniel. "Against the World: The Doctrine of Separation within the Political Context of the Origins of Swiss Anabaptism." *Baptist Heritage and History* 54, no. 1 (Spring 2019): 38–53.
Říčan, Rudolph. *The History of the Unity of the Brethren: A Protestant Hussite Church in Bohemia and Moravia*. Translated by C. Daniel Crews. Bethlehem, PA: Moravian Church in America, 1992.

Richards, Helen. "Distant Garden: Moravian Missions and the Culture of Slavery in the Danish West Indies, 1732–1848." *Journal of Moravian History* 2 (2007): 54–74.

Salter, E. Gurney, trans. *The Legend of Saint Francis by the Three Companions*. London: J. M. Dent & Co., 1902.

Sattler, Michael. "The Schleitheim Confession." In *Creeds of the Churches: A Reader in Christian Doctrine from the Bible to the Present*, edited by John H. Leith, 282–92, 3rd edition. Atlanta: John Knox, 1982.

Shantz, Douglas H. *An Introduction to German Pietism: Protestant Renewal at the Dawn of Modern Europe*. Baltimore: Johns Hopkins University Press, 2013.

Simons, Menno. *The Complete Writings*. Translated by Leonard Verduin. Edited by John C. Wenger. Scottdale, PA: Herald Press, 1956.

Šmahel, František. *Husitská revoluce*. 4 vols. Prague: Univerzita Karlova, 1995–96.

———. *Jan Hus: život a dílo*. Prague: Argo, 2013.

Smith, John Howard. *The Perfect Rule of the Christian Religion: A History of Sandemanianism in the Eighteenth Century*. Albany: State University of New York Press, 2008.

Spener, Philip Jacob. *Pia Desideria*. Translated by Theodore G. Tappert. Minneapolis: Fortress Press, 1964.

Spinka, Matthew. *John Amos Comenius: That Incomparable Moravian*. Chicago: University of Chicago Press, 1943.

———. *John Hus: A Biography*. Princeton, NJ: Princeton University Press. 1968.

———. "Peter Chelčický, the Spiritual Father of the Unitas Fratrum." *Church History* 12, no. 4 (1943): 271–91.

Stanglin, Keith D., ed. *The Reformation to the Modern Church: A Reader in Christian Theology*. Minneapolis: Fortress Press, 2014.

Stayer, James M. *The German Peasants' War and Anabaptist Community of Goods*. Montreal: McGill-Queen's University Press, 1991.

Steinmetz. David C. *Reformers in the Wings*. Philadelphia: Fortress Press, 1971.

Tanner, Norman, and Sethina Watson. "Least of the Laity: The Minimum Requirements for a Medieval Christian." *Journal of Medieval History* 32, no. 4 (2006): 395–423.

Tourn, Giorgio. *You Are My Witnesses: The Waldensians across 800 Years*. Turin: Claudiana Editrice, 1989.

van Braght, Thieleman J. *The Bloody Theatre or Martyrs' Mirror of the Defenseless Christians*. Translated by Joseph F. Sohm. Scottdale, PA: Herald Press, 1951.

Verduin, Leonard. *The Reformers and Their Stepchildren*. Grand Rapids: Baker, 1980.

Wagner, Murray L. *Petr Chelčický: A Radical Separatist in Hussite Bohemia*. Scottdale, PA: Herald Press, 1983.

Walker, Williston, Richard A. Norris, David W. Lotz, and Robert T. Handy. *A History of the Christian Church*. 4th edition. New York: Scribner's, 1985.

Wesley, John. *The Journal of the Rev. John Wesley, A. M. in Four Volumes*. London: J. M. Dent & Sons, 1913, 1915, 1916.

Westin, Gunnar. *The Free Church through the Ages*. Translated by Virgil A. Olson. Nashville: Broadman, 1958.

Williams, George Huntston. *The Radical Reformation*. 3rd edition. Kirksville, MO: Sixteenth Century Journal, 1992.

Wilson, Derek. *Luther, Out of the Storm*. Minneapolis: Fortress Press, 2007.

Woodbridge, John D., and Frank A. James III. *Church History*. Volume 2: *From Pre-Reformation to the Present Day*. Grand Rapids: Zondervan, 2013.

Yoder, John Howard. *The Priestly Kingdom*. Notre Dame, IN: University of Notre Dame Press, 1984.

Zeman, Jarold K. "Restitution and Dissent in the Late Medieval Renewal Movements: the Waldensians, the Hussites and the Bohemian Brethren." *Journal of the American Academy of Religion* 44, no. 1 (1976): 7–27.

Zwingli, Huldrych. "Of Baptism." In *Zwingli and Bullinger*. Volume 24 in *The Library of Christian Classics*, edited by G. W. Bromiley, 129–75. Louisville, KY: Westminster John Knox, 2006.

———. "On the Lord's Supper." In *Zwingli and Bullinger*. Volume 24 in *The Library of Christian Classics*, edited by G. W. Bromiley, 185–238. Louisville, KY: Westminster John Knox, 2006.

———. *Selected Works of Huldreich Zwingli*. Edited by Samuel Macauley Jackson. Philadelphia: University of Pennsylvania Press, 1901.

www.ingramcontent.com/pod-product-compliance
Lightning Source LLC
Chambersburg PA
CBHW020524080526
44583CB00013B/733